WHO SUPPORTS THE FAMILY?

*Gender and Breadwinning
in Dual-Earner Marriages*

WHO SUPPORTS THE FAMILY

?

*Gender and Breadwinning
in Dual-Earner Marriages*

Jean L. Potuchek

Stanford University Press, Stanford, California

1997

Stanford University Press
Stanford, California
© 1997 by the Board of Trustees of the
Leland Stanford Junior University

Printed in the United States of America

CIP data are at the end of the book

For my parents, Anita and Conrad Maigret,
with thanks for a lifetime of support and encouragement

Acknowledgments

A research project that extends over more than a decade is possible only with the help and support of friends, family, colleagues, and institutions. I cannot possibly thank everyone who has contributed to the completion of this project. I will try, however, to express my thanks to those whose contributions have been most important to me and trust that anyone who has been inadvertently omitted will know that I thank them, too.

My thanks go first of all to the students in my 1982 sociological research methods course at Bates College whose research triggered my interest in this subject. I'm sure they had no idea how much their work would affect my life! Thanks, also, to students at both Bates College and Gettysburg College whose responses to my ideas have further stimulated my thinking about the social construction of gender.

Bates College, where I was employed during the initial research design and data collection periods of this project, helped to defray some of the costs of the research through Schmutz faculty research grants. More importantly, a grant from Bates College and the Charles A. Dana Foundation provided me with the invaluable help of an undergraduate research assistant from 1986 to 1988. Gettysburg College provided a supportive atmosphere and funds for an undergraduate research assistant during the data analysis and writing stages of this research. In addition, grants from the college's faculty research funds and from the Lutheran Brotherhood Fund of the Evangelical Lutheran Church in America made it possible for me to take a leave from teaching to write the book manuscript. Gettysburg College's Friday Faculty Lunch series also provided me with a forum for presenting parts of my analysis as it developed. Special thanks are due to the Center for Research on Women at Wellesley College, which provided me with space, a supportive environment, and intellectually stimulating colleagues at two critical points in this project: the early phase of editing, coding, and preliminary analysis of the interview data, and the final period of revisions to the book manuscript.

I am particularly grateful to the many family members, friends, and colleagues who regularly asked about this research and listened with patience and interest while I answered in greater detail and at greater length than they necessarily wanted. Special mention is due to Charlotte Armster, Ann Ayoub, Temma Berg, Len Burman, Kathy Cain, Bev Clark, Roger Clark, Steve Crawford, Danny Danforth, Alice Dean, Darcy Donahue, Gove Effinger, Charlie Emmons, Birgitte Ginge, Dennis Grafflin, Mary Harrison, Barbara Heisler, Don Hinrichs, Steve Hochstadt, Mary Hunter, Kathy Iannello, Claudia Isaac, Sharon Kinsman, Beth Kosiak, Jean Kuebler, Nadine Lehr, Frank Loveland, Maureen Maigret, Paula Matthews, Linda Meier, Michael Murray, Georgia Nigro, Susan Pearce, Jan Powers, Rachel Rabinowitz, GailAnn Rickert, Janet Riggs, Peggy Rotundo, Ann Scott, Joyce Sprague, Anne Thompson, Liz Tobin, Amy Trevelyan, Sheryl and Fred Walters, and Anne Williams. Jo Ann Citron and Delia Sherman not only asked and listened but provided moral support, stimulating conversation, and housing during my fall 1988 semester at the Center for Research on Women. Barbara Thomas and Wesley Wallace welcomed me into their family and provided a home away from home during my 1995–96 stay at Wellesley.

Still others have read work from this project and provided me with critical comments on it over the years. They include Bruce Baum, Liliane Floge, Judy Gerson, Sandy Gill, Becky Graham, Elaine Hall, Beth Hess, Jane Hood, Laura Kramer, Jan Phillips, Betty Robinson, Carol Small, Lena Sorensen, and Joan Spade. Fran Goldsheider provided good advice about sampling and research design and some helpful references during the planning of the study. Myra Marx Ferree graciously added the role of unofficial mentor to all her other responsibilities and could be counted on for support, sound advice, and thoughtful feedback throughout this project. Joyce Seligman not only filled the role of closest friend and primary support person through the ups and downs of this research, but also acted as writing consultant, reading drafts of several chapters of the manuscript and providing advice on how to make the book accessible to a nonspecialist audience. I owe an enormous debt of gratitude to Rosanna Hertz, who read the entire manuscript and provided a substantive and incisive review at a critical point in its development.

This project could not have been completed without the help of my undergraduate research assistants. Tonia Trodahl, at Gettysburg College, provided steady and thoughtful help with data analysis and took primary responsibility for the follow-up survey. Special thanks are due to Lisa Blake, my research assistant for two years at Bates College, who worked on the design of the interview schedule, did much of the sampling, and was responsible for one-third of the interviews. Without her capable help, this study would never have gotten off the ground.

Portions of Chapter 3, including Tables 1, B1, and B2, previously appeared in Jean L. Potuchek, "Employed Wives' Orientations to Breadwinning: A Gender Theory Analysis," *Journal of Marriage and the Family* 54, no. 3: 548–58 (1992). Copyrighted 1992 by the National Council on Family Relations, 3989 Central Ave. NE, Suite 550, Minneapolis, Minn. 55421. Reprinted by permission.

Lewiston-Auburn, Maine, turned out to be a wonderful place to do research. It is a tribute to the openness and friendliness of Lewiston-Auburn residents (and perhaps also to the fact that telemarketing had not yet reached the area) that people were routinely gracious about the intrusion of my random-digit dialing into their lives; I can remember only two or three occasions when someone hung up on me. More often, people who did not fit the requirements of the study offered to help locate potential interviewees!

My most profound thanks go, of course, to that special group of Lewiston-Auburn residents, the women and men who welcomed me into their homes and their lives and participated eagerly and thoughtfully in this research. Without them, my questions about breadwinning would have remained only questions.

J.L.P.

Contents

Tables

WHO SUPPORTS THE FAMILY?

Gender and Breadwinning
in Dual-Earner Marriages

1

Introduction
Rethinking Breadwinning

This book and the research on which it is based grew from a question raised in a college classroom one April morning in 1982. When I walked into class that day, the room was buzzing with excitement. This was a course on sociological research methods, and I was a newly minted college professor in my first year of full-time teaching. Back at the beginning of the term, I had divided this class of 35 students into three groups and assigned each group a research topic. The three groups had designed research projects to study their topics, carried out the research, and analyzed the data they had collected. On this morning, members of one group would present the results of all their hard work to their classmates, to me, and to a few faculty colleagues whom I had invited to sit in on the presentation.

I slipped into a chair at the back of the room and waited for the eleven students in charge of the day's presentation to begin. It was an unaccustomed role for them and they seemed nervous and a bit unsure of themselves, but they were also very proud of the work they had done. Assigned to study college students' expectations about their future work and family lives, they had created a carefully designed sixteen-page questionnaire and administered it to a randomly chosen sample of 100 of their schoolmates. They had paid particular attention to the effect of gender on expectations about the future.

I wasn't expecting any surprises from the presentation; sociology of gender was one of my areas of specialization, and I knew something about research on these issues. Like other students of gender at the time, I "knew" that gender expectations were undergoing fairly dramatic change from traditional to more egalitarian forms, that it was primarily women who were pushing for these changes, and that the young, the well-educated, and upper-middle-class "dual-career couples" were at the vanguard of change. We could therefore expect that the upper-middle-class, 18–22-year-old college students in this study would have fairly egalitarian gender expectations and that the women students would be significantly more egalitarian than their male peers. I did not know that, before the hour was over, those assumptions would be challenged.

The student researchers described their study and began to go through their questionnaire page by page, presenting results that were interesting but fairly predictable. And then, a little more than halfway through the class period, they reported a finding that riveted my attention. They were discussing a pair of questions that focused on the work expectations of their peers and were asked of those who expected to be married in the future. "Assuming your spouse earns a sufficient income," the first question asked, "would you expect to work?" There were no differences between male and female students' responses to this question; virtually all (over 90 percent) of the students surveyed answered yes. The young women in this sample seemed to have egalitarian expectations of a future in which they, like their husbands, would combine families with careers. The second question in the pair, however, got strikingly different responses from men and women. "Assuming that you earn a sufficient income," the questionnaire asked, "would you expect your spouse to work?" Most of the young men (about two-thirds) chose the response "spouse's decision"; if they could earn enough to support their families, they didn't have strong feelings about whether or not their wives were employed. But over 80 percent of the women students surveyed said yes in response to this question; they expected their husbands to work regardless of their own incomes.

In the days and weeks that followed, I found I could not put those young women and their expectations out of my mind. Why were they so much less willing than their male peers to leave their future spouses' options open? Why were these apparently egalitarian young women so unyielding about their husbands' work? Long after the semester had ended and the final papers for the course had been graded, I kept puzzling over these surprising responses. As I tried to concentrate on other work, they gnawed at the edges of my consciousness. Finally, I decided that the only way to get past this distraction was to address it; I would do some systematic reading and research about women's and men's expectations regarding paid work. Several weeks and many books and articles later,

I had some glimmer of understanding. Like many people, I had been conflating two very different things, employment and breadwinning.

Employment and Breadwinning

To disentangle breadwinning from employment, we must go back to the industrial revolution and look at its effects on patterns of work. Preindustrial households were domestic economies in which every member of the family contributed to the production of whatever goods the family needed to ensure its survival (Tilly and Scott, 1978); domestic and work responsibilities were part of a seamless whole. As the economy became industrialized, however, the production of goods used in everyday life moved out of the household and into the factory. Workers in factories produced goods not for their own use or for barter with neighbors, but for sale in an expanding money economy. For their efforts, they were paid wages that could be used to purchase goods in the market.

As the production of goods moved out of the home, home and work came to be defined as "separate spheres," and, over time, women and men developed distinctive responsibilities for these spheres (Tilly and Scott, 1978). Women now bore primary responsibility for a domestic sphere in which housework and child care took on a new centrality, and women's attendance to these tasks was defined as something other than "work" (Margolis, 1984). At the same time, women's domesticity was made possible by the special responsibility of men for earning an income in the sphere of paid work outside the home. The idea of "the breadwinner" was born with this special male responsibility for providing an income. Sociologist Jessie Bernard has argued that breadwinning first emerged as a distinctive male responsibility in the United States in the 1830s and that, from then until the late 1970s, a *good* provider (or breadwinner) was defined as "a man whose wife did not have to enter the labor force" (Bernard, 1981: 2).

The male breadwinner who was the sole economic provider for his family was, however, always more of an ideal than a reality. In many families, male wages had to be supplemented by the earnings of wives or of children. It was not unusual for a wife to generate income by taking in laundry or sewing, renting out spare rooms to boarders, or doing "homework" for local industries, activities that could be combined with her domestic responsibilities. By the end of World War II, wives' income-generating activities had typically moved outside the home and more often involved formal participation in the paid labor force. In the 1960s and 1970s, married women's paid employment became increasingly visible, and by 1980, more than half of all husband-wife households with employed husbands also had employed wives.

Much of the writing on wives' labor force participation has assumed that these employed wives were breadwinners. But is this assumption accurate? Breadwinning involves not only paid employment, but also the day-to-day obligation to earn money for the financial support of a family. The breadwinner has a duty to work, and leaving the labor force (even temporarily) is not an option. While the young college women my students surveyed generally did not grant their future husbands the option to leave the labor force, the young men did grant this option to their future wives. Both the men and the women seemed to assume that husbands would continue to bear special responsibility for breadwinning.

Thus, although paid employment may be a necessary condition for being a breadwinner, it is not a sufficient condition. This is because breadwinning is not just a matter of behavior (being employed) but also a matter of the meaning attached to that behavior. An example will help to clarify this distinction: Imagine that you are standing out on a sidewalk in a residential neighborhood on a dark evening, looking up at lighted windows in two adjacent houses. In each of those windows, you can see an adult bathing a small child and getting the child ready for bed. The behavior of the two adults is the same. But in one house, that behavior is defined as parenting, the routine day-to-day care of a child; in the other house, the same behavior is defined as babysitting, temporarily taking over the care of a child because the person normally responsible for such care is absent or otherwise unable to meet that responsibility. Similarly, two people may both hold paid jobs, but the meanings attached to their wage earning may differ. One person may be carrying out his or her routine, day-to-day responsibility for providing financial support for a family; the other may be earning an income for personal use or may be contributing to the family's financial support temporarily because the person normally responsible for such support is incapacitated or unemployed. Only in the first instance would the wage-earner be a breadwinner.

As I read the research literature on wives' labor force participation, I began to find evidence that both women and men attach different meaning to the employment of wives than to the employment of husbands. Reports from men indicated that, even when their wives were employed, they still felt a special obligation to provide (K. Gerson, 1993; Lein, 1983; Rodman and Safilios-Rothschild, 1983; Smith and Reid, 1986).

Attitude surveys showed that both men and women generally attributed greater responsibility for family support to men than to women. In a study of Yakima County, Washington, residents, for example, Slocum and Nye (1976) asked respondents how they would act toward a man who did not do his best to support his family. About three-fourths of both men and women reported that they would not choose such a man as a close friend, while fewer than 20 percent responded that it wouldn't matter to them. Significantly, when the researchers used hypothetical situations to probe for evidence of a similar obligation for women to support their families, they came up virtually empty-handed; the only situation in which they could find any evidence of such an obligation was the case of a woman who had no husband to support her. It is not surprising, then, that in a small study of sixteen families in which stay-at-home wives had reentered the labor force, Jane Hood (1983) found that the newly employed wives were not automatically defined as family breadwinners; rather, the meaning of their employment was subject to negotiation. Moreover, in another small study, Linda Haas found that, even among a carefully selected sample of egalitarian couples committed to role sharing, almost one-third reported "some difficulty adjusting to the idea that the wife should be as obligated as the husband to work" (Haas, 1982: 750).

Other studies provide further evidence that wives' employment is not always defined as breadwinning. Sociologist Ellen Rosen studied New England factory women, dual-earner wives who made substantial financial contributions to their families. Rosen's interviewees were married women with children, who "earned almost half the family income" and whose families depended on their incomes "to maintain their standard of living" (Rosen, 1987: 98). As she interviewed them, however, Rosen was struck by the contradictions in these blue-collar women's views of their employment. On the one hand, they were quite clear that their families' need for money was their primary motivation for working and that working to provide for their children was part of being a good mother. On the other hand, these women downplayed the importance of their jobs and defined their husbands as primary breadwinners, the ones "whose income 'really supports the family.'" With more than a hint of irony, Rosen noted their insistence that "the husband's income is for 'essentials'; it goes into the bank to pay the mortgage and the other inevitable monthly bills—fuel and electricity, insurance and car payments. The wife merely works for 'extras' like gas, groceries, things for the children, or savings" (Rosen, 1987: 103). The women in Rosen's study may have been working because their families needed the money, but they did not define themselves as breadwinners.

About the same time that Ellen Rosen was interviewing women on the East Coast, sociologist Rosanna Hertz (1986), halfway across the country in Chicago, was also conducting a study of dual-earner families. At first glance, however, the high-powered dual-career couples whom Hertz was interviewing seemed to have nothing in common with the blue-collar women in Rosen's study. The *individuals* in Hertz's study had higher incomes than the couples in Rosen's, and where Rosen's families managed to raise their incomes above the national median only by combining two full-time jobs, Hertz's couples had combined incomes that were, on average, more than three times the national median. While Rosen's interviewees maintained that it was their husbands who "really" supported the family, Hertz found that the career commitment and high earning power of the women in her study more often forced a rethinking of the assumption that the man is the breadwinner. But Hertz, too, found some resistance to thinking of women as breadwinners; in a sizable minority of these dual-career marriages, wives downplayed their financial contributions just as the wives in Rosen's study did. Nor was this simply a matter of protecting their husbands' egos. In several cases, the wife actively resisted taking responsibility for financial matters despite her husband's urging that she do so. These women, too, it appeared, had some stake in defining men as family breadwinners.

In the San Francisco Bay area, yet another study of dual-earner families was being conducted by sociologist Arlie Hochschild (1989). In her analysis of data from a (mostly) middle-class sample of working couples with children, Hochschild was concerned primarily with women's responsibility for what she called the "second shift" of household work that remained to be done at the end of the day. But her case studies also reveal the staying power of male responsibility for breadwinning. Over and over in Hochschild's book, women resolved the tension between home and work by cutting back on their work hours or switching to part-time jobs. In only one case did a husband cut back on his work hours to devote more time to domestic responsibilities. Even when the wife earned more than her husband, both husband and wife seemed to grant special status to the husband's job.

All three of these studies, carried out in different parts of the country and among different classes of families, point to the disjuncture between employment and breadwinning. They show that employed wives are not automatically defined as breadwinners, even when family finances are their primary motivation for employment and their jobs account for a substantial portion of the family income. Somehow, even in a society of dual-earner families, breadwinning retains its association with men. Why is this the case? Why does the distinction between employment and breadwinning persist? How widespread is it? And what factors shape the meaning attached to a wife's (or husband's) paid employment? These are the questions that this book will address. I will consider both how the responsibility for breadwinning is allocated in dual-earner marriages and why it is allocated that way. In doing so, I will locate the issue of breadwinning within the broader context of the social construction of gender.

The Study

I have studied the issue of breadwinning by interviewing a sample of married couples with both husband and wife in the paid labor force. By limiting my study to dual-earner couples and thereby holding wives' paid employment constant, I have been able to focus on the meanings attached to that employment. Whereas many other studies have focused on dual-career couples (those highly educated, committed professional couples who are often assumed to be in the vanguard of egalitarian lifestyles and consciousness), I have chosen to look at a more broadly representative group, including older as well as younger couples, part-time as well as full-time workers, blue-collar workers as well as professionals. I have focused on dual-earner couples in a single community—Lewiston-Auburn, Maine—a decision that made it possible for me to select participants for the study randomly, through a process called random-digit dialing. (For a more complete discussion of sampling and methodology, see Appendix A.)

Lewiston-Auburn is an urban industrial center in south-central Maine. As defined by the U.S. Census, the Lewiston-Auburn Metropolitan Statistical Area consists of the cities of Lewiston (on the east bank of the Androscoggin River) and Auburn (on the west bank) and a number of nearby towns and villages. Lewiston-Auburn is known in the region as the "twin cities" or, sometimes, tongue-in-cheek, as "L-A." With its combined population of over 88,000, it is one of only three metropolitan areas in a largely rural state; Lewiston alone (population 39,800) is the second largest city in Maine, and Auburn (population 24,300) is the fourth largest.

Although the Lewiston-Auburn area was settled in the eighteenth century, it achieved most of its growth during the industrial revolution. Sitting astride the Androscoggin River at one of its major falls, Lewiston and Auburn were natural sites for industrialization. A system of dams and canals developed during the 1840s to harness the water power of the Androscoggin made Lewiston-Auburn a prime site for the development of huge mills, which were devoted principally to the manufacture of textiles and shoes. The twin cities grew rapidly during the second half of the nineteenth century, and by the opening of the twentieth they were booming, dynamic industrial centers (Leamon, 1976; Rand, 1975). Production reached an all-time high during World War I, and in a single year (1918), Lewiston-Auburn produced 160 million yards of cloth and 40 million pairs of shoes (Rand, 1975).

As Lewiston-Auburn grew into an industrial center, it also became more ethnically diverse. Of particular importance was the influx of French Canadians. In the late 1860s, mill owners in Lewiston-Auburn, as elsewhere in New England, began to send agents to nearby Quebec to recruit mill workers. The French Canadians were considered highly desirable employees both because they had large families that could provide many workers and because they had a reputation for working very hard and not causing trouble (Hareven, 1982; Leamon, 1976). By 1880, 35 percent of Lewiston's population of over 19,000 was foreign-born, mostly French-Canadian (Leamon, 1976). A 1908 census of Maine's French population counted over 14,000 French-speaking residents in Androscoggin County, primarily in Lewiston (Rand, 1975).

The French Canadians brought more than added numbers to Lewiston-Auburn; they also brought a distinctive culture. More and more, particularly in Lewiston, French was heard on the streets. Catholic churches were established and grew. The new residents also founded their own schools, social clubs, and life insurance associations. For over 80 years, from the 1880s to the 1960s, Lewiston had its own French-language newspaper, *Le Messager* (Rand, 1975). The American artist Marsden Hartley, a Lewiston native, described the changes that the French Canadians brought to the community in his poem "Lewiston Is a Pleasant Place":

> The Canadians came to the city—giving it new
> life, new fervors, new charms, new vivacities, lighter
> touches, pleasant shades of cultivation, bringing no
> harm to the city, bringing what it now has—a freshening
> of city style, richer sense of plain living.
> Recently I walked the streets of my native city
> and there was gaiety in the air.
>
> *(Hartley, 1940: 6–7)*

By the 1920s, the twin cities were a socially vibrant urban center, with a cosmopolitan air, a wide variety of entertainment opportunities, and a well-developed public transportation system that provided links to the rest of New England and the nation.

By the 1930s, however, Lewiston-Auburn was in decline. World War II brought some reprieve, but textile mills and shoe factories continued to close down, cut back, or move south through the 1950s, 1960s, and 1970s. Despite recent attempts to diversify the economy and some success at attracting new industries, the twin cities today wear the somewhat dejected air of an industrial center left behind by a postindustrial age. It's not just factories and mills that have closed; a walk through downtown reveals a number of empty storefronts and little of the office-building expansion that has characterized larger metropolitan areas. As is the case throughout much of the industrial Northeast and Midwest, central-city populations have been shrinking. Lewiston reached its peak population of almost 42,000 in 1970 and has been declining steadily since. Auburn, with a larger land area and more suburban neighborhoods, remains stable at about 24,000.

It is from this faded industrial center that I chose my sample of dual-earner couples. The sample consisted of 153 randomly chosen couples representing a broad spectrum of ages, education levels, occupations, and incomes. In many ways, they were similar to dual-earner couples throughout the United States. The median family income of couples in the sample was $40,500 in 1987–88, compared with a national median of $46,340 for dual-earner couples in 1989 (U.S. Bureau of the Census, 1993b: table 37). Eighteen percent of the husbands and 28 percent of the wives in this study were professionals, and 49 percent of the husbands and 23 percent of the wives were in blue-collar occupations. The comparable national figures for all employed civilians, age sixteen and over, in 1988 were 12 percent of employed men and 14 percent of employed women in professional occupations, and 50 percent of men and 29 percent of women in blue-collar jobs (U.S. Bureau of the Census, 1990: table 645).

In its ethnic composition, however, this sample bears the stamp of the community from which it was drawn. It reflects the existence of a distinctive regional minority group in northern New England, Franco-Americans (Americans of French-Canadian ancestry). Marsden Hartley's positive assessment of the French Canadians and their contribution to the community has not always been widely shared. Just as the francophone people of Canada have traditionally been regarded as inferiors by their English-speaking compatriots, so have the Franco-Americans of New England; the phrase "dumb Franco" is a common epithet. Until recently, Franco-Americans have maintained their distinctive language and culture, and, as is the case with other non-English-speaking minority groups, language has often been a lightning-rod issue. In the early twentieth century, many New England employers of Franco-Americans instituted rules against speaking French in the workplace; until the 1970s, speaking French on school grounds was a disciplinary offense at many schools in Maine (Nyhan, 1984). Because the study community is one of the largest centers of Franco-American population in New England, Franco-Americans make up approximately one-third of the sample. National minority groups, however, are largely absent from this study. The population of northern New England is overwhelmingly white, and, as a consequence, this sample includes very few African Americans and no Asians or Hispanics. We can be most confident that the results of this study reflect the lives of white working- and middle-class Americans; caution should be exercised in generalizing from this to other racial groups.

For a couple to be included in this study, they had to be married, both husband and wife had to be currently employed, and both had to agree to be interviewed. Couples meeting these criteria were interviewed in person, with separate interviews for husbands and wives. I personally conducted about two-thirds of these interviews, and a student research assistant conducted the remaining third. Most of the participants were interviewed in their homes, although some found it more convenient to be interviewed at their places of employment, and a few chose to come to our research office for their interviews. Sometimes husbands and wives were interviewed simultaneously, by different interviewers, in separate rooms. In other instances, the interviews were scheduled back-to-back. Less often, the two interviews were arranged for different days and times. Each interview began with some routine questions about age, education, marital history, and household composition; moved on to a detailed work history; and then focused primarily on the meanings attached to the husband's and wife's employment (see Appendix A). Most questions were closed-ended, with a limited choice of responses, but interviewees were encouraged to elaborate on their responses. In addition, a few open-ended questions provided an opportunity for more free-ranging commentary. The length of the interviews ranged from twenty minutes to almost two hours, but the average interview lasted about 35 minutes.

These interviews were unusual in the way that they combined structured and in-depth interview strategies. One perennial concern in social science research has been the problem of "reflexivity," the ways that research subjects may react to the process of being researched and alter the very phenomenon under study. Research methods texts in the social sciences typically offer considerable advice about how to minimize this problem. In interview studies like this one, interviewers are advised to be vigilant about any aspect of their behavior or demeanor that might influence the responses of interviewees. One often-mentioned mechanism for avoiding such influence is the standardization of interviews so that all participants are asked the same questions, in the same order, worded in exactly the same way, and extraneous conversation is, insofar as possible, eliminated from the encounter (Babbie, 1986).

The principle that underlies all this advice is the ideal of scientific "objectivity." The basic assumption is that phenomena under study are best understood from the "outside" by a neutral observer who maintains a proper scientific distance. But this position has been the subject of a developing critique. Research participants have long complained that standardized interviews and questionnaires "force them into boxes" and distort the meaning of what they are trying to say. More recently, scholars, particularly feminist scholars, have questioned both the possibility and the desirability of objectivity and have sought research methods that would allow room for subjectivity and the inclusion of research participants as agents rather than objects of study (Oakley, 1981; Reinharz, 1992).

This study is informed by the critique of objectivity. At first glance, it seems to observe the rules of objective interviewing; it is based on a structured interview design in which all the participants answered the same questions in the same order and, in doing so, usually had to choose from a very limited list of possible responses. The interviews departed from the typical standardized design, however, by setting those questions in the context of a conversation—one in which respondents elaborated on and qualified their responses, sometimes changed their minds, and occasionally wandered fairly far afield from the original questions. This interviewing strategy yielded two very different types of data for analysis, the standardized and easily quantifiable responses to standardized questions and the narrative constituted by respondents' commentary on and conversations about those responses. The standardized responses have been coded numerically and provide the data for the quantitative statistical analyses in this book. In most structured interview studies, the surrounding narrative would be treated as static that interferes with the clear, crisp reception of respondents' quantifiable responses. Here, however, such comments have been treated as orchestration that enriches the standardized responses. As such, they provide the basis for the qualitative analysis presented in the case studies that form the heart of the book.

Perhaps because of this conversational interviewing technique, participants in the study often asked if they would hear from me again and expressed an interest in learning about the results of the research. In response, I sent out a follow-up mailing to all participating couples in the late fall and winter of 1992–93, approximately five years after the original interviews. This mailing included a summary of preliminary findings from the study and two brief follow-up questionnaires, one each for husband and wife (see Appendix A). Twenty-five of the original couples could not be located and their mailings were returned undelivered. Of the remaining 128 couples, 72 husbands and 73 wives returned their questionnaires.

The chapters that follow present data from both the original interviews and the follow-up questionnaires. These data take the form of both numerically coded, standardized responses, which have been subjected to statistical analyses, and narrative responses, which have been analyzed qualitatively. To keep the book accessible to readers who are not knowledgeable about statistics, the statistical analyses and their results have been described in easily understood language, and statistical tables have been kept to a minimum. Readers who would like more detailed information about the statistical analysis will find it, along with statistical tables, in Appendix B. The text of the book is organized primarily around qualitative analyses of representative cases, which both illustrate and extend the results of the statistical analyses. Through these case studies, you will meet many of the women and men who participated in this study and come to understand how they grapple with the issue of breadwinning. Whenever possible, these research participants have been allowed to speak for themselves, using words tape-recorded during their interviews. Names and identifying details have been altered to protect their privacy.

Theoretical Framework

My purpose in this book is not just to describe the allocation of breadwinning responsibility in the dual-earner marriages of Lewiston-Auburn, but also to explain that allocation, to illuminate how and why breadwinning is distinct from paid employment. Such elucidation requires both a set of empirical observations (in this case, the data from the interviews and follow-up questionnaires) and a theoretical framework for interpreting those observations. The theoretical framework that guides this analysis is one that views gender as a process of social construction. Using this framework, I examine the process through which husbands and wives construct gender by attaching gendered meanings to their paid employment. In particular, I look at the ways that they use breadwinning as a *gender boundary* that distinguishes men from women.

Social scientists have long defined gender as socially constructed, as a product of culture rather than of nature. For many readers, the idea of gender as socially constructed will call up one particularly well known version of this theoretical approach, the *gender roles model*. Gender roles theory distinguishes between sex, the biologically given categories of male and female, and gender, the culturally elaborated and learned sets of appropriate behaviors, attitudes, and personality traits attached to those biological categories. It assumes that these culturally prescribed behaviors, attitudes and personality traits constitute "gender roles" or "sex roles" that are learned (and internalized) primarily during childhood, forming unified wholes that are relatively stable once internalized. When people argue that changes in gender relations depend on "raising our children differently," they are drawing on the gender roles model. This understanding of gender has spread well beyond the community of social scientists; the concepts of gender roles or sex roles and discussions of role models and gender socialization are now part of common parlance.

The gender roles model is not the only theoretical explanation of the social construction of gender, however. Indeed, while it is the most prevalent understanding of gender among the general public, it has been widely critiqued by social scientists, and a number of alternative theoretical approaches have been developed to challenge it (Carrigan, Connell, and Lee, 1987; Connell, 1987; Ferree, 1990; Ferree and Hess, 1987; Hall, 1994; Lopata and Thorne, 1978; Lorber, 1994; Stacey and Thorne, 1985). It is one of these alternatives, which I refer to as the *gender construction model*, that provides the theoretical framework for this book.

The gender construction model differs from the gender roles model in many ways, but one of the most important is its treatment of the biological foundations of gender. Where the gender roles approach assumes that culturally defined gender roles rest on a foundation of natural sex categories, the gender construction model questions the naturalness and inevitability of sex categories and argues that the categories themselves must be created and given meaning through a process of social construction. Proponents of the gender construction model argue that there is no biological criterion that neatly divides human beings into the two exhaustive and mutually exclusive categories that we label "men" and "women" (Kessler and McKenna, 1978). Ferree (1990) points out that men and women are more like one another than either of them is like any other species, and notes that there are at least as many differences within the categories of male and female as there are between them. How is it, then, that the categories of male and female loom so large in our existence? Why is it that the first thing we want to know about a newly born human being (even before we ask whether it is whole and healthy) is whether it is a boy or a girl? How does gender come to be at the core of our experience? The gender construction model answers these questions by examining the routine and continuous construction of gender in the social interactions of everyday life.

The process of social construction by which gender becomes central to our experience of self and others can be divided into two distinct but related dynamics, gender differentiation and gender integration. Gender differentiation is the process by which human beings who are both similar and different in a myriad of ways are organized into the two distinct, highly salient, and nonoverlapping groups of male and female. Gender differentiation is not "natural"; children must learn this process. At an early age, they come to understand that gender is central to their self-definition in a way that other characteristics on which they differ from one another (e.g., eye color, hair color, height, age) are not. Only race assumes a similar importance. A number of years ago, while on a weekend visit to the home of friends, I spent a Saturday morning playing with their three-and-a-half-year-old twins, a boy and a girl. The little boy was endlessly fascinated with issues of gender and spent much of the morning repeatedly presenting me with a riddle that asked me to choose which "one of these things is not like the others." The answer he was looking for was that he was "not like the others" because he was a boy while his twin sister and I were both girls. Time after time, I playfully challenged this assumption and suggested alternative constructions of the situation: His sister was the one who was different because she was blonde, while he and I both had brown hair. He was the one who was different because he was wearing sneakers with Velcro closings while his sister and I were both wearing tie shoes. I was the one who was different because, while he and his sister were both children, I was a grown-up. And on it went. Throughout this game, my little friend never wavered in his insistence that gender was a much more fundamental difference than any of these others and that my alternatives were "silly" rather than serious responses to his riddle; he was practicing the process of gender differentiation.

In that process, we emphasize characteristics and experiences that are seen as distinctly masculine or feminine and generalize them in a way that masks the great variation within each gender group and obscures similarities between men and women. The construction of gender boundaries that distinguish "real men" from "real women" is critical to this process and a routine part of our daily lives. Children have difficulty learning how to construct gender boundaries "correctly." The distinctions seem capricious and arbitrary to them, and adults may be both amused and bemused as children draw rigid and exaggerated gender boundaries or just "get it wrong." I once had occasion to overhear a father and his five-year-old son in an altercation that hinged on just this kind of misapprehension of gender boundaries. The father had bought a new set of underwear, printed with a space exploration theme, as a special treat for his son, who was interested in space travel to the point of obsession. But, rather than being thrilled by his new undershirt and shorts, the son was refusing to wear them. The father cajoled; the son demurred. The father insisted; the son dug in his heels. As I listened, the battle escalated, until the child was sobbing and raging and the father was barely managing to control his temper. Finally, in exasperation, the father said, "I just don't understand why you won't wear these, Ricky; I thought you would like them. Explain it to me." "They have stars on them," Ricky wailed, "and stars are for girls!"

We associate this kind of confusion about gender boundaries with childhood. By the time we are older, we are no longer so self-conscious or troubled about the construction of gender; we have learned to take gender differentiation for granted. I often begin college classes on the social construction of gender by asking students to list differences and similarities between men and women. Invariably, they produce long lists of differences, but have trouble naming similarities. It is not that they are unaware of any similarities between men and women, but they have learned the lesson of gender differentiation, that to think about gender is to focus on difference (Bem, 1993).

The social construction of gender is not just about the differences between men and women, however; it is also about the relationship between the two gender groups. Gender integration is the articulation of a system of relationship between categories of people who have been constructed as different. The process of gender integration may specify how the distinct characteristics of each gender are to be combined in interpersonal relationships. If, for example, men are defined as physically strong and women as physically weak, an important part of a male-female relationship may be the man's responsibility to protect and help the woman. If women are defined as emotionally adept and "in touch with their feelings" in a way that men are not, the woman may bear responsibility for the emotional quality of a relationship and for helping the man to understand both her emotional responses and his own. If men are defined as having more urgent sexual needs than women, the rituals of heterosexual courtship may include the man's right to push for sexual satisfaction and the woman's responsibility to keep things from "going too far."

Gender integration involves not just individual male-female relationships, but also relations between the two gender groups. In our own culture, inequality is a defining element in those relations. It is because of this basic inequality that one can effectively insult a man by saying he is "like a woman," but that describing a woman as "like a man" is sometimes a compliment. Sociologist Barrie Thorne's research on gender relations among schoolchildren provides numerous examples of the processes of gender integration. In her observations of elementary school playgrounds, for example, Thorne has noted that boys' participation in girls' games almost always takes the form of a disruption in which the boys assert their superiority by expressing contempt for the girls and their game. By contrast, when girls join boys' games, their participation is generally earnest, and being accepted as good enough to play is a source of pride (Thorne, 1993). A similar, but more subtle, dynamic often governs informal interaction among adults. In a workplace cafeteria, when a lone woman sits down at a table where a group of men are engaged in conversation about a "male" topic (e.g., sports), the conversation usually continues, and the woman may try to join it by proving herself knowledgeable. When a lone man sits down with a group of women who are discussing a "female" topic (e.g., child rearing), however, the conversation is more likely to stop. The women will then introduce a new, more gender-neutral topic or allow the man to initiate a new topic himself.

The dynamics of gender differentiation and integration shape interaction within each gender group as well as between the two groups. All-male groups, for example, may engage in "hypermasculine" displays, using language and posture to highlight their differences from women and emphasizing their dominance over women by recounting heterosexual exploits in ways that render women as sexual objects rather than sexual partners. After all, men are more often called on to "prove their masculinity" to other men than to women. All-female groups also engage in the construction of gender. Groups of married women may express mystification at the behavior of their husbands, arguing that men are "like children." Women may also emphasize their reproductive difference from men by discussing (depending on their ages) menstruation, pregnancy and childbirth, or menopause. Because gender differentiation universalizes the characteristics of a gender group and masks differences within that group, a woman who is not married, does not menstruate, has never been pregnant, or has not yet reached menopause can be included in such conversations; but a man cannot.

You will notice that all these examples focus on everyday social interactions. This is not coincidental. The gender construction perspective argues that gender must be continually created and re-created in everyday life (West and Zimmerman, 1987) through a dynamic and often contentious process of interaction and negotiation. Thus, it is not just that gender differentiation and integration *affect* interactions like those described above, but also that such interactions constitute gender differentiation and integration. As we interact with one another every day, we continually and actively construct gender categories, delineating their characteristics, their importance, and their relationship to one another.

This book examines the routine construction of gender in the everyday lives of 306 ordinary women and men, focusing particularly on their use of breadwinning as a gender boundary. It demonstrates that these dual-earner couples are not simply enacting gender scripts that were learned during childhood, but are actively constructing gendered meaning. They do so through a dynamic process of negotiation, collaboration, and contestation, a process in which they must deal with gender ideologies, the institutionalization of gender in social structures, and the ever-changing material conditions of their own lives.

Plan of the Book

The chapters that follow analyze breadwinning as part of the routine social construction of gender, considering how the meaning attached to husbands' and wives' employment and the use of breadwinning as a gender boundary contribute to the dynamics of gender differentiation and integration. Chapter 2 develops the theoretical framework of the analysis, presenting the gender construction perspective in more detail and elaborating the theoretical concept of gender boundaries.

Chapters 3 and 4 use case studies to examine how dual-earner wives and husbands, respectively, construct the meaning of the wives' employment and the allocation of breadwinning responsibility in their marriages. These chapters define typical constructions of breadwinning, consider the factors that influence these constructions, and develop an analysis of breadwinning as a gender boundary. Chapter 3 focuses on wives' orientations to breadwinning, examining the persistence of breadwinning as a gender boundary, the variety of ways in which these women actively construct that boundary, and the importance of adult experiences and circumstances in shaping those constructions. Chapter 4 undertakes a similar analysis for husbands. Here, I argue that the persistence of breadwinning as a gender boundary constrains men's constructions, and I focus on the role of husband-wife negotiations in the construction of gender.

Chapters 5 and 6 further explore these dynamics of gender construction by taking couples, rather than individuals, as the unit of analysis and by examining changes over time in couples' use of breadwinning as a gender boundary. Chapter 5 examines the extent to which the construction of gender is a collaborative process, focusing on couples who have developed a shared understanding of the meaning of breadwinning in the system of gender relations. Using data from the follow-up study, this chapter also explores the surprising plasticity of these constructions of breadwinning. Chapter 6 investigates contention in the construction of gender. It concentrates on couples who disagree about the use of breadwinning as a gender boundary, and it further develops our understanding of how and why constructions of gender change over time.

Chapters 7 and 8 move the analysis to a broader plane. Chapter 7 considers the place of breadwinning in a larger system of gender boundaries by exploring the relationship between breadwinning and mothering. This exploration demonstrates the subtle interaction of collaboration and contention in the social construction of gender. Finally, in Chapter 8, I return to the questions with which this book began, consolidating our understanding of breadwinning as a gender boundary and further developing a more general theory of gender construction.

2

Gender Boundaries and the Social Construction of Gender

No fact, empirical observation, or set of data ever stands alone; it is always interpreted. Theories are interpretive tools, cognitive frameworks that we can use to understand and make sense of our experiences and observations. What's more, theories also guide our observations, telling us what questions to ask and what phenomena to pay attention to.

This is true of both formal scientific inquiry and the less systematic observations of daily life. Suppose, for example, that you find yourself suffering from a stomachache. You will consider whether the cause is likely to be indigestion, a hangover, the flu, food poisoning, or appendicitis. You will look for evidence to support or refute any of these possibilities, and, based on your analysis, you will decide whether to ignore the pain, take an over-the-counter medicine, crawl into bed, go to the doctor, or call an ambulance. The questions you ask yourself and the observations you make as part of this decision-making process will be shaped by a medical theory that interprets pain as a symptom of illness or injury. Imagine, however, that the theoretical framework you brought to this situation was not medical, but spiritual—one that regarded physical pain as punishment for a moral transgression. In that case, you would ask very different questions, make different observations, and consider different options for responding to your stomachache.

Our understandings of gender are similarly shaped by theoretical frameworks. Whether we even see a phenomenon like breadwinning as gendered, what questions we ask about it, which observations we make, and how we understand those observations will all depend on the theoretical framework that guides the inquiry. Let us turn, then, to the theoretical perspective that I think best illuminates breadwinning as a gendered phenomenon, gender construction theory.

Gender Construction Theory

As we saw in Chapter 1, gender construction theory focuses on the processes of social construction that create gender as a fundamental feature of social life. Such processes are assumed to be ubiquitous and embedded in the daily round of routine interactions. Gender construction theory thus conceptualizes gender as a system of social relations, not as a characteristic or attribute of individuals.

There are several forms of gender construction theory, and one way these vary is in the extent to which they regard the social construction of gender as resting on a foundation of "natural," biological sex difference (Nicholson, 1994). The account I am developing here assumes that the gender system does *not* rest on a stable biological foundation—in other words, that biological characteristics do not divide human beings neatly, inevitably, and immutably into the two distinct, exhaustive, and non-overlapping categories of male and female (Kessler and McKenna, 1978). On the contrary, it is the very existence of these seemingly natural, non-overlapping, and immutable categories that is produced through social construction. Even if biological measurement could identify two distinct categories, this biological information is not usually accessible as part of social interaction and cannot explain the social importance of gender. (We do not routinely check one another's genitals, gonads, chromosomes, or hormone levels.) Gender, then, is not a set of categories in which membership is automatically ascribed, but a system of categorization that must be achieved, constructed through social interaction (West and Zimmerman, 1987).

I am not arguing here that biological sex *characteristics* are a social fiction; it is the organization of those characteristics into strictly dichotomous sex *categories* and the importance attached to those categories in social interaction and social structure that I am concerned with. A comparison with another set of biological characteristics may help to clarify this point. Let's consider eye color. Like sex characteristics, eye color is biological, largely beyond the control of the individual. And, like sex characteristics, eye color tends to divide the population into two broad categories, those with light eyes (in the United States, predominantly blue) and those with dark eyes (in the United States, primarily brown). Here, however, the similarity ends. We do not define eye color as a fundamental human characteristic. Although we could, we don't divide ourselves into two, and only two, eye color categories. We don't assign people to one category or the other in infancy, make a big deal about which eye color category they're in, give them names that reflect their eye color, or expect eye color category to shape virtually every aspect of their lives. We don't find it impossible to interact with people if we can't tell their eye color (e.g., on the telephone), and we aren't scandalized if people alter their eye color (e.g., with tinted contact lenses). Rather than finding anomalous eye colors (e.g., green) a source of discomfort, we are likely to find them attractive. Gender construction theorists would argue that the organization of social life around sex characteristics is no more inevitable than the organization of social life around eye color. A system of social relations based on sex characteristics (the gender system) does not naturally happen; it is something we must work to create.

But gender categories and gender relations are a fundamental part of social structure and social interaction. By this I mean that they seem to be built into every aspect of our society. Our major social institutions—family, work, politics, religion—are all structured by gender: We have different expectations of mothers and fathers; women and men work at different kinds of jobs; men make up the vast majority of public officials (although they are a minority of voters); and many organized religions limit women's access to positions of authority. Our everyday interactions are also structured by gender. If you've ever been in the situation of being unsure whether another person was a man or a woman, you probably found it very difficult (if not impossible) to interact with that person until this question had been resolved. Even our interactions with infants often begin with an attempt to determine whether they are boys or girls.

If gender categories are not biologically given but are fundamental to society, then the process of gender construction must be central to social life. Sociologist Myra Marx Ferree (1990: 868–69) has argued that "the fundamental question [of the gender construction model] is how the illusion of a gender dichotomy is constructed and maintained in the face of between-sex similarity and within-sex difference." The answer, according to gender construction theory, is that the gender system must be continually created and re-created. Theorists Candace West and Don Zimmerman have emphasized the active nature of this process by using the phrase "doing gender" to describe it. "Doing gender," they explain, "means creating differences between girls and boys and women and men, differences that are not natural, essential, or biological" (West and Zimmerman, 1987: 137). In studying this process of "doing gender," gender construction theorists often focus on routine, everyday social interaction. It is not that such interaction is the only, or even the primary, site of gender construction; institutional arrangements are also critical to the construction and maintenance of the gender system. But it is in the examination of routine, everyday experience that we begin to see just how ubiquitous the process of constructing gender is.

As an example, let's consider some of the routine experiences of my own life. I begin the day by getting showered and dressed. This involves removing my nightgown (a garment with a tucked bodice and a wide ruffle at the hem that would only be considered appropriate for a woman), washing with a delicately rose-scented soap, and dressing in garments that were chosen from the women's racks of my favorite store and that are designed in a style and color that would be considered inappropriate for a man. I put some moisturizer (a product designed to stave off wrinkles and marketed specifically for women) on my face, add a touch of eye shadow and some lipstick, and put on my glasses (in frames styled specifically for women). I get to my office about an hour before my first class meets and spend the time completing my class preparation; this involves, among other things, taking notes in a handwriting that most observers would label distinctly "feminine." As I teach my class, I stand, move, and use language and gestures in ways that distinguish me from my male colleagues. As I meet with students during my office hours, my posture also marks me as a woman; I sit with my legs crossed at the knees or ankles, or with legs together and one foot slightly in front of the other—but never with my knees spread wide apart, a posture common among the male students who come in to meet with me. At a committee meeting in the late afternoon, I continue to display appropriately feminine posture, language, and gestures, and I also raise a concern about how a proposed new policy will affect women faculty. As I ride a crowded bus home at the end of the day, I keep my knees together, my elbows close to my body, and my briefcase and purse on my lap, so as to make myself small and infringe as little as possible on the space of the stranger who sits beside me. This contrasts noticeably with the behavior of my male seatmate; he sprawls, knees apart, one arm resting on the back of the seat, expanding, claiming his rightful portion (and then some) of our shared space.

Throughout the day, even as I carry out activities that are not obviously gendered (dressing, preparing for class, teaching, meeting with students, attending meetings, riding public transportation), I "do gender," constructing myself as a woman and helping to create a system of gender relations that rests on gender difference. Nor am I unusual in this; an analysis of your own activities would undoubtedly reveal similar practices. The construction of gender is embedded in the routines of our daily lives.

To say that the construction of gender is routine, however, is not to say that the gender system is inevitably and invariably reproduced. On the contrary, it is a contested system that is open to challenge and redefinition, and, as such, a system that depends on the active involvement of individuals for its shape and its maintenance. Thus, although my routine construction of gender may seem automatic, I am an active agent in the process; I have some choice about the ways in which and the extent to which I construct myself as womanly. I may or may not choose to act as an advocate for women at committee meetings (although, if I am the only woman on the committee and others repeatedly ask me for "the woman's perspective," I may find it difficult to demur). Over the years, I have rebelled against some of the routines of "doing" femininity: I have rejected high-heeled shoes, elaborate hairstyles, most makeup, and other elements of feminine dress and grooming that I find uncomfortable and a nuisance. On occasion, I have even been known to "accidentally" elbow the stranger sitting next to me on the bus as he sprawls across the center line of the seat. Even as I make sure that those around me know that I am a woman, I may challenge what it means to be a woman.

Because the gender system is open to challenge, the construction of gender involves negotiation (Gerson and Peiss, 1985). This negotiation may be quite explicit (as when a husband and wife sit down to discuss the division of household labor), or it may be indirect (as when my seatmate and I jostle to determine our relative shares of space on the bus). Negotiations may be carried out between individuals (a man and woman deciding who will pay for a dinner date) or between groups (elementary school boys and girls working out the gendered allocation of playground space). They may be informal discussions between those involved or a matter for some kind of official arbitration or mediation (as when a group of women brings a class action to gain membership in an all-male organization).

Although gender is created through a continual process of negotiation and social construction, however, men and women are not completely free agents in this process. There are constraints that limit their choices. Those who contest the system of gender relations may find themselves subject to negative social sanctions. Moreover, because the gender system is a system of inequality, some parties come to gender negotiations with more resources and bargaining power than do others. Individuals are also constrained because the existing gender system is institutionalized in the form of social structures. So, when gender construction theorists emphasize human agency and negotiation as important factors in the creation of the gender system, they do not mean that the wage gap between men and women or employed women's disproportionate responsibility for housework and child care are simply the consequences of individual choice. A woman who earns $15,000, compared with her husband's $25,000, may feel that her substantial financial contribution entitles her to more help from him with housework, and she may try to negotiate a more equal sharing of domestic labor. At the same time, though, the realization that she could barely support herself and her children above the poverty level without her husband's income will probably keep her from pushing her challenge if it seems to risk the stability of the marriage. The occupational structure that pays her clerical occupation less than his blue-collar trade, the greater negotiating power that his higher income confers, and the social stigma and financial hardship that accompany divorce for women all constrain her ability to contest and renegotiate the construction of gender.

Nevertheless, even here, the processual nature of gender construction is evident. The structural constraints that limit challenge and negotiation are themselves contested and open to redefinition. Economic inequality between men and women has been one of the most powerful constraints on women's ability to negotiate gender change, but that economic inequality has itself been contested by women. Indeed, challenging economic inequality has been one of the central foci of the late-twentieth-century feminist movement, and that challenge has succeeded in diminishing some forms of inequality, thus reducing the structural constraints on women.

The gender system as conceived by the gender construction model is dynamic. It is always being challenged, contested, renegotiated, dismantled, and reconstructed. We can take "snapshots" of the system as it is in a given historical moment, social location, or situation, but we should not mistake these freeze-frames for a representation of a stable, reified structure. The amount of ferment in the system may vary across time and space, but, according to gender construction theory, the gender system is always being constructed and reconstructed because gender is, by definition, a process.

The theory of gender presented here is very different from the one that guides much lay thinking about gender. That theory, the gender roles model, locates the roots of the gender system in "gender roles" or "sex roles," culturally defined sets of behaviors, attitudes, and personality traits prescribed as appropriate for members of a particular sex category. Gender roles, according to the most widely held version of this theory, are culturally defined and vary greatly from one culture to the next, but they often seem "natural" because they are holistic, encompassing virtually all aspects of our lives, and because they are learned and deeply internalized during the process of childhood socialization (Oakley, 1972). Because gender role socialization begins at an early age and encompasses so much of the child's life, this theory argues, gender roles are deeply rooted and resistant to change. As a result, an individual's gender role behaviors, attitudes, and personality traits are not only generally consistent with one another, they are also fairly stable once formed. Like other aspects of culture, gender roles change in a process that is usually slow and incremental, most often as members of each generation teach their children somewhat different gender attitudes than the adults have themselves been able to enact and as those new attitudes are subsequently reflected in the next generation's behavior. Such change is likely to be uneven, with some segments of society adopting the changed roles before others do (Young and Willmott, 1975).

It is important to emphasize that the gender roles and gender construction models are theories, sets of propositions that we can use to make sense of reality. And, like all theories, they are judged by how useful they are for explaining the world around us. The gender roles model caught on rapidly in the 1970s and has persisted since then because it resonates for us, helping us to make sense of our own experiences. However, many aspects of gender have not been well explained by the gender roles model. For many of these, the gender construction model proves to be more illuminating.

Because the gender construction perspective that guides this inquiry into breadwinning makes very different assumptions, asks different questions, and highlights different phenomena than does the more conventional gender roles perspective, readers who are not familiar with the gender construction model may find a systematic comparison of these two theoretical frameworks useful. Both assume that gender is a social product, something that is culturally, not biologically, defined. Beyond this shared basic assumption, however, the two models part company.

Where the gender roles model focuses on the culturally defined *content* of gender difference (the behaviors, attitudes, and personality traits that constitute the masculine and feminine roles), the gender construction model is concerned primarily with the *process* of gender differentiation (the continual creation and re-creation of gender difference through social interaction by active agents). To the extent that the gender roles model emphasizes process, it is a process of childhood socialization in which individual children are viewed more often as objects than as active agents. Gender roles theory posits a relatively stable gender system, one based on holistic, all-encompassing gender roles made up of internally consistent and mutually reinforcing behaviors, attitudes, and personality traits. The gender construction model, however, envisions a dynamic, fragmented gender system that is full of contradictions and inconsistencies. The content of gender difference is contested, shifting, subject to continual challenge and negotiation, and always in the process of creation and re-creation. The only constant in this system is the process of gender differentiation itself. Moreover—unlike gender roles theory, which sometimes sees men and women as equally constrained by gender socialization—the gender construction model never loses sight of the proposition that gender is, at its base, a system of inequality. Although both men and women are active agents in the construction and negotiation of gender, they are not equal agents. Gender construction takes place in a context of unequal power and of social structures that institutionalize and reinforce male hegemony.

If we wanted a visual image to represent the gender system as conceived by the gender roles model, we might choose two profiles in silhouette, one of a man and the other of a woman. Each figure is a separate whole, indicating both the distinct biological categories on which gender roles are assumed to be built and the holistic nature of these roles. The two profiles face each other, reflecting the construction of the masculine and feminine roles as opposites. The image itself is static.

The image presented by the gender construction model is strikingly different. We can replace the facing profiles with the visual image of a web. The strands in the web are gender boundaries, and they are myriad. Although each boundary is distinct, they are linked in complex and inconsistent ways. Some run parallel and reinforce one another; others seem to run at cross-purposes and to contradict one another. The web does not provide the solid distinction between men and women that the two profiles do. It is diaphanous and permeable. Moreover, this is not a static image, but a motion picture. As if stirred by a breeze, the web remains anchored in place, but is fluid and moving. Boundaries shift; some strands break. At the same time, the web is always under construction; old strands are repaired or reinforced and new ones are added. The web varies across time, space, and circumstances not only in content, but also in density (the number of individual boundaries that are simultaneously deployed) and in the thickness and rigidity of individual boundaries. Thus, it may be almost impenetrable in some times, places, and circumstances, while it creates only the barest differentiation between men and women in others. This is a dynamic image, one that emphasizes contradiction, challenge, and change.

Gender Boundaries

In drawing the image of a complex and dynamic web to represent the gender construction model, I identified the strands of this web as gender boundaries. Because these boundaries are central to the process of gender construction, an understanding of that process requires further development of the gender boundaries concept.

The concept of gender boundaries was introduced in 1985 by Judith Gerson and Kathy Peiss, who defined them as "the complex structures— physical, social, ideological, and psychological—which establish differences and commonalities between women and men, among women, and among men" (Gerson and Peiss, 1985: 317). They argued that viewing gender in terms of boundaries provided a number of advantages, including the ability to conceptualize a multiplicity of boundaries rather than bifurcated gender categories and the suggestion of permeability rather than rigid gender differences. Gerson and Peiss's conceptualization of gender clearly struck a chord with many scholars; their article is frequently cited, and it has become commonplace for gender scholars to invoke "boundaries" as a metaphor. However, few have worked on the theoretical development of the boundaries concept or used it systematically in their analyses. (For important exceptions, see Epstein, 1989, 1992, and Thorne, 1993.) In this book I intend to do both, furthering the development of the gender boundaries concept as I use it to illuminate the gendered construction of breadwinning.

In my development of gender boundaries as a theoretical concept, I both build on and depart from Gerson and Peiss's formulation. A pivotal departure is my definition of the concept; I define a gender boundary as anything that marks, and thereby constructs, the difference between "real men" and "real women." I argue that these boundaries are thus central to the process through which (1) human beings in all their variety are divided into the two sharply distinct categories of "men" and "women," (2) that division is made a fundamental feature of society and social interaction, and (3) relations between these two groups are defined so as to create a system of inequality. Like Gerson and Peiss, I believe that we must conceptualize the boundaries that construct gender difference as multiple; I also believe that we must think about these various gender boundaries as in dynamic relationship to one another. Individual strands (gender boundaries) in the web of gender difference can be moved, re-arranged, or even broken without necessarily weakening the structure as a whole.

Gender boundaries are ubiquitous, a part of much of our daily life experience, and come in a variety of types. One of the most visible types is that which marks a particular space as men's or women's "territory." One obvious example of a spatial boundary is the distinction between men's and women's public rest rooms. Even when, as is often the case in restaurants and at service stations, there are only two rest rooms, they are identical, and each can only be used by one person at a time and can be locked while in use, they are almost always marked as one for men and one for women. This spatial differentiation does not simply acknowledge biological difference between men and women; rather, it *creates* a sense that women and men are fundamentally different. So powerful is the sense of difference thus created that, if two women or two men approach two such empty bathrooms, they will almost always take turns using the appropriately marked one, even as the other stands empty.

There are many other gender-marked spaces, most of them less explicit. I remember my acute embarrassment when, as a twelve-year-old, I was assigned the task of taking my two-year-old brother for his first haircut and thus was required to enter the male space of the barbershop. A man may feel similarly uncomfortable going into a hairdressing establishment, even though there is no sign on the door that says Women Only. Observers of schoolchildren have long noted their propensity for creating spatial gender boundaries by demarcating girls' and boys' sections of the playground or by establishing separate girls' and boys' tables in the cafeteria (Thorne, 1993). Similarly, male and female factory workers stepping outside during a break may claim separate corners of the building as gendered space.

Such spatial gender boundaries are just the proverbial tip of the iceberg. We also use occupational boundaries to distinguish men from women. Nursing, secretarial work, hairdressing, social work, and nursery school teaching are all female-marked occupations. It is not that men can't enter these occupations; they can and do. But, where a woman's choice of such an occupation is unremarkable and confirms her womanliness, a man in one of them is likely to find that his manliness is suspect and that he is called on to explain his choice. Similarly, such occupations as carpenter, surgeon, boilermaker, police officer, and prize-fighter are marked as male, and a woman who crosses one of these occupational gender boundaries may find she must make extra efforts to demonstrate that she is a "real woman."

We also divide women and men in terms of interests and skills. Three friends of mine, two men and a woman, once found themselves in a car that had broken down on the way home from work. The woman, the owner of the car and long accustomed to its idiosyncrasies, got out to look under the hood and see if she could remedy the problem. The two men were left sitting inside, feeling discomfited and a bit "unmanly" because knowledge about cars is supposed to be a men's skill. As a way of easing the tension, one turned to the other and quipped, "Aren't we supposed to talk about clothes or something?" In this way, he noted that they were on the right side of one gender boundary (interest in fashion) even though another (knowledge about cars) was being breached.

Personal qualities and personality traits are additional boundaries used to differentiate men and women. We may define women as more intuitive or emotionally expressive, men as more competitive and aggressive. Such personal qualities are deeply held and strongly resonant gender boundaries for many in our culture, and they loom large on the lists of gender differences that my students produce in class. Indeed, the importance of these boundaries is reflected in the enormous impact of a number of books that have provided social science affirmation of them—books such as Nancy Chodorow's (1978) *The Reproduction of Mothering* (about male-female personality differences), Carol Gilligan's (1981) *In a Different Voice* (about men's and women's different approaches to moral reasoning), and Deborah Tannen's (1990) *You Just Don't Understand* (about men's and women's different communication styles).

It could be said, however, that none of the gender boundaries discussed thus far is as pervasive as our use of appearance and personal grooming to distinguish between "real men" and "real women." These visible boundaries assume a particular importance because we often use them to assign individuals to one or the other gender category as a prelude to social interaction. We expect women and men to look different—to wear different articles of clothing (skirts and scarves versus business suits and neckties), different styles of clothing (wing tips versus high heels), and different colors of clothing (hunter green, burgundy, russet tweed, and charcoal heather sweaters for men; lilac heather, rose heather, and light yellow for women).* We also make distinctions in grooming habits (women shave leg and underarm hair, but men don't; men shave facial hair, but women who have facial hair use a different method of removal; women pluck their eyebrows, but men don't) and in the use of cosmetics (for the most part, women use them, but men don't). We differentiate women and men by their hairstyles and by their use of jewelry (different styles of watches, rings, and necklaces; women can wear hair adornments, but men can't). Indeed, when we go to the optician to have a new prescription for eyeglasses filled, we take it for granted that the eyeglass frames are organized not by head size, but by gender!**

Grooming is a form of behavior, and other types of behavior, too, are used as boundaries in the construction of gender. Women and men walk differently, sit differently, use different gestures when they speak. Crying may be marked as a womanly behavior, emotional stoicism or direct expression of anger as manly. If a man who is insulted by another man responds with a punch to the mouth, he may be regarded as a hothead, but not as unmanly. A woman who rears back and throws a punch at someone who insults her, however, will provoke more than raised eyebrows and may find that her womanliness is called into question. Fist fighting is a behavioral gender boundary that distinguishes men from women.

Even when men and women routinely engage in the same behavior, that behavior may be perceived and interpreted differently. This is the most subtle type of gender boundary. During the 1980s, a number of women's magazines called attention to such gendered interpretation of behavior by publishing tongue-in-cheek analyses of how to tell a businessman from a businesswoman, based on work by Natasha Josefowitz (1980). These offerings typically consisted of one page divided into two columns in which differently gendered interpretations of the same behavior were presented side by side. "He's not in the office; he must be meeting customers," one column would say, and the parallel would read, "She's not in the office; she must be out shopping." "He recognizes a good opportunity," one column would offer as an explanation of leaving for a better job, while the other column would assert, "She's undependable."

---

* L. L. Bean catalog, fall 1995.
** A national chain of "eyewear" retailers recently introduced (and extensively advertised) the practice of sizing their eyeglass frames. A customer entering the store, however, quickly discovers that, while the sizes are marked on individual frames, these are distributed randomly on shelves that are organized not by size, but by men's styles and women's styles.

Such gendered interpretations are pervasive as well as subtle and seem to begin virtually at birth. During the 1970s, a number of social scientists conducted experiments which demonstrated that adults reacted to infants differently depending on whether they thought the infants were boys or girls. In one study, the subjects were shown a videotape that included a sequence of an infant crying. Over and over again, those who were told the infant was a girl interpreted the crying as fear, while those who were told it was a boy interpreted the crying as anger—although all had seen the same tape (Condry and Condry, 1976).

Nor are such differential interpretations limited to babies; they also shape our perceptions of adults. Let's return to the example in Chapter 1 of the two lighted windows in which we can see adults putting small children to bed. Now let's suppose that one of these adults is the mother of the child she is tending, and the other is the father of the child he is caring for. Does it seem obvious to you that the mother is engaging in routine parenting and the father is "babysitting"? If so, you are using different interpretations of the same behavior to construct a gender boundary.

Dividing gender boundaries by type is just one way of classifying and analyzing them. Epstein (1989) has suggested that gender boundaries may operate on a number of different levels, including social-psychological (where they may become incorporated into the sense of self), structural (where they may be institutionalized), and cultural (where they may be enmeshed in larger cultural patterns and enforced by informal sanctions). Thus, an individual woman may actively construct gender by wearing "feminine" clothing to work because (1) she chooses such clothes to express her sense of self, (2) such clothes are mandated by a formal dress code that, for example, prohibits slacks as "unprofessional" dress for women, or (3) this is the prevailing and expected style of dress for women at her place of employment and to dress otherwise is to create problems in her interactions with superiors, co-workers, and clients or customers. Being aware of the various levels on which gender boundaries operate can help us to identify both elements of choice and elements of constraint or coercion in the construction of gender.

We can also analyze gender boundaries by comparing them in terms of a number of important variables. Individual gender boundaries may differ, for example, in the extent to which they are institutionalized, or built into the social structure. Men's and women's rest rooms create a highly institutionalized gender boundary. They are formally demarcated, expected in public places (as contrasted to private homes, which, even if they have two bathrooms, do not have them marked Men and Women), and in some cases even required by law. The use of hair ornaments is a much less institutionalized gender boundary; although their advertising, the pictures on their packages, and their location in stores often mark hair ornaments as being for women, the wrapping or tag doesn't actually say For Women, and there are certainly no laws prescribing or prohibiting their use.

Institutionalization is not a stable feature of a gender boundary; it can change over time. Occupational gender boundaries, for example, are much less institutionalized today than they were 30 years ago, when newspapers routinely printed separate "help wanted" sections for men and women and employment agencies kept separate listings of male and female jobs. Indeed, one could argue that occupational boundaries have been deinstitutionalized in the sense that such practices have since been declared illegal.

Gender boundaries also vary in permeability. "Permeable" is a term that is often used to describe membranes in the body; although they act as partial barriers, certain substances can pass through them. When we say a gender boundary is permeable, we mean it is not an impregnable wall separating men from women, but more like a national border, a boundary that can be crossed. And just as some national borders are more easily crossed than others, some gender boundaries are more permeable than others. If we think about clothing, for example, it is quickly apparent that the wearing of neckties is a more permeable gender boundary than the wearing of skirts. Similarly, while both police work and prizefighting are occupational gender boundaries, one is more permeable than the other; a woman will have an easier time getting accepted into the police academy than onto the pro boxing circuit.

To say that a gender boundary is permeable is not necessarily to say that it can be crossed equally easily in both directions. On the contrary, most gender boundaries seem to be asymmetrically permeable, more open to crossing in one direction than the other. The wearing of skirts is a case in point; a woman can cross this boundary by wearing pants and still be considered a "real woman," but a man who crosses it will find it almost impossible to retain the status of "real man."*

---

* The exception is in cases where gender boundaries are crossed in a ritual or joking way that clearly marks the act as exceptional (e.g., a man goes to a Halloween party dressed as a woman). Thorne (1993) refers to this kind of marked crossing of gender boundaries as "borderwork" and distinguishes it from "real crossings." Borderwork, she argues, actually serves to highlight and reinforce gender boundaries.

Related to both institutionalization and permeability is yet another dimension that we can use to analyze gender boundaries: how severely a breaching of a boundary will be sanctioned. Parents whose son repeatedly shows up at nursery school wearing barrettes in his hair may well be reprimanded by the teachers, but they probably won't be asked to remove their child from the school. Parents who routinely send their son to nursery school wearing a dress, however, can expect swifter and more severe reprisals. They may be presented with an ultimatum of dressing their child "appropriately" or having him barred from the school. And if they insist on their right to let him wear dresses, they may be reported to the authorities as unfit parents. Some spatial boundaries may also carry more severe sanctions than others. At the college where I teach, a "faculty lounge" is used regularly as a gathering place by a group of faculty men; its use has created a spatial boundary that differentiates men from women. A faculty woman who enters the lounge will be ignored and made to feel that her presence is unwelcome, but she will not experience any overt threats, and no one will ask her to leave. A woman entering some male bars, by contrast, may find herself threatened with sexual violence that the men in the bar consider justified by her invasion of "their" space. A man who enters a women's rest room may find that someone calls the police.

Gender boundaries also vary by how universally they are used as markers of gender difference within a society. In the United States, for example, the wearing of skirts is almost completely limited to women and girls. When men or boys do wear something that looks like a skirt, the occasion is usually ceremonial and the garment will probably be called by a different name (e.g., the "christening gown" worn by a baby boy for his baptism, the "kilt" worn by a bagpiper in a parade, the "cassock" worn by a Catholic priest during religious rites). Other gender boundaries, however, may be less universally imposed, deployed by some groups within the society but not by others. Earrings provide an interesting example. It used to be the case that only women wore earrings as a routine part of their attire, making earrings a fairly universal gender boundary. Among some groups in the culture, earrings continue to be regarded as feminine accessories. Among other groups, however, male use of earrings has become commonplace.* Some gender boundaries may be

---

* Since, even here, men wear earrings differently from women, it would be more accurate to say that this gender boundary has been moved in these groups than that it has been eliminated.

available as part of the cultural repertoire, but whether or not they are invoked may be a matter for negotiation at the interpersonal level. Some formerly all-male voluntary organizations, for example, may now let local chapters decide whether they will retain their masculine character or open up their membership to women. Similarly, whether or not a father's care for his young child is defined within the family as indistinguishable from the mother's care or is clearly differentiated as "babysitting" will probably be decided primarily by negotiation between the two parents.

Thus far, we have been considering institutionalization, permeability, sanctions, and universality as characteristics that differentiate gender boundaries from one another. It is also possible, however, to analyze how the construction of gender boundaries differs from one situation to another. This is the issue of salience. Thorne (1993) discusses salience at some length, arguing that in some situations, gender difference is important and gender boundaries are deployed, while in other situations, gender difference is unimportant and gender boundaries are not deployed. Her analysis of salience thus treats the situation as the unit of analysis and gender boundaries as collective. We can take the analysis further by considering the interaction between the situation and the individual boundary; it seems likely that the situation will influence which gender boundaries are more important to the construction of gender difference.

While variability in type, institutionalization, permeability, sanctions, universality, and salience is important in analyzing gender boundaries, we should not lose sight of the common features that define those boundaries. First, gender boundaries are always used to differentiate "real men" and "real women." Second, they are never absolute barriers; they are always, to some extent, permeable (although the degree of permeability varies). Third, they are not fixed; they are always actively constructed as part of a dynamic system of gender construction, and, as such, they are open to challenge and subject to negotiation. Fourth, although we can highlight individual gender boundaries for purposes of analysis, a gender boundary never stands alone; it is always part of a web of interconnected boundaries.

Breadwinning as a Gender Boundary

How does the gender boundary of breadwinning fit into the more general analysis provided above? First of all, it is one of those most subtle of gender boundaries that differentiate men and women by interpreting similar behavior (in this case, paid employment) differently. There is evidence that, once breadwinning became defined as a distinctively male responsibility in the nineteenth century, the belief that men should be breadwinners began to color interpretations of men's and women's employment. For example, sociologist Christine Bose (1987) has noted that U.S. census enumerators of the late nineteenth century asked not whether a respondent was employed, but what his or her "usual task" was. As a consequence, many employed wives were recorded as housewives, and census data systematically underestimated the extent of women's wage earning. The result was to emphasize differences between men and women, to minimize the importance of wives' wage earning, and to exaggerate and help to institutionalize male financial responsibility for families.

The use of breadwinning to differentiate men's and women's employment persists in the late twentieth century, but how prevalent is it, and what are the factors that shape its construction? In the early years of the twentieth century, the breadwinning boundary was reinforced by structures that institutionalized it: protective labor laws that limited women's occupations, work hours, and working conditions and established lower minimum wages for women than for men; a family wage movement that worked for a male wage sufficient to support a family; and laws that held men responsible for support of their families. Institutionalization of male responsibility for breadwinning has lessened considerably in the years since, but some forms of it remain. It is easier for a wife than for a husband to bring a suit for nonsupport; welfare laws in most states continue to define a woman as eligible for Aid to Families with Dependent Children only if she has no husband to support her; and traces of protective labor laws and the family wage movement persist in the forms of marked occupational segregation by gender and the wage gap between men and women.

This book, however, focuses not so much on the structural aspects of breadwinning as a gender boundary as on the construction of that boundary in interpersonal interaction. I will show that the use of breadwinning as a gender boundary is common, even among dual-earner couples, that the meanings these husbands and wives attach to their employment are actively constructed through a complex process of negotiation, and that maintaining the breadwinning boundary often involves making it permeable. Breadwinning is often a contested boundary, and its construction is remarkably plastic. The salience of breadwinning as a gender boundary and the negotiations about its construction are shaped by the circumstances of couples' lives.

3

Employed Wives'
Constructions of Breadwinning

Let us examine how gender construction theory highlights aspects of wives' employment that other perspectives on gender have obscured. During the heyday of the gender roles model, students of gender paid little attention to the issue of breadwinning. Indeed, when feminist scholars began to explore changes in gender-specialized family roles, they focused almost entirely on the female homemaker role, generating a whole host of studies considering whether, when, or under what circumstances men take on the traditionally female responsibilities for housework and child care (Berk, 1985; Hochschild, 1989; Model, 1982; Pleck, 1983, 1985).

It is not that gender roles theory rendered breadwinning itself invisible. On the contrary, scholars using the gender roles perspective helped us to see responsibility for providing as a socially prescribed part of what it means to be a man (Bernard, 1981; Filene, 1981; Grønseth, 1972; Hood, 1983; Slocum and Nye, 1976). But the underlying assumptions of gender roles theory tended to deflect attention away from systematic study of changes in gendered responsibility for breadwinning. Remember that this model emphasizes the congruence of behavior, attitudes, and personality; the importance of childhood socialization; and the stability of individuals' approaches to gender. This perspective led researchers studying the growing numbers of women (particularly married women with children) in the paid labor force in the 1970s to assume that they were observing a new breed of women who had been socialized into an egalitarian version of gender roles. Because behavior and attitudes were assumed to be congruent, the very presence of these women in the work force was seen as evidence that they rejected the traditional gender specializations of homemaker and breadwinner. As a result, considerable research focused on the childhood conditions that predicted adult labor force participation for women, but little research asked what that participation meant to this new group of workers. Employed wives were simply assumed to be family breadwinners.

Because gender construction theory does not share these assumptions, it regards employed wives' orientations to breadwinning as an issue to be studied. Its focus on the active construction of gendered meaning highlights the distinction between paid employment and breadwinning and raises questions about the meanings that wives attach to their employment. In this chapter, I address these questions by analyzing data from interviews with 153 dual-earner wives, interviews that focused specifically on the issue of breadwinning.

These wives are a fairly heterogeneous group. When they were interviewed in 1987–88, their ages ranged from 20 to 59 with a median of 37, and their educations ranged from less than eighth-grade level to graduate and professional levels, with a median of thirteen years of formal schooling. They lived in households with annual incomes ranging from less than $20,000 to more than $200,000. Characteristics of their employment also varied greatly: Some worked as few as 4 hours per week, others as many as 75. Most, however, held full-time jobs, and the median number of hours worked per week was 40. About 37 percent of these wives held professional or managerial positions, another 40 percent held clerical or sales positions, and the remainder worked at blue-collar or service jobs. Their earnings also spanned a fairly wide range, from the absence of income reported by two small businesswomen (who were forgoing any salary in order to build their businesses) to the $125,000 annual salary reported by one corporate executive. Most were nearer the low end of this range, however, and the median annual income of these wives was only $13,700. Their husbands' annual earnings were, on average, $11,000 more than their own, and the average husband earned 1.7 times what his wife earned. Some of these women had been married only a year, others 30 years or more; the median length of marriage was 14 years. Most of the women (81 percent) had children, and the average number of children per family was two. Some of the children were infants, while others were grown and gone with children of their own, but the average woman in the study had school-age children living at home.

Dimensions of Breadwinning

In her study of gender boundaries in the workplace, Epstein (1989, 1992) argued that a gender boundary is likely to have a number of dimensions (e.g., behavioral and conceptual) that may vary independently.

Because many studies have used a woman's employment status as the sole indicator of whether she is a breadwinner (Pleck, 1983; Smith and Reid, 1986), they have not been able to tap such dimensions. This study, however, following the advice of Hood (1986), has incorporated a variety of measures and is thus able to analyze breadwinning as a multidimensional phenomenon. The indicators available in this study include questions about both the wife's and her husband's motivations for being in the paid work force, questions about the relative importance of various social roles played by both husband and wife, questions about the number of hours per week worked by each partner and about how family finances are arranged, questions about the sense of obligation to earn money and about whose job is more important in the family, a direct question about who the financial provider for the family is, and a question about who, ideally, should be the financial provider for the family.

To identify dimensions of breadwinning, I have used a statistical technique called factor analysis that is designed to examine patterns of relationship among a number of items. Factor analysis of wives' responses to the items outlined above has revealed three distinct dimensions in their orientations to breadwinning. (For a more complete discussion of the factor analysis, the items included in it, and its results, see Appendix B, particularly Table B1.) The first dimension concerns the extent to which a woman defines her employment as something she does to contribute to the financial support of her family. Four indicators contribute to this dimension. Two of these are from a series of questions, asked early in the interview, that presented respondents with a list of seven reasons why a person might work for pay and asked them (1) to rate the importance of each one as a personal reason for working (very important, somewhat important, or not important) and (2) to rank them in order of importance. One of the items on this list was earning money for basic family needs; the more important a woman said this reason was to her and the higher she ranked it in relation to other reasons, the more she was emphasizing her contribution to the financial support of her family. Later in the interview, respondents were presented with a list of social roles they might play and asked to rank these in order of personal importance. How high a woman ranked financial provider for the family relative to the other roles on the list (wife, mother, worker or professional, friend, daughter, houseworker) also taps the extent to which she was interpreting her employment as financial support. The fourth measure of this dimension of breadwinning is the extent to which a woman's income was actually being used to meet basic family expenses; I ascertained this by asking women to provide fairly detailed descriptions of their family financial arrangements.

The second dimension of breadwinning, how central a woman's employment is in her family's experience, is related to the financial support dimension but is also distinct from it. One of the three measures of this dimension—a woman's response to the question, "Who is the financial provider for your family?"—clearly taps issues of financial support. This is not surprising; it seems likely that a woman will regard her job as more important to her family if she defines herself as a financial provider than if she does not. The other two measures that cluster with this one, however, are not financial. One of these is the number of hours per week that a woman works. It is easy to see that a family's experience will be more strongly shaped by a woman's employment if she works 50 hours per week than if she works 10. The third measure is a woman's response to the direct question, "Whose job would you say is considered more important in your family?"

Whereas the financial support and job centrality dimensions of breadwinning focus on a woman's interpretation of her employment behavior and what it means to her family, the third dimension is a conceptual one, measuring her beliefs or norms about breadwinning as a gender-specific activity. Does she believe that breadwinning should be used as a gender boundary? This dimension is measured by a woman's response to a single question: "Ideally, who do you think should be the financial provider for your family?" Possible responses range from "husband only" to "wife only" and tap the extent to which a woman thinks breadwinning should be a masculine responsibility, something that distinguishes her husband's employment from her own.

A woman's positions on these three dimensions of breadwinning may be complementary and mutually reinforcing, but this is not necessarily the case. Indeed, contradictions are common. Later in this chapter, I will return to the ways that dual-earner wives combine these various dimensions of breadwinning. First, however, I want to consider how positions on these dimensions are formed.

Influences on the Dimensions of Breadwinning

If breadwinning is a gender boundary that is actively constructed by daily social interactions, then positions on the dimensions of breadwinning should be shaped by the situational context of those interactions. The gender construction perspective thus points to the circumstances and experiences of adult life, rather than to childhood socialization, as a primary influence on constructions of gender.

I have used the statistical technique of multiple regression analysis to examine the factors that shape women's approaches to breadwinning. This type of analysis makes it possible to sort out the effects of a fairly large number of factors, measuring both the overall explanatory power of a group of variables and the independent contribution made by each specific variable. Because they are so much a part of the prevailing "commonsense" understanding of gender, I have begun this analysis with variables suggested by gender roles theory: the background characteristics of age and education, variables to represent childhood socialization (including whether or not the respondent was assigned sex-atypical chores as a child and her mother's employment status), and variables to measure attitudes toward gender equality. After the explanatory power of these background, socialization, and attitude variables has been taken into account, I have included variables to tap the adult experiences and circumstances highlighted by gender construction theory. These include measures of the woman's and her husband's earnings, her occupation and the extent to which her paid employment has been continuous or interrupted, the length of her current marriage, the number of children she has, her stage in the family life cycle, and the amount of role conflict she experiences. Since the three dimensions of breadwinning are not necessarily consistent with one another, I have done this analysis separately for each dimension. (For a more detailed account of the regression analysis, see Appendix B.)

The results of this analysis provide support for the gender construction model's emphasis on adult circumstances and experiences (Appendix B, Table B2). For the financial support and job centrality dimensions of breadwinning, the background, socialization, and attitude variables have virtually no effect, and the absence of any influence from the socialization measures is particularly striking. The important influences are, instead, those predicted by gender construction theory. For the financial support dimension, it is length of marriage that is by far the most important influence; the longer a woman has been married to her current spouse, the less likely she is to interpret her employment as financial support of her family. Being in a clerical or sales occupation and having a high-earning husband also decrease the likelihood that a woman will define her employment as financial support, while having a high income herself increases that likelihood. For the job centrality dimension, the most important influences are a woman's income and her stage in the family life cycle. The more she earns, the more likely she is to define her job as important in her family's experience, but having a high-earning spouse or having children of any age in the home decreases that likelihood.

It is only when the analysis turns to the conceptual dimension, norms about breadwinning, that the socialization and attitude variables emerge as important influences and the adult situation variables add little to the explanation. Even here, however, it is not socialization variables that are most critical, but attitudes toward gender equality. In particular, women who disagree that making important decisions in the family should be a male prerogative and those who agree that "a woman who works full time can establish just as warm and secure a relationship with her children as a mother who does not work" tend to believe that breadwinning responsibility should be shared. Such egalitarian attitudes are often assumed to be products of childhood socialization. There is no evidence here to support that assumption, however; these attitudes are equally likely to be responses to adult experiences.

The results of this analysis, then, validate the emphases of gender construction theory. Women's approaches to breadwinning are not unidimensional, and none of the dimensions of breadwinning identified here is shaped primarily by childhood socialization. Rather, the meanings that employed wives attach to their paid work are actively constructed through the interactions of adult life and are influenced by the situational context of those interactions. A better understanding of this process requires a closer look at the ways that women and men construct gender in their daily lives.

Breadwinning as a Gender Boundary: Eight Approaches

Each of the three dimensions of breadwinning tells us something about the extent to which an individual woman constructs breadwinning as a gender boundary. The higher her score on a particular dimension, the more she defines her own employment as breadwinning rather than seeing breadwinning as a distinctly male activity. The lower her score, the more she defines breadwinning as something that distinguishes her husband's employment from her own. Combining the three dimensions provides an even better depiction of the variety of dual-earner wives' constructions of breadwinning. If each dimension is divided into two categories (high and low), the possible combinations of high and low scores yield eight distinct approaches to breadwinning (Table 1). I now turn to

TABLE I
A Typology of Wives' Approaches to Breadwinning

Type	Financial support	Job centrality	Norms	Number of cases	Pct. of cases
Employed homemakers	Low	Low	Low	32	21%
Co-breadwinners	High	High	High	23	15
Helpers	High	Low	Low	29	19
Supplementary providers	High	Low	High	19	12
Reluctant providers	High	High	Low	21	14
Reluctant traditionals	Low	Low	High	18	12
Family-centered workers	Low	High	Low	7	5
Committed workers	Low	High	High	4	3
TOTAL				153	101%

examples of these eight approaches: eight representative dual-earner wives, each of whom deals differently with the issue of breadwinning.

Sally — An Employed Homemaker

The most common approach to breadwinning among the dual-earner wives in this study is that of the *employed homemakers* (21 percent of the women interviewed). These are women who rank low on all three dimensions of breadwinning: They do not define their employment as something they do to contribute to the financial support of their families; they do not see their jobs as occupying a central place in the lives of their families; and they do not consider breadwinning a responsibility that they should appropriately be sharing with their husbands. In other words, despite their employment, they maintain breadwinning as a gender boundary that differentiates men from women.

A number of characteristics distinguish the employed homemakers from other women in the study. They tend to be older than average (median age = 41.5 years) and to be in marriages of longer duration (median = 20.5 years). Almost all of the employed homemakers (94 percent) have children, who tend to be somewhat older than average. The employed homemakers have somewhat less education than other women in the sample (median years of school = 12), are much less likely to hold professional or managerial positions (28 percent do so), and are considerably more likely to be in clerical or sales jobs (59 percent). They tend to earn less than other women in the study (median annual earnings = $8,900), and most are married to high-earning husbands whose incomes are, on average, more than three and one-half times their own.

Sally provides a good example of an employed homemaker. I have driven out to Sally and John's house on the outskirts of the city on a balmy evening in late August. Sally has greeted me at the door, proudly showed me the view out over nearby apple orchards from their hillside patio, and then led me into the living room. As I set up my tape recorder on the coffee table, I can't help noticing the family photographs that hang on the walls and cover the mantel over the fireplace. The pictures include Sally and John, her husband of 25 years; their two sons, both now in their early twenties and still living at home; and Sally's and John's parents and siblings. The pictures contribute to an atmosphere of warmth and seem to speak about the importance of family.

At 44, Sally is a vital and energetic person who gives the impression of being pleased with the world and with her place in it. She is alert and eager to participate in the interview, despite the fact that it is Friday evening and the end of a busy workweek for her. Like the majority of employed homemakers, Sally has a full-time job, as senior secretary at a small insurance agency. She has been employed almost continuously, in a variety of clerical positions, since she graduated from high school. She left the labor force during both of her pregnancies, but in each case found a new job when the baby was about six months old. Sally has changed jobs often over the years, gradually working her way up to positions of greater responsibility.

Sally's college-educated husband works as a midlevel manager at a local bank and earns two and one-half times what she does. Nevertheless, given her continuous work history and a fairly sizable income of $15,000 a year, one might expect Sally to define her financial contribution to the family as significant. But that is not the way she sees it. Instead, in a pattern that is typical of employed homemakers, she de-emphasizes her earnings and describes her employment as something she does for herself. When presented with a list of seven possible reasons for her being employed, Sally singles out earning money for basic family needs as the only one that is not at all important. She does rate earning money for family extras as a very important reason for working, but she ranks it as less important than the feeling of accomplishment and the personal independence provided by a job. Over and over, throughout the interview, she emphasizes the psychological benefits of her employment. When discussing her reasons for being employed, she states simply, "I love working." When I ask what she would do if she won a $3 million state lottery jackpot, she says, "I would quit my present job, but I would find something else to do. I would find a part-time job. I like working too much to be home all day."

It is clear that this emphasis on the personal rewards of working is a way that Sally distinguishes her employment from her husband's. When discussing his reasons for being employed, she rates the "self" reasons of having a feeling of accomplishment, being independent, and having contact with other people as very important to him, but she also notes that earning money for basic family needs is by far the most important. She highlights this distinctive feature of her husband's employment throughout the interview. When asked who the financial provider for the family is, she replies unhesitatingly, "My husband," and she responds to a question about who feels an internal sense of obligation to support the family with a quick and firm, "Him." She also notes that his job is considered more important to the family than her own.

Sally once again makes the distinction between John's employment and her own when discussing their social roles. Presented with a list of seven roles that she might play, she ranks financial provider for the family dead last, even after houseworker, a role she has already described as of little importance to her. Despite her love of working, she also gives worker or professional a low ranking, choosing instead to emphasize the importance of personal relationships by ranking wife, mother, daughter, and friend as most important. When asked to rank her husband's roles, however, she ranks financial provider second, just after husband and ahead of father, son, and friend. This distinction between the meaning of Sally's employment and the meaning of John's is given form in their system of family finances. They use a pattern that is common among couples in which the wife is an employed homemaker: John's income is used for basic family expenses and Sally's is earmarked for extras, special projects, and so forth. As she describes it, "I mostly use mine for a second car, gifts . . . some savings."

From Sally's point of view, all this is as it should be. Another woman might read a shared responsibility for breadwinning into a work history like hers, but Sally, like all of the employed homemakers, believes that men should be responsible for the financial support of families. When asked about a hypothetical dual-earner family in which the wife earns somewhat more than the husband and in which an ill child needs extended care at home, she puzzles for a moment over what is clearly a difficult situation, but then responds firmly, "Well, I would think that the wife would stay home and take care of the child." Although Sally sees benefits from a relaxation of gender distinctions—she believes that husbands of employed wives should share housework and child care and that professions should be open to women—she also believes that men should be men and women should be women and that breadwinning is an important way of differentiating the two gender groups.

Terry—A Co-breadwinner

A striking contrast to Sally's approach to breadwinning is provided by Terry, a *co-breadwinner*. Terry is one of the 15 percent of women in this study who rank high on all three dimensions of breadwinning. These women define financial support of their families as a primary motivation for working, see their jobs as central in the lives of their families, and believe that all this is as it should be, that breadwinning ought to be just as much the responsibility of women as of men. These women do not assign a distinctly different meaning to their own employment than to their husbands'; they do not use breadwinning as a gender boundary that differentiates men and women.

The co-breadwinners are the most highly educated women in the sample (median years of school = 15) and are much more likely than average to be professionals or managers (56.5 percent). They are also among the highest-earning women in the study (median annual income = $20,000) and are married to men whose earnings are similar to their own. The co-breadwinners tend to be younger than other women in the sample (median age = 33), are likely to be in more recent marriages (median length = 8 years), and are particularly likely to have no children (only 56.5 percent do).

Terry provides a good example of a co-breadwinner. She and I are sitting at her dining-room table on a cool, rainy morning in late May. We try to keep our voices low so as not to wake her husband, Richard, an actor with a regional theater company, who had a performance the night before and is sleeping in another part of the house, but Terry's quick smile and wry sense of humor make it difficult. Her responses to interview questions frequently leave us laughing.

Terry and Richard are older than average for co-breadwinners; they are both about forty and have been married for seventeen years. Like many of the co-breadwinners, however, they have no children. Terry, who is college-educated, has had a varied work history. After trying her hand at teaching, banking, and her own small business, she recently moved into a career in retail computer sales. She has been selling personal computers for two years now and enjoys the work. Although her hours are flexible and she has been able to free up time this morning for the interview, her career is clearly an absorptive one. Twice during the interview she is interrupted by business-related telephone calls, one from a customer and one from a supplier.

Terry thinks it is important to find work that one enjoys doing, but, unlike Sally, she does not see personal gratification as the primary purpose of employment; rather, she defines paid work as one of the inevitable responsibilities of adulthood. When asked to rank her reasons for being employed, her top three all involve financial responsibility: Like 75 percent of the co-breadwinners in the study, she ranks earning money for basic family needs as her single most important reason for working. She ranks second a reason not on the standard list: her obligation to support the horses that are her passion. Her third priority is earning money for family extras. The two reasons for employment that were most important to Sally, personal feelings of accomplishment and independence, are the least salient for Terry. The contrast between Terry's and Sally's interpretations of their employment is even more apparent when we look at their rankings of the social roles they play. Where Sally ranked financial provider for the family last, Terry ranks it first.

The dramatic differences in Terry's and Sally's approaches to breadwinning do not simply reflect different employment experiences. While Terry is currently earning more than Sally ($22,000 compared to Sally's $15,000), her work history also shows more discontinuity and a less clear sense of progression. After she graduated from college, Terry went to work as an elementary school teacher. She spent four years in this position and then left it to travel with her husband. A year later, she returned to teaching briefly, spending one academic year as a teacher's assistant before deciding on a career change and enrolling in a master's program at a local business college. After six months of business courses, she returned to the labor force with a job in the mortgage department of a bank. She was steadily employed for the next eight years, first at the bank and then as the owner of her own small business. She closed the business after three years, when her husband's work required a temporary move to another state, and spent the next year and a half, as she puts it, "hanging out at the barn." It was after this period of "hanging out" that she began her current career in computer sales.

The gaps and changes of direction in Terry's work history, however, are matched by her willingness to allow her husband the same kind of freedom. After a four-year stint in the army, Richard took some time off and then joined the National Guard, first on the active duty roster and then in the reserve. For eight years, he used his reserve pay as a supplement to his earnings as a fire fighter for the city. Richard's true love, however, has always been the theater, and although he has been active in amateur community theater groups, he has always dreamed of a professional acting career. About a year ago, he and Terry decided it was time to take the plunge; Richard quit his job with the fire department to devote his energies to acting. Although Richard still has earnings from the National Guard and receives a small veteran's benefit for a service-related disability, he is now bringing in less income than Terry. As she discusses their current situation, she gives a definite sense that she is taking her turn to provide financial support for her spouse's career change.

Throughout the interview, Terry presents her marriage to Richard as a partnership in which each supports the other's aspirations and "expensive hobbies" and in which financial and other family responsibilities are shared. When asked, "Who is the financial provider for your family?" she replies, "I'd say it's about equal." She also reports that her own and her husband's careers are considered equally important, that they feel equally the obligation to earn money to support the family, and that, ideally, they should be sharing financial responsibility equally. When asked if she can "imagine any circumstances, other than serious illness, under which you would leave the labor force and your husband would be the sole financial provider for the family," Terry responds with a laugh, "Sure, if he made enough money, I'd hang out at the barn—which I have done before." When asked about circumstances under which Richard might leave the labor force, she says, "To act. He actually *has* left the labor force; it's just fortunate that he's in the National Guard so he still gets an income." She makes it clear, however, that such circumstances would have to be temporary, that Richard will have to give up his dream of being a professional actor if he cannot make it pay after several years, that over the long haul the responsibility for financial support must be shared. Terry also emphasizes the importance of shared responsibility in her response to the hypothetical situation about the family with a sick child. After enumerating a number of possibilities, including leaves of absence from work and hiring someone "exceedingly responsible" to care for the child, she decides that the best solution would be for both parents to make some kind of work-sharing arrangement that would allow them to reduce their hours, "because then they would have responsibility for their own child, but it wouldn't fall totally on either one or the other."

Nothing in Terry's interview suggests that she thinks it is important to differentiate women from men. She gives egalitarian responses to all of the gender attitude items at the end of the interview. In her portrayal of marriage as a partnership, Terry emphasizes similarity rather than difference—similarity of needs and similarity of responsibilities. Unlike Sally, she sees no need to distinguish her employment from her husband's by assigning it a different meaning. Although Terry presents herself and her husband as different from one another, the differences she describes are not gender-based. In describing the money management system that she and Richard use, for example, Terry attributes difference to practical considerations, not to gender: "I have a regular income; I know that every Thursday I'm going to get paid. Richard's income is very erratic. . . . So we use my income to take care of the steady bills—like car payments and all that stuff—and when his income comes in, we pay the lump sum things." But, she emphasizes, both incomes are used primarily to meet basic family expenses. For Terry, breadwinning is not a meaningful boundary in the construction of gender.

Charlene — A Helper

Sally and Terry represent pure, consistent approaches to breadwinning; their positions on all three dimensions point in the same direction. Most of the women in this sample, however, are not so consistent; their approaches to breadwinning are, in some sense, more complex. One of these complex constructions, that of the *helpers*, is the second most common approach to breadwinning among the wives in this study (19 percent). Like the employed homemakers, the helpers emphasize their husbands' responsibility to provide for the family. Unlike the employed homemakers, however, they identify their own financial contributions as necessary for their families and as their primary motivation for working.

The helpers are typical of women in the study in age, education, income, and husband-wife wage ratio. They are, however, less likely than average to hold professional or managerial positions (25 percent) and more likely to work part time (median hours of work per week = 37).

I have come to interview Charlene on a crisp evening in late September. We sit in her living room, I on the sofa and she in a wooden rocking chair by the fireplace. Periodically, she leans forward to toss another log on a fire that burns in the grate and takes the autumn chill off the night air. The firelight gives the room a cozy glow and is supplemented only by a discreet lamp by my side that allows me to take notes. I quickly learn that Charlene is open and friendly, and I often feel as though I am chatting with an old friend. She responds expansively to my questions, making the interview an easy one.

Charlene and her husband, Don, a welder at a nearby shipyard, are younger than is typical for the couples in which the wife is a helper; they are in their early thirties and have been married six years. They have one child, a three-year-old daughter on whom Charlene clearly dotes. Charlene is a licensed practical nurse. She used to work at a full-time hospital job, but since her daughter's birth, she has been working about twenty hours per week as a home-duty nurse for the local hospice organization. Charlene has strong religious convictions, and as she talks about her work, it is clear that she values the contribution it makes to people in need. It is also clear that her work is a source of personal pride; she describes herself as a "very good nurse." Yet, when she is asked about her reasons for being employed, Charlene subordinates the social contribution and personal rewards of her job to her family's need for her wages. Her most important reason for working, she says, is to earn money for basic family needs. She ranks independence second in importance, but she isn't referring to her own personal independence. Rather, she is concerned that she and Don be able to maintain their financial independence as a family, that they "stand on [their] own two feet."

Despite the need for her income, however, Charlene downplays the importance of her job for the family. She identifies Don as the primary provider, says it is he who feels the obligation to go out and earn money to support the family, and describes his job as more important to the family than hers, explaining, "We could get by just on what he makes, but we couldn't get by just on what I'm making right now." She emphasizes this disparity again in describing their financial arrangements; Don's paycheck, she explains, is used for the "major payments" while hers is used for the "little piddling bills." The distinction is not entirely obvious to an outsider, however, since the "major payments" include telephone and electricity as well as the mortgage and the "little piddling bills" include both the car payment and food. Charlene's insistence on the relative insignificance of her paycheck becomes even more surprising when one looks at her actual income; she earns far more per hour than her husband, and her part-time employment grosses only $5,000 less per year than his full-time job.

These seeming inconsistencies make more sense when we realize that Charlene believes husbands *should* be the breadwinners for their families. When asked about her ideal situation, she replies, "I would like for Don to be the sole provider, but I know at this time he can't handle it." So, in an interpretive move characteristic of the helpers, she defines her financial contribution not as breadwinning, but as helping Don with *his* responsibility for breadwinning.

This approach to the issue of breadwinning helps Charlene to resolve a whole host of contradictions in her life. The evangelical church to which she and Don belong teaches that complementary but distinct roles for husband and wife are a critical element of Christian family life. Charlene's endorsement of this position is clearest when she is asked about the hypothetical situation of the dual-earner family with a sick child. She responds unequivocally: "Family comes before the job, regardless of whether the woman is making the most money. I would think that her husband could find a part-time job with his other job to make up for the deficit, but I think the woman should stay with the child, very strongly." At the same time, however, Charlene has some feminist impulses.* When read the list of six gender attitude items, she gives definitely egalitarian responses to two, disagreeing strongly that "women should take care of running their homes and leave running the country up to men" and agreeing strongly that "if a wife works on the job as many hours as her husband, he should spend as much time in housework and child care as she does." Most telling, however, is her response to the item, "Most of the important decisions in the life of the family should be made by the man of the house." "Well," she says, laughing, "it hasn't been easy for me, but I have to agree with that." She is committed to the tenets of her religion, but they don't always go down easily.

The contradictions of Charlene's situation go beyond the internal tension between her egalitarian streak and her church's prescription of conventional gender inequality. There is also the matter of how well she and Don fit the gender distinctions prescribed by their church. Husbands are supposed to be the financial providers for their families, but Don lacks the kind of ambition that is needed to play this role well. Several times during the interview, Charlene hints that she has had to push Don in this regard. In discussing his role as primary provider, she notes, "He has a far better job than when we first got married, which is good." Later, she volunteers that "he was a financial fiasco before we got married. . . . He's really made some great financial strides . . . with a lot of guidance from me." At the same time, although Charlene believes that mothers should be home with their children, she loves her work. In describing her ideal of Don as sole provider, she adds, "I love nursing; I'd probably go and volunteer every weekend"; and when asked if she would quit her job if she won a lottery jackpot, she contradicts her earlier responses, saying,

---

* For an analysis of feminist beliefs among evangelical Christian women, see Stacey, 1990.

"I don't think I would. . . . I really value the contribution that I'm making. . . . I'm not in nursing for the money."

Charlene is a woman who loves her work and is married to a man who does not particularly care about his, but she is also a woman who is ideologically committed to conventional gender boundaries. She manages these contradictions by maintaining those boundaries but defining them as permeable. When she contributes to the financial support of the family and when Don contributes to housework ("He helps me quite a lot," she says), they are not breaching those boundaries, they are just helping one another. And what could be more appropriate in a loving, Christian family than just this kind of mutual help?

Barbara — A Supplementary Provider

Another approach to breadwinning, that of the *supplementary providers* (12 percent of the women studied), looks very much like that of the helpers. The supplementary providers, too, define their financial contributions as important to their families but name their husbands as primary providers. However, the supplementary providers believe that breadwinning responsibility ought to be shared, and this belief leads them to a quite different interpretation of their own employment.

The supplementary providers are fairly typical of women in this study in age, income, and occupation, but their educational level is somewhat lower than average (median years of school = 12). Although their current marriages are somewhat more recent than is typical for the sample (median = 11 years), their children tend to be older than average, which suggests that many of them have children from previous marriages. Barbara provides a good example.

Barbara and I are sitting at her kitchen table on a weekday evening in early September. She is in her late thirties and works full time as a bank teller. Barbara and her husband, Paul, a textile mill foreman, have been married only one year, but both have been married before and both have children from their previous marriages. Barbara's two youngest children, aged ten and twelve, live with them. Barbara is a no-nonsense person who speaks emphatically and exudes a sense of self-assurance. She and the children have been cleaning up the dinner dishes while I interviewed Paul in the living room, and now it is her turn. She has shooed husband and children into the living room and closed the door on the din of television and children's chatter about new teachers and classmates. "It tends to get a bit rowdy around here," she comments. Periodically during the interview, her husband or a curious child wanders into the kitchen, but she firmly sends them out again. "This is private," she says. It is clear that she is enjoying this opportunity to sit back and reflect on her life.

As her story unfolds, I realize that Barbara has achieved her self-assurance through years of struggle. When she was barely seventeen and a junior in high school, she found herself pregnant. "I got caught first thing," she notes wryly. She left school, married the father of her child, and settled down to be a housewife. Very soon, however, financial need and her own restlessness pushed her into the labor force. During this period of her life, she worked sporadically at a series of unskilled jobs. "My first husband was really jealous of my working," she explains, "so I'd work for a while and stay home for a while." After six years and two children, the marriage ended in divorce. Barbara spent one year at home with her children, supported by AFDC, before she married again. During her second marriage, she earned her high school equivalency degree and helped her husband run a small business in which she did a variety of jobs. After five years and two more children, that marriage, too, ended in divorce. What followed was a very difficult period for Barbara. With low earning ability and four children to support, she went back on welfare—this time for seven years. When the youngest child started preschool, Barbara began to do volunteer work for her local Head Start program and was eventually accepted into an employment training program for welfare mothers. Three years ago, that program placed her in a job as a clerk-typist, and she has been employed full time ever since. Barbara is ambitious; when asked about her aspirations for advancement, she replies simply, "I want my boss's position." At one point, she even enrolled in college, but she discovered after one semester that she couldn't handle either the time pressures or the costs.

Two divorces and years of struggling to get by on AFDC have left Barbara profoundly convinced of the importance of a good income. Although she describes the feeling of accomplishment that her work provides as "tremendously important" ("It's a kind of high to me," she says), she makes it clear that her primary motivations for being employed are financial. When asked to rank her reasons for working, she ranks both earning money for basic family needs and earning money for family extras ahead of the feeling of accomplishment that work provides. Of her social roles, she ranks financial provider third, just after mother and wife. The importance of her contribution is also clear when she describes the organization of family finances. She and Paul have decided to maintain separate accounts and to each take responsibility for specific bills; her responsibilities include rent, utilities, and groceries.

Yet, when she is asked who the financial provider for her family is, she replies instantly, "My husband, definitely," and adds, "He's great." She also identifies Paul's job as "definitely" more important for the family than her own and says that he, much more than she, feels the obligation to provide. What is going on here? Part of the explanation is that Paul earns about 50 percent more than Barbara does, and she has learned from hard experience the precariousness of trying to survive on her own earnings. Of her husband's social roles, she ranks financial provider for the family as the most important to her. Her sense of financial dependence on Paul is intensified by the special financial responsibilities that he has taken on. Barbara entered the marriage with a backlog of sizable debts, some of them left over from the business she ran with her second husband. "Paul has paid up a lot of them," she explains; "he's helped me get out of a lot of debt." She's also grateful that Paul is there to fall back on when her own income doesn't quite stretch to meet her designated expenses. After listing the bills that he covers, she adds, "And he helps me with all those other things when I run out."

Unlike Charlene, however, Barbara is not underemphasizing her own role as provider because she thinks that role is inappropriate for her. On the contrary, Barbara believes that responsibility for breadwinning should be shared, not used to differentiate men from women. When asked about her ideal allocation of responsibility for providing, she responds that, ideally, she and Paul would do it "together, about equally." These ideals also come through in other parts of the interview. She can't imagine any situation other than being "totally disabled" in which she would leave the labor force and Paul would be sole provider; and, when she is presented with the hypothetical situation about the sick child, she states unhesitatingly that "the one with the lesser income"—in this case, the husband—should stay home with the child. As far as she is concerned, gender has nothing to do with such decisions.

For Barbara, breadwinning is not a prescriptive gender boundary, but a descriptive one. She understands that, in the real world, men earn higher wages than women and that this enables men to support families in ways that most women cannot. She can imagine a world in which breadwinning would no longer distinguish men from women, but she realizes that she does not live in that world. In her own life, she has not been able to eliminate breadwinning as a gender boundary; she has succeeded only in moving the location of that boundary. For now, Barbara sees breadwinning as a responsibility that is shared, but shared unequally. Primary responsibility is gendered male and supplementary responsibility is gendered female.

Marie — A Reluctant Provider

Perhaps the most theoretically interesting of the "mixed" approaches to breadwinning are those in which interpretations of behavior are at odds with beliefs. The *reluctant providers* constitute the larger group of this type (14 percent of the women interviewed). These women look very much like the co-breadwinners in the way they interpret their employment. They recognize the importance of their incomes and the centrality of their jobs in the lives of their families. They are also like the co-breadwinners in age (median = 34), education (median years of school = 14), occupation (55 percent are in professional or managerial positions), earnings (median = $17,000), and similarity between their incomes and their husbands' (median husband-wife wage ratio = 1.1:1). But the reluctant providers differ from the co-breadwinners in one very important way: They don't consider their responsibility for breadwinning appropriate. Rather, they think that their husbands should be the financial providers for their families.

Marie, a junior high school teacher in her late thirties, fits into the category of reluctant provider. She and her husband, Eugene, a surgical nurse at one of the local hospitals, have been married eighteen years and have two children, a fifteen-year-old daughter and a twelve-year-old son. They live in an older single-family house on a busy street. I have arrived there to interview them on a frigid Thursday evening in midwinter. The welcoming light by the back door indicates that this is the way I should enter, and Marie greets me at the door, invites me into the kitchen, and introduces me to Eugene. We agree that she will be interviewed first, and I set up my tape recorder on the kitchen table. I am grateful to be in out of the cold and wind, and as Marie sets down steaming mugs of tea and as her cat, a big gray tabby, wanders back and forth between us, winding around our legs, putting his head up to be petted, and purring loudly, I am filled with a sense of warmth and well-being. Marie, however, is visibly tired; it is late in the evening, the end of a busy week of teaching, and, like many of her students, she is nursing a cold. Nevertheless, she seems pleased to be participating in the study and gives thoughtful responses to my questions.

Except for a three-year hiatus when her children were small, Marie has been working full time throughout her adult life, and she clearly regards her employment as breadwinning. She left the labor force during her first pregnancy, planning to stay home with the children until they were ready to go to school. But she returned to the classroom when her second child was less than a year old because "when I stayed home, it was difficult for us financially." When asked to rank her reasons for working, Marie, like more than 80 percent of the reluctant providers, names earning money for basic family needs as her most important motivation. Her annual salary is only $2,000 less than her husband's, and their family financial arrangements reflect the importance of her income. Her pay, like Eugene's, is deposited in a joint account and used to meet family expenses. So it is not surprising that, when asked who the financial provider for her family is, Marie replies that she and Eugene share providing equally. Nor is it surprising when she reports that both jobs are considered equally important in the family. It is Marie who makes budgeting decisions and handles family finances, and when I ask who feels an obligation to earn money to support the family, she responds, "We both feel the need together, but sometimes I think I feel it more because I'm the one who pays the bills."

And yet, while Marie feels the responsibility to provide, she is reluctant to embrace this responsibility. When asked to rate the importance of her various social roles, she describes those of wife, mother, and friend as very important, but rates financial provider for the family as only somewhat important, a response typical of the reluctant providers. Yet, when asked to rank these social roles in order of importance, Marie ranks financial provider first, ahead of wife, mother, and friend, and explains the apparent inconsistency by saying, "I guess I'll have to put financial provider first because I really feel that my job is necessary for us to survive comfortably." Marie's reluctance to grant breadwinning this priority becomes clear when she is asked about her ideals for her family. She is quick to say that, ideally, her husband should be the primary provider.

Many of the reluctant providers in this study dislike their jobs and yearn for the chance to leave the paid labor force and stay home. This is not the case for Marie. She likes her work and would continue teaching even if Eugene were earning enough to support the family. But, she notes, "I think I would work more for my own independence." Although Marie considers earning money for basic family needs to be her primary reason for being employed, she ranks the feelings of accomplishment and the contact with others that work provides close behind. When asked if winning a $3 million lottery jackpot would lead her to quit her job, she has no trouble answering, and her answer is no. "I like what I do," she explains. "When I stayed home those three years, it was nice being home with the children, but I missed that contact with other people and being my own professional person."

Marie's reluctance focuses not on working, but on the responsibility to provide. She is quite willing to help out with wage earning, but she wants to maintain the conventional gender boundaries of homemaker and breadwinner. She would like to have the option of leaving the labor force if her family needed her at home, and she makes this preference clear when I ask if she can imagine any circumstances under which she would leave the labor force and her husband would be the sole financial provider for the family. "If something happened with the children," she responds. She expands on this theme when presented with the hypothetical situation about the dual-earner family with a sick child: "Well, having a strong maternal instinct, I would say the mother should take a leave of absence. . . . I just feel children, at that age especially, need Mom." Marie is not committed to firmly segregated roles for men and women. She gives moderately egalitarian responses to the gender attitude items. But she is also not interested in eradicating the gender boundaries that differentiate men and women. Indeed, she would like to use breadwinning as one of these boundaries, albeit a permeable one, and is frustrated that circumstances do not allow her to do so.

Kate — A Reluctant Traditional

If the reluctant providers have been pushed into a position of responsibility for breadwinning that they would rather not have, the *reluctant traditionals* (12 percent of those studied) are not acting as providers for their families, but wish they could be. Despite their egalitarian norms about breadwinning, these women neither regard their jobs as central in the lives of their families nor report financial need as a primary motivation for their employment. Indeed, the reluctant traditionals are more tenuously attached to the labor force than other dual-earner wives in this study. Most work part time, typically as clerical or sales workers, and their yearly earnings are among the lowest in the sample (median = $9,200). Moreover, they are in long-standing marriages (median length = 21 years) to high-income husbands who outearn them almost four to one. All of these women have children, usually adolescents or older, and their families tend to be somewhat larger than average (median number of children = 3). Kate, a substitute teacher who works fewer than twenty hours per week and earns less than $10,000 per year, is a good example of a reluctant traditional. Her low earnings, as is typical for this group, contrast with the very high income of her husband, Ed, a partner with a local law firm.

I have arrived at Kate's restored Victorian home on a sunny morning in early June to find her working energetically in the garden behind the house. At 49, she is fit and trim and looks as though she spends a great deal of time outdoors. After we have introduced ourselves, she tosses her work gloves into a box of gardening tools and suggests that we take advantage of the wonderful weather by sitting out on the porch to do the interview. I am more than happy to concur.

Kate reports that she and Ed were college sweethearts who married the day after graduation in the chapel of their midwestern college and then drove halfway across the country to the East Coast university where Ed had been accepted into law school. Kate quickly landed a full-time job in the university library and helped to support her husband's legal education. By the time Ed received his degree three years later, she was pregnant with the first of their four children. First came three boys, spaced evenly two years apart, and then, after a seven-year gap, a daughter. During the early years of Ed's career, when the boys were small, Kate interspersed periods of staying home with periods of employment at part-time jobs that averaged fewer than ten hours per week. By the time Eliza was born, they had moved to the community where they now live; when her daughter was a year old, Kate got herself onto the substitute teacher list for the local school system. When Eliza was three, Kate began to work full time, first as a teacher's assistant and then as a classroom teacher in the local elementary school. She continued this full-time employment until a little over a year ago, when she went back to part-time substitute teaching because she felt that her daughter, now fourteen, needed more of her attention.

Kate does not define her employment as breadwinning. When asked how important earning money for basic family needs is to her as a reason for being employed, she replies, "I'm sure we'd survive without me working." Instead, she highlights the personal benefits of employment and the importance of the work itself, noting, "I am not a career-oriented person, but I do feel a real commitment to contribute to the community." Despite these emphases, however, she names a financial reason, earning money for family extras, first when she is asked to rank her reasons for being employed, and she explains that her pay is helping to finance her children's college educations. Her family financial arrangements provide a direct expression of this: Kate never sees her paycheck; it is deposited directly into a special savings account that is used only for paying college bills. Since Kate's earnings are insufficient to cover all of the children's education expenses, some of Ed's earnings are also used for this purpose. Most of his pay, however, goes into a joint checking account that is used for all their regular expenses.

Since basic family expenses are covered entirely by Ed's earnings, it is not surprising that, when asked to name the financial provider for her family, Kate replies, "My husband," and that, of her social roles, she ranks wife, mother, and daughter first and financial provider next to last. Nor is it surprising that, when asked whose job is considered more important in the family, she says that Ed's is—although she qualifies this by noting that it is so "just because of the economic benefits." What is surprising is her response to the question, "Who in your family do you think feels an *obligation* to earn money to support the family?" She replies that they both feel this obligation equally.

Kate's feeling of obligation to contribute to the support of her family may be a reflection of the importance she attaches to the college educations that her income helps to finance. When asked if she can imagine any circumstances under which she would leave the labor force, she responds that she can imagine this happening after the children are all through college. "If it were not a question of income, I could pretty much be a volunteer."

It is also likely, however, that her feeling of obligation reflects her belief that men and women *ought* to share such responsibilities. She does not have any commitment to dividing up family responsibilities on the basis of gender. When asked about her ideal allocation of responsibility for breadwinning, she responds, "Whoever is most able." "Suppose both are able," I rejoin. "Then they should share the responsibility equally," she concludes. Her sense that gender is largely irrelevant in such matters also colors her response to the hypothetical situation about the sick child. She enumerates a number of variables that would have to be considered: Are both parents career-oriented? Could one person get a leave? Does one parent have a special relationship with this particular child? and concludes, "And if none of these things can be worked out, then I say hire in a nurse."

It is clear from her responses that Kate is not committed to the use of gendered family responsibilities as a way to differentiate men from women. On the contrary, she is in favor of gender equality and of the eradication of some of the gender boundaries that have supported inequality. Like all the reluctant traditionals, however, she finds herself living in a very traditional arrangement that seems at odds with her convictions. If the reluctant providers have been pushed into breaching a gender boundary that they would like to maintain, Kate and the other reluctant traditionals seem to have gotten stuck in a gender-differentiated existence that they no longer believe in.

Elise — A Family-Centered Worker

The six constructions of breadwinning already discussed account for 93 percent of the women interviewed for this study. Two other types are logically possible, however, although they are relatively rare among these dual-earner wives. The more common of the two approaches is that of the *family-centered workers* (5 percent of those studied). These women resemble the employed homemakers in the low emphasis they put on their own financial contributions to the support of their families and in their belief that men have a special responsibility for breadwinning. They differ from the employed homemakers, however, in that they regard their work as important in the lives of their families.

The family-centered workers are also quite different from the employed homemakers in demographic characteristics. They are considerably younger (median age = 35) and have fewer children. Moreover, all of these women have full-time jobs, their earnings are much higher than those of the employed homemakers (median = $16,000), and all but one of them bring in a significant portion of the family income (on average, more than 40 percent). Elise provides a good example.

I have gone out to interview Elise on a raw, rainy evening in early November, and I am being warmed by an old-fashioned woodstove as we talk in the kitchen of her apartment. Elise and her husband, Gerard, live on the first floor of a well-maintained building near the center of the city. They are in their mid-twenties, have been married for a little over a year, and have no children. Gerard is an automobile salesman at a local dealership; Elise is a registered nurse and has been working in a hospital surgical ward since she finished nursing school three years ago. She readily admits that she finds the work stressful, and she seems tired at the end of the day.

Like Sally, the employed homemaker, Elise puts little emphasis on basic financial needs when she discusses her motivations for employment. She says that earning money for basic family needs is not important to her as a reason for working, and she ranks contact with people, a feeling of accomplishment, and earning money for family extras (in that order) as her three most important reasons for being employed. When asked to rank her social roles, she identifies wife, daughter, and friend as most important and, like Sally, ranks financial provider last. Elise and Gerard's financial arrangements reflect these priorities. Their basic pattern is to use his income to live on and use hers for special items or savings. Indeed, for the first year of their marriage, they have put virtually all of Elise's earnings into a savings account earmarked for a house down payment. Recently, they have found a house they want, have made an offer, and are in the process of negotiating a final price. They are clearly excited about the prospect of owning their own home, and they are now setting aside Elise's income to "buy things for the house."

Elise and Gerard's pattern is particularly interesting because Elise, in fact, earns somewhat more than her husband. She acknowledges this when asked who the financial provider for the family is, responding that they share providing equally. She suggests that this is a temporary aberration, however, when she is asked whose job is considered more important in the family. "At this point," she says, "it's both." Even now, when Elise is earning more, she reports that Gerard, somewhat more than she, feels the obligation to provide. And this makes sense to her, because Elise believes that, ideally, her husband should be the primary provider for the family.

It is not that Elise is strongly committed to conventional gender arrangements. When I present her with the series of six gender attitude statements, she gives mildly egalitarian responses to all of them. And, when presented with the hypothetical situation of the dual-earner couple with a sick child, she responds that the parents should provide the care, but she doesn't have an opinion about how they should divide it up.

In her own life, however, Elise wants to reserve the right to subordinate financial to domestic responsibilities. When asked if she plans to work outside the home continuously until retirement, she replies, "I don't plan on it, no." When I ask why she would leave the labor force, she responds simply, "Family." Upon further reflection, she considers it more likely that she will continue to work part time after she and Gerard start a family, but it is clear that this is something she imagines fitting in around her primary responsibility as caretaker for her children. But Elise can only subordinate financial responsibility to caring for children if Gerard bears primary responsibility for breadwinning, and it is important to her that he do so. She ranks his social role as provider second in importance to her, just after husband.

Elise's identity is centered in family relationships. She is quite willing to add her earnings to the family's assets for the time being, but she insists that they not depend on her income for basics, and she reserves the right to cut back on her employment when more important family responsibilities claim her time. Like Charlene, Elise maintains breadwinning as a gender boundary by defining this distinction between men and women as permeable. But where Charlene downplays the importance of her job and defines her considerable financial contribution as "helping," Elise acknowledges the current importance of her job but defines this as a temporary situation.

Diane — A Committed Worker

The least common approach to breadwinning among the dual-earner wives in this study, that of the *committed workers*, characterizes only 3 percent of the women interviewed. Like the co-breadwinners, the committed workers regard breadwinning as something that should appropriately be shared, and they see their own jobs as central in the lives of their families. However, they do not define their employment as something they do primarily to contribute to the financial support of their families. Because this is such a small group, it is difficult to describe these women in terms of "average" characteristics. They do share some distinctive features, however: They tend to work long hours; all have earnings above the median for the sample; each of them earns a significant proportion of total family income; and all but one of them have no children living at home. Diane is one of the committed workers.

I have driven out to the country to interview Diane and her husband, Leo, on a crisp, sunny Saturday in mid-October. They have only been living in their newly constructed two-story colonial, high atop a ridge, for two months; the property, which has not yet been landscaped, has a raw, unfinished look. On this morning, however, the view out over the autumnal scarlets and golds of the surrounding hills is so breathtaking that landscaping seems irrelevant. It is Leo who meets me at the door and organizes introductions; Diane is shyer and more soft-spoken than her husband. They agree that she will be interviewed first, and Leo goes off to work on a project in his garage workshop while Diane and I settle into overstuffed chairs in a corner of the living room.

Diane and Leo are in their mid-thirties, have been married for fifteen years, and have no children. He holds a supervisory position in a nearby electronics plant, while she is employed full time as a legal secretary. Diane is a very busy person. She often works overtime to keep up with the needs of the lawyers in her small firm. In addition, she is a part-time student, working toward a college degree at the nearest branch campus of the state university.

Diane has been working full time since she graduated from high school sixteen years ago. In that time, she has worked doggedly at improving herself and her employment, moving from a low-level job in a fast-food restaurant to the position of considerable responsibility that she now holds. When I ask why she left one of her jobs, as a receiving clerk in a warehouse, she replies, "One does want to advance, but you can't do it in a warehouse—that's for sure." When asked about her aspirations for advancement, she responds without hesitation that she wants "to advance as far as possible." The college degree she is pursuing is clearly part of this plan.

Given her career orientation and the fact that she earns slightly more than her husband, Diane's answer to the question, "Who is the financial provider for your family?" is not surprising; she and her husband, she says, share providing equally. When asked whose job is considered more important in the family, she hesitates a bit and finally decides the honest response is that hers is more important. All this makes sense in terms of her beliefs. She believes in gender equality and gives emphatically feminist answers to most of the gender attitude items. When asked about the hypothetical situation of the dual-earner couple with the sick child, she answers instantly, "I think the man should stay home." Diane doesn't see any reason why breadwinning should be related to gender, and she says that her current situation of equally shared responsibility for providing is her ideal.

And yet, financial responsibility is not central in Diane's motivation for working. She says that earning money for basic family needs is only somewhat important as a reason for her to be employed. Her number one reason for working, she explains, is the financial and personal independence that the work makes possible. This is followed by the feeling of accomplishment that the work provides and the family extras that her income buys. It is her husband, she notes, who strongly feels the obligation to earn money to support the family, a difference between them that is reflected in their financial arrangements. His paycheck, she says, is used to cover all the regular monthly bills, while hers is used for groceries, "fun money," and extras (although those extras include major items like the down payment for their new house and payments on the truck that they have just purchased).

The complexities of Diane's feelings about work become clearer when she is asked if she would quit her job after winning a $3 million lottery jackpot. She laughs and responds, "Of course I would; I'm no fool!" "Why would you quit?" I prompt. "Oh, honestly," she says wistfully, "there are so many things that we have yet to see and do." For some committed workers, it is the intrinsic rewards of particular jobs that are critical. For others, like Diane, it is extrinsic rewards that make their jobs so important to them. While all the committed workers share a basic belief in gender equality and a willingness to have their families depend on their incomes, their motivations for employment have much less to do with the responsibility to provide than with the personal rewards they reap through their participation in the labor force.

Conclusion

The women whose approaches to breadwinning have been presented in this chapter are not simply describing a set of facts about their lives and work; rather, they are actively constructing the meaning of their employment. Sally, the employed homemaker, combines her paid work with her belief that providing is a masculine responsibility by defining her employment as a source of personal satisfaction that has nothing to do with breadwinning. Marie, the reluctant provider, also sees breadwinning as a male responsibility, but she defines her wage earning differently from Sally, as something she does ambivalently and out of economic necessity. Charlene, the helper, interprets her employment in a way that helps her resolve the contradictions between her egalitarian inclinations and the strict gender differentiation prescribed by her church.

All of the women we have met in this chapter are employed. Yet, with the exception of Terry, the co-breadwinner, all of them use breadwinning as a gender boundary that distinguishes their husbands' employment from their own. Sally maintains breadwinning as a strict barrier separating men's work from women's work. Charlene and Elise (the family-centered worker) have maintained the distinction between men's and women's wage earning, despite their own significant earnings, by defining breadwinning as a permeable boundary. Diane, the committed worker, does not express an ideological commitment to the maintenance of this gender boundary, but she implicitly maintains it by de-emphasizing her own contributions to family financial support. Barbara, the supplementary provider, has redefined the nature of the boundary (both men and women are providers, but men are primary providers) while acknowledging its continued existence. For both Kate, the reluctant traditional, and

Marie, the reluctant provider, the breadwinner boundary is a source of strain. Kate is committed to the eradication of such gender distinctions, but she has not succeeded in eradicating them in her own marriage. Marie wants to maintain the boundary, but her efforts to do so are undermined by the economic realities of her life.

The variation in these dual-earner wives' constructions of breadwinning reflects the fact that breadwinning is still an implicit gender boundary in American culture, one that is assumed unless it is explicitly questioned and that is part of what makes a man a real man. But in a time of gender change, such boundaries are increasingly open to challenge. There is no evidence here that such challenges result primarily from orientations to gender learned in childhood. On the contrary, the most important influences seem to be adult experiences and circumstances—things like income, occupation, work history, stage in the family life cycle, and, interestingly, length of marriage. Breadwinning is challenged as a gender boundary when circumstances or experiences either raise questions about a husband's ability to fulfill the responsibility for breadwinning or increase the value and importance accorded to a wife's work.

A comparison of the co-breadwinners and the reluctant traditionals highlights these processes. Both groups of women express an ideological commitment to the elimination of breadwinning as a gender boundary. But while the co-breadwinners are in situations that support a challenge to this boundary and encourage its renegotiation, the reluctant traditionals' circumstances inhibit such redefinition. First of all, the co-breadwinners' husbands tend to have relatively low earnings, a factor that undermines the assumption of male responsibility for breadwinning. Moreover, these women are in circumstances that encourage them to place a high value on their own paid work: They tend to be in professional or managerial occupations; they have higher average earnings than most women in the sample; they are in relatively recent marriages; and almost half have no children. The reluctant traditionals, by contrast, are more often in clerical jobs, have low earnings, are in long-standing marriages to very high-earning husbands, and have larger than average numbers of children. Thus, Terry, the co-breadwinner, has been supported in her tendency to define breadwinning as a shared responsibility by her own high earnings, by the absence of responsibility for child rearing, and by the fact that Richard wants to pursue a not very lucrative acting career. Kate, the reluctant traditional, on the other hand, no longer believes in the conventional gender bargain that she made over 25 years ago, but she has no leverage to negotiate a change. Her responsibilities for raising four children have kept her earnings low over the years, and since her husband's income is quite high (more than five times hers), there has been no need to look to hers as a source of financial support.

If Terry's and Kate's approaches to breadwinning have been influenced by their adult experiences and circumstances, however, they have also been formed through interaction with their husbands. For the construction of gender is not something that each individual does in isolation. Rather, it is an interactive process in which the nature, location, and meaning of gender boundaries are created through negotiation. A complete examination of the construction of gender in dual-earner marriages, then, requires an understanding not only of how employed wives approach the issue of breadwinning, but also of how dual-earner husbands interpret the meaning of their wives' employment.

4

Dual-Earner Husbands' Constructions of Breadwinning

Breadwinning, as I noted earlier, came to be defined as a male responsibility in the mid-nineteenth century. To say that breadwinning was *a* male responsibility, however, understates the case. At least in the context of the urban industrial family, it is probably more accurate to say that breadwinning was *the* male responsibility: To be a good husband, a man had to be a good provider for his wife; to be a good father, he had to be a good provider for his children. A man's roles as worker and as breadwinner for his family, then, were at the center of his existence, critical parts of what it meant to be a man. In other words, for much of the nineteenth and twentieth centuries, breadwinning was a very important gender boundary.

In the United States of the late twentieth century, however, it is no longer clear that breadwinning is a distinctively male responsibility. Women's labor force participation has been increasing, and by 1992, 70 percent of husband-wife families with employed husbands also had employed wives (U.S. Bureau of the Census, 1993a: 133). What, then, has happened to breadwinning as a defining element of manhood? The analysis in Chapter 3 demonstrated that most employed wives, at least to some extent, continue to use breadwinning as a gender boundary, assigning different meanings to their husbands' employment than to their own. But what about the husbands? To what extent do they continue to construct breadwinning as a gender boundary? Are they, as some have argued (Ehrenreich, 1983), more than happy to escape this responsibility, replacing it with other, more pleasurable emblems of manhood? Or do they experience a breaching of this boundary as a threat to their manhood, and are they, as other observers have suggested (Slocum and Nye,

1976), even more resistant than their wives to relinquishing it? These are some of the questions this chapter addresses.

This analysis, like that of wives' constructions of breadwinning in Chapter 3, considers both behavioral and conceptual dimensions and explores the factors that influence husbands' use of breadwinning as a gender boundary. Once again, representative case studies provide an in-depth examination of characteristic approaches to breadwinning. This chapter pays particular attention to the process by which these men develop such approaches, focusing especially on the role of husband-wife negotiation in the construction of gender within the family.

The 153 husbands interviewed for this study are, like their wives, a varied group. At the time of their interviews in 1987–88, their ages ranged from 24 to 62, with a median age of 41. Their years of formal schooling varied from a low of 7 to a high of 25, with a median of 13. Sixteen percent had never had children, and 31 percent currently had no children living at home. The number of hours that these husbands worked varied from the 5 hours per week that one disabled man put in at a small part-time business to the 120 hours per week reported by a self-employed construction contractor. Almost all of these men, however, held full-time jobs, and they tended to work longer hours than their wives (median hours per week = 48). Forty-nine percent of the husbands were in blue-collar occupations, and 35 percent were professionals or managers; the remaining 16 percent\ held lower-level white-collar positions. Their annual incomes ranged from less than $10,000 to more than $140,000, with a median of $24,000. On average, a husband in the study brought in 63 percent of his family's total income.

Dimensions of Breadwinning

As was the case with wives, husbands were asked a variety of questions about breadwinning and factor analysis was used to identify distinct dimensions of breadwinning in their responses. The questions used to measure breadwinning for husbands, however, are not identical to those used for wives. Some measures that were important for wives were not useful for husbands, simply because virtually all of the men answered them in the same way. For example, 90 percent of the husbands interviewed said that earning money for basic family needs was a very important reason for being employed, and 79 percent ranked it as their single most important reason. Eighty-four percent reported that being good financial providers for their families was very important to them. At the same time, some measures that were not useful for differentiating wives from one another (e.g., the ranking of the spouse's financial provider role) proved important for husbands.

Seven indicators of breadwinning were included in the husbands' factor analysis, and, as was the case for wives, the analysis revealed both behavioral and conceptual dimensions in husbands' use of breadwinning as a gender boundary. But husbands' orientations to breadwinning turned out to be less complex than those of their wives. You will remember that the factor analysis of wives' responses, reported in Chapter 3, identified three distinct dimensions of breadwinning: financial support, job centrality, and norms about breadwinning. The factor analysis for husbands, however, revealed only two dimensions, one interpretive and one conceptual (Appendix B, Table B3). The first of these, behavioral interpretation, represents the extent to which a husband interprets his wife's employment as breadwinning (or, conversely, the extent to which he maintains breadwinning as a boundary that distinguishes his employment behavior from hers). Five of the seven indicators of breadwinning contribute to the measurement of this dimension. These include two of the same variables that measured job centrality for wives: whom a man identifies as the financial provider for his family, and whose job he says is considered more important in the family. They also include one of the measures of the wives' financial support dimension—the extent to which the wife's earnings are used to meet basic family expenses—and two indicators that were not included in the factor analysis for wives: whom the respondent reports as feeling an obligation to financially support the family, and where he ranks his wife's financial provider role in importance relative to her other social roles. The second dimension, norms, measures the extent to which a husband believes that breadwinning *should* be a boundary distinguishing men from women. Two indicators contribute to this dimension: his response to a question about who, ideally, should be the financial provider for his family, and where he ranks his financial provider role in importance relative to his other social roles.

Paradoxically, the greater simplicity of husbands' approaches to breadwinning reflects the greater power of this gender boundary in their lives. For wives, there is a question whether or not their employment constitutes breadwinning, and their behavioral interpretation dimensions revolve around the meanings they attach to that employment. There is no question for these husbands, however, that their own employment is breadwinning; abdicating this responsibility is not a serious option. Because breadwinning is a less permeable boundary for husbands than for wives, husbands have fewer possibilities available to them in constructing this boundary.

Closer comparison of husbands' and wives' breadwinning dimensions helps to elucidate the ways that the breadwinning boundary is less permeable for men. The behavioral interpretation dimension for husbands overlaps more with the job centrality dimension for wives than with the wives' financial support dimension. The two variables that were most important in measuring the financial support dimension for wives—their ratings and rankings of earning money for basic family needs as an important reason for being employed—were not included in the analysis for husbands. This is not because these variables were unimportant for husbands but because they lacked variation; the vast majority of husbands gave them the highest possible ratings. This highlights the continued importance of breadwinning as a gendered phenomenon. Husbands' and wives' constructions of breadwinning differ precisely because breadwinning is still an important gender boundary in American culture; it is taken for granted that husbands should contribute to the financial support of their families.

Factors That Influence Husbands' Use of the Breadwinning Boundary

The analysis in Chapter 3 found that the extent to which wives use breadwinning as a gender boundary is best explained by the circumstances and experiences of their adult lives, a finding consistent with gender construction theory. In this section, I once again use multiple regression analysis, this time to examine factors that influence husbands' approaches to breadwinning. As before, I have done a separate regression analysis for each dimension of breadwinning. I have again begun each analysis with background, socialization, and attitude variables and then included the situational variables that are central to gender construction theory.

In this analysis, however, I also want to consider how the construction of this gender boundary is shaped by husband-wife negotiation. Thus, after the situational variables have been allowed to explain as much of the variation as possible in husbands' scores on each dimension, I have added measures of negotiation to the analysis. These include a man's wife's norms about breadwinning and attitudes toward gender equality (as measured by the six gender attitude items). I am assuming that any influence of a wife's norms and attitudes on her husband's use of breadwinning as a gender boundary results from some kind of negotiation. These are, admittedly, indirect measures and, as such, may leave much negotiation unaccounted for. But more direct measures (for example, direct observation of husband-wife negotiations or direct questions about such negotiations) are also problematic* and were not included in these interviews.

The results of the multiple regression analysis show that for husbands, as for wives, adult circumstances and experiences are very important predictors of the meaning attached to a wife's employment (Appendix B, Table B4). Once again, background and socialization variables have virtually no effect on the behavioral interpretation dimension of breadwinning. One of the gender attitude items, whether a woman who works full time can establish a warm and secure relationship with her children, is important; a husband who agrees that she can is more likely to define his wife's employment as breadwinning. But it is the situational factors that add dramatically to our understanding. Income is particularly important here; the more a man earns, the more likely he is to use breadwinning as a boundary that distinguishes the meaning of his work from the meaning of his wife's. This effect is modified, however, by his wife's income; as her earnings go up, he becomes more likely to interpret her employment as shared breadwinning. Other situational factors further complicate the picture: Dual-earner husbands who have children (especially of elementary school age) are more likely to use breadwinning as a gender boundary than are those who do not have children, but once the presence of children is controlled, greater numbers of children increase the likelihood that a man will interpret his wife's employment as breadwinning (presumably because of the greater level of financial need that more children represent). A wife's work history also influences her husband's interpretation of her employment; the more discontinuous that employment has been, the less likely he is to define it as breadwinning. Once these situational influences have been accounted for, the measures of negotiation do not add anything significant to our understanding of this dimension, although there is some suggestion that a husband is more likely to define his wife's employment as breadwinning if she believes that a mother's full-time employment does not harm her relationship with her children.

---

* Direct observation is most often carried out in laboratory simulations, and there are questions about how similar these are to real-life negotiations. Direct questions about negotiation carry the risk that husbands and wives will give idealized responses, describing how they think they should negotiate rather than how they actually do.

When we turn to the conceptual dimension of breadwinning, a somewhat different picture emerges. As was true in the analysis for wives, the gender construction model does not explain norms about breadwinning as well as it explains interpretations of employment behavior. Once again, overall attitudes about gender equality are important predictors of norms. Husbands who believe that married women have a right to work outside the home and those who agree that husbands of employed wives should share responsibility for housework and child care are more likely to embrace ideals of shared breadwinning. However, situational variables also prove to be significant influences. A wife's occupation is the most important factor here; if she works at any kind of white-collar job (but especially a professional or managerial one), her husband is less likely to believe that breadwinning should be a distinctively male responsibility than if she works at a blue-collar job. This relationship is modified somewhat by characteristics of the husband's job. Interestingly, both high earnings and a blue-collar occupation increase the likelihood that a man will express ideals of male breadwinning.

Even after the influence of situational factors has been taken into account, two indicators of negotiation contribute significantly to explaining dual-earner husbands' norms about breadwinning. One of these is a wife's norms; not surprisingly, if she believes that breadwinning should be a male responsibility, her husband is more likely to express that same belief. This suggests that husband and wife work together to construct gender definitions in their marriage. The other significant effect, however, seems to contradict this conclusion. Wives' responses to one of the gender attitude items, "Most of the important decisions in the life of the family should be made by the man of the house," are related to their husbands' norms about breadwinning in a surprising way: When wives take an egalitarian stance on this item, their husbands are more likely to claim breadwinning as a male responsibility. It is hard to know how to interpret this result, but it seems to point to contention in the process of negotiating gender boundaries.

What the multiple regression analysis shows us, then, is that for husbands, as for wives, the extent to which breadwinning is used as a gender boundary is influenced primarily by adult experiences and circumstances. Such situational factors are particularly important in explaining husbands' interpretations of their wives' employment, but they also have a significant effect on norms about breadwinning. While variables related directly to the wife's work—her occupation, her income, and the continuity of her work history—loom especially large in this analysis, the husband's income and occupation and the couple's family circumstances are also important. The measures of negotiation have much less effect than the current situation variables, and the effect they do have is primarily on norms, not on behavioral interpretation. However, it would be premature to conclude that the gender construction model's emphasis on negotiation is misplaced. The measures of negotiation used here are weak ones; husbands' use of breadwinning as a gender boundary may be influenced by forms of negotiation that are simply not tapped in this analysis. Fuller consideration of the effects of negotiation therefore requires a more sensitive form of analysis. Such an analysis is provided below by detailed case studies of four husbands with different constructions of breadwinning.

Husbands' Constructions of Breadwinning

Husbands, like wives, can be divided into two categories on each dimension of breadwinning, those who scored low on that particular dimension (male breadwinning) and those who scored high (shared breadwinning). And husbands, like wives, can be cross-classified on these dimensions to identify distinctive approaches to the use of breadwinning as a gender boundary. This cross-classification yields four basic approaches, as depicted in Table 2 and described in the following case studies.

Roger — A Traditional Breadwinner

The largest group of men in the sample, 36 percent of the total, fall into the category of *traditional breadwinners*. Although their wives are employed, most often at full-time jobs, the traditional breadwinners do

TABLE 2

A Typology of Husbands' Approaches to Breadwinning

Type	Behavioral interpretation	Norms	Number of cases	Pct. of cases
Traditional breadwinners	Low[a]	Low	55	36%
Role sharers	High[b]	High	40	26
Reluctant co-providers	High	Low	35	23
Uncommitted providers	Low	High	23	15
TOTAL			153	100%

[a]Low scores denote male breadwinning.
[b]High scores denote shared breadwinning.

not interpret that employment as shared breadwinning. Rather, they retain breadwinning as a distinct gender boundary in their families.

These men are somewhat older than average for the sample (median age = 43), are in longer-standing marriages (median length = 18 years), are more likely to have children (91 percent), and have somewhat older children than average (typically adolescents). The traditional breadwinners are less likely than average to be managers or professionals (29 percent) and more likely to be blue-collar workers (56 percent), but their annual earnings are somewhat higher than average (median = $26,000). Their wives, however, have unusually low earnings (typically less than $10,000), so the average man in this group outearns his wife three to one. Roger, a 39-year-old lineman for the electric company, provides a good example.

I have driven out to Roger's small ranch-style house, in a mixed residential and commercial area near the edge of the city, on a late afternoon in early February. Midwinter days are short at this northern latitude and, as I pull into the driveway, it is already getting dark and the snow in the front yard is rosy with the glow of twilight. Roger's interview has been difficult to schedule because he works long hours and his time is heavily committed. Finally, though, he has managed to fit me into a small window of time between his arrival home from work and the family's dinner hour. It turns out that I have arrived just behind Roger, who is getting out of his pickup truck. I introduce myself and accompany him through the back door and into the kitchen. While Roger goes off to change out of his work clothes, I exchange greetings with Francine, his wife of seventeen years, and their three children—all of whom I met a week ago when I was here for Francine's interview. This is a busy time of day in a busy household and, as Francine cooks dinner in the kitchen, the children gather around the table at one end of the combined living/dining room. The two younger children (ages eight and twelve) are playing a board game on one side of the table while their teenage sister works on her homework on the other side. Roger and I settle down in living-room chairs at the other end of the room and, trying to shut out the clatter and buzz of all this household activity, begin the interview.

Roger could aptly be described as a "superprovider." He has been continuously employed since he finished school twenty years ago, working long hours at his regular job and moonlighting as well. Before going to work for the electric company, he worked for only one other employer, and he went directly from one job to the other without missing even a single day of work. Moreover, although his job with the electric company averages 50–60 hours per week, he supplements it with service in the army reserve and with a variety of odd jobs that he takes on from time to time. Indeed, two of his three weeks of summer "vacation" each year are devoted to such moonlighting, training with his reserve unit.

All of this is not for himself, Roger emphasizes, but for his family; he has taken on such a heavy work load in order to be a good provider. He makes it clear that it is not the work itself that drives him, but the income it provides. When asked how important a feeling of accomplishment is as a reason for him to be employed, Roger seeks clarification of what I mean by "accomplishment," asking, "Because of what you get—like a house and things like that?" He responds similarly to a question about his aspirations for advancement, explaining that promotion to crew chief, a salaried position that is not eligible for overtime, would not represent a clear financial gain and concluding, "I'll take it if it comes around, but if it doesn't come around, it won't bother me." Roger's income is devoted to the needs of his family. "Whatever money I make with all the jobs that I've got," he explains, "all goes to [Francine] and she's the one who decides how it gets spent."

Throughout the interview, Roger emphasizes the importance of his role as financial provider for the family. Like the vast majority of traditional breadwinners, he names himself as primary provider, says his job is more important in the family than his wife's, and says he feels an obligation to provide that she does not. When presented with the list of reasons for being employed, Roger ranks earning money for basic family needs first and earning money for family extras second. Moreover, he unhesitatingly ranks financial provider at the top of the list of seven social roles, of more importance even than husband and father, and he justifies this ranking by noting that it's "the financial that makes the whole thing work out." He organizes his busy schedule using the principle that being a good provider is his central obligation; when I ask how rushed he usually feels, he responds, "It doesn't really matter because—see, I do a lot of side jobs. . . . Sometimes [one of my employers] wants something, my wife wants something, and there are things I have to do for myself. But I usually always go for the one that gives me the extra money first, and the rest just fall into line behind."

Being a breadwinner not only organizes Roger's life, but is also central to his sense of who he is. He tries to express the depth of his felt obligation to provide by explaining, "If I stay home, I feel like I'm cheating." When asked if he can imagine any circumstances under which he would leave the labor force and his wife would be the provider for the family, he draws a blank. In fact, he finds it hard to imagine ever leaving the labor force at all. When I ask if he would quit his job after winning a $3 million state lottery jackpot, he says no and adds, "I'm too much of a workaholic. It seems as though, when I take too much time off, I feel like I don't belong, that I should be working."

It is not that Roger discounts his wife's employment. Her job as a teacher's aide at the local elementary school brings in almost 25 percent of their total family income, and he deeply appreciates this contribution. Indeed, unlike the majority of traditional breadwinners, who would prefer to be sole providers, Roger considers this arrangement ideal. But he assigns Francine's employment a distinctly different meaning from his own. He emphasizes at every opportunity that she works not to meet basic family financial needs, but for extras. When asked how important earning money for family extras is as a reason for him to be employed, he immediately draws the distinction between his employment and Francine's, responding, "It's not that important [to me]; that's why *she* works." He reiterates this point when asked about his wife's motivations for working, rating earning money for basic family needs as not at all important to her and describing earning money for family extras as "*the* reason she works." He ranks financial provider for the family near the bottom of the list of her social roles, sixth out of seven.

Roger clearly uses breadwinning as a gender boundary, something that does and should differentiate his employment from his wife's. Moreover, he views the breadwinning boundary as an integral part of a larger system of gender boundaries. Just as he sees himself as having a special responsibility for breadwinning because he is a man, he sees Francine as having a special responsibility for home and children because she is a woman. (One of the things he likes best about her current job is that she can be at home when the children are home.) In describing this gender differentiation, Roger gives it a spatial aspect, assigning women to the "inside" domestic sphere and men to the "outside" work sphere. When explaining why it is appropriate that he be primary provider, he notes, "I can't keep the house as well as she can, so I'll stay outside." It is hardly surprising that, when presented with the six gender attitude items, Roger agrees that "there is some work that is men's and some that is women's and they shouldn't be doing each other's."

Roger draws clear gender boundaries, but he doesn't draw them unilaterally. Both his interview and Francine's make it clear that such matters are a subject of discussion and negotiation within their marriage.

Throughout their interviews, they repeatedly refer to one another's views. Indeed, Roger begins his response to my first question about breadwinning by calling attention to discussion with Francine, noting, "When we got married, we decided that I was going to be the financial provider." When Francine is asked, "Ideally, who do you think should be the financial provider for your family?" she begins by musing, "He'd probably always want to be the primary provider." Similarly, when Roger is asked if he can imagine circumstances under which Francine would leave the labor force and he would be sole financial provider for the family, he responds, "She's mentioned more than once that she'd definitely like to stay home."

For the most part, Roger and Francine have reached agreement about the construction of gender in their marriage. They agree, for example, that he is the breadwinner and that she works for extras. But their interviews also reveal some tensions in this negotiated gender order. Thus, while they both agree that he should bear primary responsibility for breadwinning, they disagree about how high a priority this responsibility should have in his life. She ranks his provider role as less important than his husband and father roles, and he ranks the provider role first, a precondition to being a good husband and father. This particular tension emerges in Roger's interview when he is asked about the importance of the various roles he plays. He says it is very important to him to be a good provider and explains, "To have peace all the way around, you have to be a good provider." A few minutes later, however, when we are discussing role conflict, he recognizes with some exasperation that devoting himself to providing does not always bring peace. When asked how often other obligations interfere with his ability to be a good provider, he responds that they never do "because I usually do the financial provider first and put everything else second." But then he adds, in a tone of injury, "That's where it comes into harassment of the husband, because she doesn't always agree with that."

Roger may not always agree with Francine's views on gender issues, but he takes them into account. When asked if he agrees that "if a wife works on the job as many hours as her husband, he should spend as much time in housework and child care as she does," Roger replies, "If you listen to my wife, that's 100 percent true." "Is that what you think?" I ask. "Well," he responds without much conviction, "to be right, that's the way it should be." When asked if he agrees that "a married woman should not work outside the home if her husband can comfortably support her," he responds, somewhat defensively, "That's what *I* think," and then adds in a conciliatory tone, "That is, if she doesn't want a career or anything."

Roger and Francine work together to construct what it means to be a man and what it means to be a woman in their marriage. For the most part, they do this collaboratively, using discussion and negotiation to deploy gender boundaries and create a gender system with which they are both satisfied. This is very much a process, however—one that is never completed and one that sometimes involves disagreement and contention.

David — A Role Sharer

While the traditional breadwinners deploy breadwinning as a distinct gender boundary, the second largest group in the study, the *role sharers* (26 percent of the sample), have relinquished this boundary. They define their wives' employment as shared breadwinning, and they express an ideological preference for this arrangement.

The role sharers are somewhat younger than the traditional breadwinners (median age = 39), are in more recent marriages (median length = 10.5 years), and are less likely to have children (75 percent). They also tend to be more highly educated (median years of school = 14) and are much more likely to be professionals or managers (47.5 percent) and less likely to work at blue-collar jobs (27.5 percent). At the same time, though, their incomes are lower than those of the traditional breadwinners (median = $21,000) and their wives' incomes are higher (median = $17,700). David, our representative role sharer, is a 34-year-old carpenter who works in the maintenance department of the local college. He is also a part-time college student. He and his wife, Molly, a registered nurse, have been married eight years and have two preschool-age children.

I have arrived at David and Molly's house on a beautiful Monday afternoon in early October. The sun is shining, the sky is the deep blue that is characteristic of October in New England, and the temperature is an unseasonably warm 70 degrees—one of those rare "Indian summer" days that provide a brief respite before the onset of winter. David and Molly have opened windows to take advantage of the warm air, and since theirs is one of the few private residences left on a main artery out of the city, the dull roar of rush-hour traffic provides a steady backdrop to the interviews. I have set up my tape recorder on the kitchen table and interviewed Molly while David played with the children in the living room. Now Molly has taken over child minding and it is David's turn to be interviewed.

At first glance, David seems to have much in common with Roger, the traditional breadwinner. Both men work in skilled, blue-collar trades. Both have been steadily employed without a break since they finished full-time schooling. Both have young children and wives who work about 30 hours per week at jobs that fit well with the demands of child care. Both lead very busy lives, Roger because he works long hours and David because he combines a full-time job with part-time schooling.

But these similarities are far outweighed by the striking contrasts in the ways that these two men interpret their situations. Where Roger focuses on the differences between his wife's employment and his own, David emphasizes the similarities. Like all the role sharers, he defines breadwinning as a shared responsibility. Although Molly is currently working part time and earning several thousand dollars per year less than he is, David does not use breadwinning as a boundary that differentiates his work from hers. Instead, he says that they share providing equally; that both feel the obligation to provide; that her income, like his, is critical for meeting basic family needs; and that, ideally, responsibility for breadwinning ought to be shared by husband and wife. David and Roger's different emphases are particularly apparent when they describe their family finances. While both men turn their paychecks over to their wives, they interpret this arrangement very differently. Roger defines his wife's handling of finances as part of her responsibility for the female domestic sphere, but David chalks it up to personality differences that have nothing to do with gender. "We'll sit down and do budgets pretty good on paper," he explains, "but put a dollar in my pocket and it's gone. So she takes care of the whole financial thing."

David's responses to interview questions make it clear that breadwinning is not central to his conception of himself as a man. Although he does work primarily to earn money for basic family needs, he does not consider his role as financial provider very important relative to his other social roles and ranks it sixth out of seven, again in sharp contrast to Roger. Moreover, unlike Roger, David gives as much importance to his wife's providing as he does to his own. Thus, he ranks earning money for basic family needs as the most important reason for her employment as well as his, he says that her job is somewhat more important than his in the family, and he gives her provider role a slightly higher ranking than his own, fifth on the list of seven roles. When asked who the financial provider for the family is, he volunteers that "if she goes to work full time, it will be her," and he does not seem threatened by Molly's greater earning potential.

Like Roger, David finds it hard to imagine leaving the labor force permanently, but it is the sense of accomplishment that holds him, not the personal importance of his role as provider. David ranks a feeling of accomplishment as a very close second to earning money for basic family needs on his list of reasons for being employed, and that need for accomplishment would keep him in the paid labor force even if he won a $3 million lottery jackpot. "I'd still need something to do," he explains. "I would think about it, and I might leave that position to do something else, but I'd still continue to work." At the same time, though, because breadwinning is not central to his sense of self, David can imagine being supported by Molly temporarily—if, for example, he decided to go to school full time to finish his degree. He can also imagine supporting her temporarily if she decided to take some time off to have another baby. In the long run, however, he expects that responsibility for breadwinning should be shared, that it should not distinguish him from his wife.

David and Molly seem to be in basic agreement about the use of breadwinning as a gender boundary—she, too, reports that they share breadwinning equally and that this is the way it ought to be—but there is no evidence here of the kind of explicit negotiation that shows up repeatedly in Roger's and Francine's interviews. David and Molly do not allude to one another's opinions or refer to previous discussions they have had about issues. They don't begin their responses to interview questions by considering what the other would say. It may be that, since they are already in agreement, there is no need for discussion and negotiation.

But David and Molly don't seem to be in complete agreement about the social construction of gender. Many role sharers would like to minimize all gender difference, but David is not one of these. His responses to the gender attitude items indicate that, even as he relinquishes breadwinning as a gender boundary, he holds on to other gender distinctions. While he is adamant that men and women should not be differentiated by paid work, for example, he does believe that women bear special responsibilities at home. Thus, he disagrees that "if a wife works on the job as many hours as her husband, he should spend as much time in housework and child care as she does," and he believes that a mother cannot work full time without impairing her relationship with her children. Molly takes very different positions on these issues, seeing breadwinning as only one of many gender boundaries that should be eliminated.

This disagreement raises another possible explanation of why David and Molly do not refer to discussion and negotiation in their interviews. Perhaps they do not explicitly discuss these gender issues because to do so would raise conflicts that they could not easily resolve.* As long as Molly is, in fact, working part time, their disagreements are only theoretical. David can maintain that a mother's full-time work harms her relationship with her children without criticizing Molly. Molly can believe that she bears most of the responsibility for housework and child care because she works fewer hours than David, while he assumes that she does so because she is a woman. Gender difference is more important to David than to Molly, although breadwinning is not one of the boundaries that he uses to construct that difference. He and his wife have worked out an arrangement that allows them to emphasize their agreement, ignore their disagreement, and live together in harmony despite their different assumptions about the social construction of gender.

Brad — A Reluctant Co-provider

Whatever the complexities in their constructions of gender, both David and Roger construct the breadwinning boundary as a consistent whole in which behavioral interpretation and norms are parallel and mutually reinforcing. For the substantial minority of men in our sample who fall in the remaining two categories, however, the use of breadwinning as a gender boundary is more complex, characterized by a contradiction between behavioral interpretation and norms. The larger of these two groups comprises the *reluctant co-providers*, who are almost as numerous (23 percent of the sample) as the role sharers and who, like the role sharers, interpret their wives' employment as breadwinning. They are unlike the role sharers, however, in their norms about breadwinning. Of all the men in the study, it is the reluctant co-providers who cling most strongly to ideals of male breadwinning.

In some ways, these men resemble the traditional breadwinners. They are of a similar average age (median = 42), typically have adolescent children, are much less likely than average to hold professional or managerial positions (20 percent), and are more likely to be blue-collar workers (69 percent). However, the reluctant co-providers tend to be in more recent marriages than the traditional breadwinners (median length = 12 years) and are much less likely to have children (77 percent). Even more importantly, they earn considerably less than the traditional bread-

---

* I am indebted to Janet Riggs and Amy Trevelyan for this insight.

winners (median = $22,000) and are married to relatively high-earning wives (median = $16,900). Brad, a 28-year-old soft-drink salesman, provides an interesting example of the complexities and dilemmas of the reluctant co-providers' approach to breadwinning.

I have driven across the river and down a road that runs along the other side to meet Brad for a late-afternoon interview. I have no trouble finding the house because it's the second time I've been here today. During the morning, I came out to interview Brad's wife of one year, Michelle, a second-shift machine operator at a plastics factory. Brad, tall and lanky and dressed in shorts and a T-shirt, greets me at the door of his second-floor apartment and invites me in. It is a hot, humid day in July, the start of one of Maine's infrequent summer heat waves, and the kitchen that was cool and inviting when I interviewed Michelle in the morning is now steamy. Brad offers me a glass of iced tea and then suggests that we conduct the interview at a picnic table in the backyard where we can take advantage of a river breeze.

As Brad begins to talk about his work, I realize it is unusual for him to be home this early in the day; he is a very hard worker who puts in an average of 55 hours per week at his sales job. Although the job does not pay particularly well, offers virtually no room for advancement, and includes relatively few fringe benefits, Brad is very grateful for the steady work and determined to be a model employee. The first four years after he graduated from high school were discouraging ones in which he alternated work at a series of unskilled and part-time jobs with periods of unemployment. During one particularly bleak period, he worked at a grueling job hauling cut timber out of the woods for a logging company—with one arm (broken in a bicycling accident) in a cast! Finally, however, he landed a job as a salesman in an auto-parts store. It was the first job he'd had that lasted more than a few months, and he did it happily for more than three years before the store's parent company went bankrupt and the store was closed. This time, however, he did not experience a period of unemployment. Helped by his sales experience, an upswing in the local economy, and a strong reference from his supervisor, he was able to find another job (his current position) immediately.

Brad is proud of having worked his way up from unskilled labor to a white-collar job, but he also readily acknowledges that his earnings are not enough to support the kind of life-style that he and his wife aspire to. Michelle's income, too, is critical. It is in this sense that Brad's responses to interview questions about breadwinning are very much like those of David, the role sharer. Like David, Brad says that he and his wife share providing equally, that her job (which pays more than his and provides their health insurance) is the more important of the two, that they both feel the obligation to provide, and that both incomes are needed to meet basic family expenses.

Unlike David, however, Brad does not embrace this sharing of responsibility. Instead, he emphasizes the lack of choice in his situation. When I ask who the financial provider for the family is, he replies, "It's a two-way thing here; we couldn't do it without one another." Similarly, he comments on his and Michelle's shared sense of obligation to provide by noting, "I think we feel it equally because we need each other's paychecks." But Brad makes it clear that this mutual dependence is not his ideal; he believes that breadwinning should distinguish men from women. Like more than two-thirds of the reluctant co-providers, he says that his ideal is to be the sole provider for his family. "If there was any way that I could get a job to do it," he asserts emphatically, "my wife would be out of work."

Brad feels that paid work is and should be central to his sense of self as a man in a way that it is not for women. Brad gives his provider role a very high ranking (second only to husband and just ahead of worker or professional), a response typical of the reluctant co-providers. But in Brad's view, work is also a central form of achievement for men. When he talks about his wife's work, he emphasizes only financial necessity; she works because she has to. When he talks about his own, he also emphasizes the feeling of accomplishment that a job provides. That feeling, Brad says, is "very important; it makes going in tomorrow worth it." Thus, if he won a lottery jackpot, he would leave his current job, but not the labor force, using the opportunity instead to increase his sense of accomplishment. "I'd quit to do something on my own," he explains. "I don't know what it would be right now, but I'd like to start a business of some kind."

Brad and Michelle, like Roger and Francine, openly discuss and negotiate gender issues. Their interviews, like those of the latter couple, are sprinkled with references to such discussions and to one another's opinions. Both, for example, respond to the hypothetical situation of the dual-earner couple with the sick child by noting that such a problem would, of course, have to be thoroughly discussed. When asked what she would do if she won a $3 million lottery jackpot, Michelle laughs and says, "Now, this question is funny, because we've talked about it a few times." At another point, she says, "I know . . . he feels basically the same as I do." But Michelle also hints that such discussions can sometimes be contentious: "I am an independent person," she says, laughing. "You can ask my husband; he'll tell you that. I make up my own mind."

What is most interesting about Brad and Michelle's negotiations is the extent to which they disagree about what it is they've agreed on. Brad defines their need for Michelle's earnings as an unfortunate necessity; she defines such sharing as appropriate and her ideal. He can easily imagine circumstances in which she would leave the labor force. "Those would be me having a very good-paying job and us having a child," he says. "I'd want her to be home. I don't know if it would be permanent, but I think we both agree on it." She, on the other hand, can't imagine any circumstances under which she would leave the labor force and plans to be employed continuously until retirement:

> There are so many things that we want and we know that there is just no way. He has a good job, but the things that we want, it will take the two of us; and we are planning on having a family as soon as possible, so that's going to take up a lot of money, too. . . . Even when I have my children—we talked about it—I don't think I'll be able to take any time off because of the way that we're going to be living.

Although they've talked about winning the state lottery "quite a few times," the fantasies they report are different; he talks about going into business for himself, while she talks about their going into business together.

Perhaps the level of unrecognized disagreement between Brad and Michelle is not so surprising. After all, this is a relatively new relationship. They have just celebrated their first anniversary and have not had the long years to work out a shared construction of gender that Roger and Francine have had. In many ways, Brad and Michelle are just beginning the process of negotiation. At this point, they agree about the importance of gender boundaries but disagree about the nature of those boundaries. While he embraces conventional definitions of "separate spheres" for men and women, she is looking for equality with difference. Thus, she agrees that "there is some work that is men's and some that is women's and they shouldn't be doing each other's" and disagrees that husbands of employed wives should fully share responsibility for housework and child care, and she explains these views by saying, "It's an equal thing, but there are just some things that women do in the household." It is very possible that, as the years go on and they continue their discussions, Brad and Michelle's constructions of gender will converge (although the content of that convergence will probably depend as much on their circumstances and experiences as on their negotiations). For the time being, Brad resolves the contradiction between his norms and their circumstances by maintaining male responsibility for breadwinning as a goal to be sought and by assuming that Michelle shares this goal.

Rod — An Uncommitted Provider

If the reluctant co-providers cherish the ideal of breadwinning as a gender boundary even as they breach that boundary in practice, the *uncommitted providers* (15 percent of the sample) distance themselves from the breadwinning boundary despite its clear presence in their own lives. Like the role sharers, the uncommitted providers profess an ideal of shared responsibility for breadwinning. But, although they are not ideologically committed to breadwinning as a male responsibility, they are, in fact, the financial providers for their families.

Like the role sharers, the uncommitted providers are somewhat younger (median age = 38) and better educated (median years of school = 14) than average for the sample. They also have a higher than average proportion of professionals and managers (48 percent) and have a higher average income (median = $31,200) than any other group in the sample. Their wives, however, earn less than average for the sample (median = $11,900), and these men are more likely than average to have children (91 percent). Rod, our representative uncommitted provider, is—like Brad, the reluctant co-provider—caught on the horns of a dilemma about the use of breadwinning as a gender boundary.

Rod is a self-employed building contractor who specializes in moderately priced, custom-built houses. At age 40, he has been married to his wife, Anita, for eighteen years and is the father of two adolescent children. I have pulled into the driveway of Rod's house in the country at 9:00 P.M. on a balmy evening in June. This is late to begin an interview, but I have scheduled it for this time at Rod's request. During his "off" hours (after he has completed his "normal" 75–80-hour summer workweek), Rod is building an addition to his own house, and he wants to take advantage of the long hours of daylight at this time of year. Rod and Anita's house is not visible from the road, and as I wend my way along the drive, I hear the sound of hammering before the house comes into view. After parking my car, I follow the hammering sounds to the new addition, and there I find Rod—a small, muscular man with skin weathered to a deep bronze—up on a ladder taking advantage of the last bit of evening light. As I call out my greetings, he climbs down from the ladder, proudly gives me a quick tour of his family-room-to-be, and then leads the way through the new construction into the house, where we sit down at the kitchen table.

An outsider looking at Rod's situation would have no hesitation in defining him as the breadwinner for his family. Last year, he brought almost $50,000 into the family from his construction business, a sharp contrast with the $4,000 that his wife earned from her part-time job as a salesclerk in an upscale clothing boutique. It is clearly his earnings on which the family depends. He acknowledges this when he ranks financial provider as the least important of the social roles Anita plays and when he says that he could imagine being sole provider for the family if his wife "just got tired of [her job] and she wanted to take some time off."

And yet, throughout the interview, Rod repeatedly understates his responsibility for breadwinning. When asked who the financial provider for his family is, he responds, "We both share." "Do you share equally," I probe, "or does one of you provide more than the other?" "No," he replies with obvious reluctance, "I would say that I provide more than she does." He is similarly hesitant when asked whose job is considered more important in the family; after a series of hedges, he finally concludes, "I would probably say that my job would be considered more important." His reluctance to claim breadwinner status appears again when he is asked to describe his family's financial arrangements. Although Anita describes their pattern as one in which they live on his earnings and she is free to spend hers however she wants, he says that both incomes are pooled to cover basic expenses. He also downplays his responsibility for breadwinning by ranking the financial provider role fifth of seven roles that he plays.

What is going on here? For one thing, Rod is not ideologically committed to the use of breadwinning as a gender boundary; he describes his ideal world as one in which he and his wife would share providing equally. It is probably also significant that his family has not always been so heavily dependent on his income. During the early years of their marriage, when he was struggling to establish himself in the construction trades, it was Anita whose full-time work as a textile-mill operative provided the steady income and the higher wages. Indeed, their current situation is fairly recent. It was not until their second child was born that Anita took any appreciable time off, staying home with the children for several years before she went back to the mills. It's only in the past five years that Rod's business has been well established and Anita has cut back to part-time work.

The most compelling explanation for Rod's reluctance to claim breadwinner status, however, may be the tensions surrounding the social construction of gender in his marriage. Rod's interview hints at such tensions, but they emerge clearly when I talk with Anita the next morning.

Although she is much more open about acknowledging the family's reliance on Rod's income (describing her own earnings as "pitiful"), she also insists on the importance of her own contributions and aspirations. She describes his job as more important financially, but asserts emphatically, "Even if I weren't working, I'd feel I was providing for the family. . . . I provide support and [all kinds of things] that make it possible for him to go out to work—and I always have." Although her wages are negligible, she considers her current work important because it allows her "to have a say, to have something to look forward to" and because, unlike the mill work she did just for money, she "loves it." She plans to continue working until retirement because "I love working [and] I don't like taking money from my husband." Moreover, Anita doesn't plan to remain a salesclerk; she has developed aspirations for a career in fashion design. "I'm just starting, for some reason," she confides, "wanting to make *my* life. . . . It took this long to see what I wanted to do in life. . . . I'm going to go as far as I can go; I'm not hesitant about it."

These aspirations have given Anita a new sense of self-confidence and have made her more assertive. She is openly questioning the gendered division of labor in her marriage and expressing resentment about the priority that Rod places on work over family. While she can't imagine ever being sole financial provider for her family, "because I could never make the money he does," she does not think such a role would be a hardship. "I would gladly give up all this responsibility and just have to worry about working 40 hours a week," she says. "To me, that's the perfect life." Indeed, she would like Rod to ease her burden now by taking more responsibility for the routine running of the household. When asked to rank his social roles, she says derisively, "Housework is going to be last because he does *nothing*." She makes this point again when asked whether she agrees that "if a wife works on the job as many hours as her husband, he should spend as much time in housework and child care as she does." "Should, but doesn't," she says tersely. Anita also wants her husband to spend more time with their children. When she is presented with the hypothetical situation of the couple with the sick child, Anita responds that the husband should stay home to care for the child and then, referring to her own husband, says with some feeling, "It would've been great if he had done it; he would've gotten to know his own kids a little better."

It is clear from Rod's interview that these are open issues in his marriage. He also expresses concern about how little time he has for his children. When asked how important it is to him to be a good father, he responds, "It's very important to me, but I don't feel I am—because I'm working such long hours." And Anita's influence is apparent when he is asked whether he agrees that a dual-earner husband should share housework and child care. He laughs ruefully and says, "He probably should, but *I don't*," and then adds, "But I would say that I agree."

Rod seems to be conflicted about the use of conventional gender boundaries to construct a gendered division of labor, particularly within the family. On the one hand, he agrees that "there is some work that is men's and some that is women's and they shouldn't be doing each other's," and his marriage seems to enact such distinctions. On the other hand, he expresses a belief that marriage should be an equal partnership in which both domestic and financial responsibilities are shared. He readily acknowledges the justice of Anita's claims for the opportunity to develop a career of her own, to "make her life," but he also realizes that she can only do so if he cuts back on his work and takes on more responsibility at home. And, when push comes to shove, Rod really does not want to reduce his absorption in his work. Asked what he would do if he won a $3 million lottery jackpot, he does not say he would hire more help and cut back on his own long hours of work; instead, he says he would expand the business. Rod and Anita do not seem close to agreement on these issues, and the construction of gender will probably continue to be a source of contention in their marriage. For now, Rod seems to be resolving the contradictions by relinquishing certain gender boundaries (including breadwinning) in theory even as he maintains them in practice.

Conclusion

The dual-earner husbands in this study, like their wives, vary considerably in their use of breadwinning as a gender boundary. They range all the way from the role sharers, who have completely relinquished breadwinning as a boundary in the construction of gender, to the traditional breadwinners, who steadfastly maintain it despite their wives' employment. Just as important as the variation that is present, however, is the variation that is missing. This analysis has revealed only half as many characteristic approaches to breadwinning for husbands as for wives. Unlike their wives, these husbands do not vary on the financial support dimension of breadwinning; virtually all of them see their work as something they do primarily to support their families.

If we assume that the "missing" dimension in husbands' constructions of breadwinning is financial support, it is possible to imagine four additional breadwinner types, made up of husbands who do not see financial support of their families as a primary, or even a very important, reason for being employed. We might find "career-committed providers" (men who, like the female committed workers, are quite happy to fill the provider role, but who work for other reasons); "advanced role sharers" (husbands who have so far relinquished breadwinning as a gender boundary that they no longer feel it as a motivation for employment); "discouraged reluctant co-providers" (men who hold an ideal of male breadwinning, but who see so little chance of ever attaining it that they have chosen to emphasize other aspects of their employment); and "reluctant providers" (men who, like their female counterparts, feel trapped by a responsibility to provide that they do not want). While we can imagine men with these approaches to breadwinning, however, their virtual absence from the sample provides yet another reminder of the extent to which breadwinning continues to serve as a gender boundary that defines masculinity.

Like their wives, the vast majority of husbands in this study (74 percent) use breadwinning in some way to create gender difference. Some, like Roger, maintain this gender boundary by relocating it—defining primary breadwinning, rather than sole breadwinning, as the distinguishing mark of manhood. Others, like Rod, keep breadwinning in place as a de facto gender boundary, although they claim no ideological commitment to it. Still others, like Brad, maintain this boundary only as an ideal, a distinction to strive for.

Both the regression analysis and the case studies show that for husbands, as for wives, it is adult circumstances and experiences—particularly husband's and wife's earnings, other characteristics of the wife's employment, and stage in the family life cycle—that most influence the extent to which these men use breadwinning as a gender boundary. And it is in shaping men's actual interpretations of their wives' employment (rather than their norms) that these influences work most powerfully. These effects are apparent when we consider the cases of Brad, the reluctant co-provider, and Rod, the uncommitted provider. Both men's interpretations of their wives' employment contradict their norms about breadwinning. Brad firmly believes that, as a man, he should be the family breadwinner, but this ideology is outweighed by his inability to earn enough money to support his desired life-style and by the fact that his wife has a more stable work history and earns higher wages than he does. Moreover, because they do not have children, Brad cannot easily use

Michelle's domestic responsibilities as the basis for an argument that her work should be regarded as secondary. In Rod's case, although he has relinquished the breadwinning boundary in theory, his high income, his wife's low income, the discontinuities in her work history, and the presence of children all militate against his interpreting her employment as shared breadwinning.

It is also clear from these case studies that these men do not construct gender boundaries in isolation. Rather, the process is an interactive and negotiated one. In three of the four cases, the interviews provide explicit evidence of negotiation. And we have no evidence that the fourth couple, David and Molly, do not negotiate; they may simply be more reserved and less willing to discuss their negotiations with a stranger who has come to interview them.

The regression analysis tells us that husbands' interpretations of their wives' employment are less susceptible to the influence of negotiation than are their gender attitudes and norms about breadwinning, and the case study of Rod bears this out. Rod may have developed a more egalitarian stance on gender issues in response to his wife's insistence that her contributions and aspirations be taken seriously, but these have not led him to interpret her employment as breadwinning. The greater influence of negotiation on attitudes than on behavioral interpretation also suggests that, of these four men, it is Brad, the reluctant co-provider, whose approach to breadwinning is most likely to be changed through negotiation. Particularly if their circumstances do not change, Michelle may well influence Brad to accept her normative stance that breadwinning should be shared, transforming him from a reluctant co-provider into a role sharer.

If wives influence their husbands to adopt egalitarian attitudes now, will this lead to egalitarian behaviors later? The evidence here is that behavior, interpretations of that behavior, and norms are all relatively independent of one another. Indeed, the case studies of Roger and Rod both suggest that changes in attitudes may be substitutes for, rather than precursors of, changes in behavior (a possibility that will be explored further in Chapter 6). Both of these men are in conflict with their wives about the high priority they place on their work and their correspondingly low involvement in domestic activity. And in their responses to the gender attitude items, both men seem to offer some egalitarian attitudes as a concession to their wives, a way of saying, "See, honey, I'm a reasonable guy; I'm willing to admit that you're right—at least in principle." But neither of them shows much inclination to change his behavior.

These case studies suggest, then, that the construction of gender in the family is a complex process, one in which conceptual and behavioral dimensions are not directly related and the use of breadwinning as a gender boundary interacts with the construction of other gender boundaries. Thus, for Roger, male responsibility for breadwinning is the complement of female responsibility for home and children; his wife's contesting of his construction of the breadwinning boundary is linked to their disagreement about other gender boundaries. Rod's contradictory position with regard to breadwinning also seems to be related to the contention about other gender boundaries in his marriage. A similar statement could be made about Brad; while he and his wife agree that gender difference is important, they disagree about which gender boundaries should be central in its construction. David, on the other hand, seems willing to relinquish breadwinning as a gender boundary precisely because other gender boundaries, particularly Molly's greater responsibility for home and children, have been maintained.

The interconnections of gender boundaries will be explored further in Chapter 7. At this point, however, it is clear that the "snapshots" of couples' relationships that these interviews provide are limited in what they can tell us about the ongoing process of negotiation. Examining how constructions of gender change over time can provide a better picture of how circumstances and negotiation influence couples' construction of gender boundaries in general and the breadwinning boundary in particular. It is this type of analysis that will provide the central focus for Chapters 5 and 6, as I supplement data from the initial interviews with information collected from follow-up questionnaires five years later.

5

Collaborative Constructions of Gender

Couples Who Agree About the Breadwinning Boundary

The gender construction model tells us that the gender system is dynamic rather than static. It is always in flux, subject to frequent challenges and continual negotiation, always being created and re-created in our daily lives. Examination of the breadwinning boundary confirms this assumption of dynamism, for breadwinning is indeed a site of challenge, negotiation, and change in the gender system. In the pages that follow, I consider two aspects of this dynamism in the breadwinning boundary: the extent to which this boundary is agreed upon or contested within dual-earner marriages, and the prevalence of stability or change over time in its use.

This analysis is based not only on data from my original 1987–88 interviews, but also on data from a 1992–93 follow-up survey. The follow-up survey was mailed out in fall 1992 to all of the original study participants. The mailing consisted of a two-page summary of preliminary study results and separate two-page questionnaires for husband and wife. These questionnaires were designed to assess change over time in constructions of breadwinning and in family, employment, and income circumstances. (For a fuller discussion of the methodology of the follow-up survey, see Appendix A.)

Not all of the original 153 couples could be included in the analysis of data from the follow-up survey. About half (76 couples) either could not be reached because their addresses were unknown or chose not to respond to the survey. Of the 77 couples who did return follow-up questionnaires, some were no longer in dual-earner marriages and others sent back incomplete questionnaires. Much of the analysis in this and the following chapter is based on a subsample of 50 couples who were in dual-earner marriages in both 1987–88 and 1992–93 and who returned completed follow-up questionnaires.

It is important to keep in mind that this 50-couple subsample, unlike the original sample, was not randomly selected. Instead, these couples selected themselves by responding to the follow-up survey, and they are likely to differ in important ways from those who did not respond. Fortunately, however, information gathered in the original interviews can be used to identify some of these differences. Thus, we know that couples of French-Canadian extraction, those in professional and managerial occupations, and those who agreed about the construction of breadwinning in 1987–88 were more likely than average to respond to the follow-up survey. In contrast, those who had no children at the time of the original interviews were less likely to respond. Even among couples who responded to the follow-up survey, some were more likely than others to be included in the subsample because they were more likely to still be in dual-earner marriages in 1992–93. Husbands and wives who believed in 1987–88 that breadwinning responsibility should be shared fall into this category and are thus disproportionately represented in the 50-couple subsample. (A more detailed comparison of the main sample and the subsample can be found in Appendix B, Table B5.)

The original sample and the subsample are also likely to differ in ways that cannot be readily measured. For example, couples for whom the issue of breadwinning is a continuing source of tension may have been less likely to return their follow-up questionnaires. Given these sources of bias in the subsample, the analysis that follows should be regarded as more tentative and exploratory than that in the previous chapters.

Agreement About the Breadwinning Boundary

One of the surprising things about the data from the original 1987–88 interviews was the relatively low incidence of agreement between husbands and wives about breadwinning in their marriages. Only 54 percent of the 153 couples were in complete or substantial agreement about the use of breadwinning as a gender boundary.

For purposes of this analysis, I consider a couple in complete agreement if husband and wife agree both on their interpretation of the wife's employment and on norms about breadwinning. Thus, a male traditional breadwinner and a female employed homemaker are in complete agreement because both report that breadwinning is and should be a male responsibility in their marriage. Similarly, male role sharers and female co-breadwinners agree that breadwinning is and should be a shared responsibility. Complete agreement does not require, however, that a couple's norms about breadwinning match their interpretations of their employment behavior. Female reluctant providers and male reluctant co-providers are in complete agreement that breadwinning ought ideally to be a male responsibility but that they are, of necessity, sharing it. Male uncommitted providers and female reluctant traditionals demonstrate the reverse form of agreement; they are completely agreed that breadwinning ought ideally to be a shared responsibility but that it is not shared in their marriage. Thirty-one percent of the couples in the original sample displayed one of these four varieties of complete agreement about breadwinning.

As noted in Chapter 4, husbands' constructions of breadwinning are less complex than wives', reflecting the restricted permeability of the breadwinning boundary for husbands. Thus, while wives' constructions of breadwinning involved two distinct dimensions of behavioral interpretation, husbands' constructions included just one. Because wives' approaches to breadwinning are more complex, not all of these approaches can be matched with corresponding types for husbands. A substantial minority of women, those whose scores on the two dimensions of behavioral interpretation are inconsistent (the helpers, the supplementary providers, the family-centered workers, and the committed workers), cannot possibly be in complete agreement with their husbands about breadwinning because there are no comparable categories for their husbands to fall into.

To deal with this difficulty, I have designated a second category of agreement about the breadwinning boundary, substantial agreement. I consider a couple to be in substantial agreement if two conditions are met: (1) their norms about breadwinning agree, and (2) one of the wife's behavioral interpretation dimensions agrees with the husband's behavioral interpretation dimension. Thus, a helper or a family-centered worker married to either a traditional breadwinner or a reluctant co-provider is judged to be in substantial agreement with him. Similarly, supplementary providers and committed workers are regarded as in substantial agreement with husbands who are either role sharers or uncommitted providers. Twenty-three percent of couples in the original study were in substantial agreement about the use of breadwinning as a gender boundary.

Examination of data from the 1987–88 interviews reveals that some breadwinner types are more likely than others to be part of a collabora-

TABLE 3

Agreement About Breadwinning by Breadwinner Types

	Pct. in complete agreement	Pct. in substantial agreement	Pct. in substantial disagreement	Pct. in complete disagreement
Wives' types				
Employed homemakers (N = 32)	69%		22%	9%
Helpers (N = 29)		69	31	
Reluctant providers (N = 21)	38		52	10
Co-breadwinners (N = 23)	52		35	13
Reluctant traditionals (N = 18)	33		50	17
Committed workers (N = 4)		75	25	
Supplementary providers (N = 19)		47	53	
Family-centered workers (N = 7)		43	57	
Husbands' types				
Traditional breadwinners (N = 55)	40	20	34	6
Reluctant co-providers (N = 35)	23	34	34	9
Uncommitted providers (N = 23)	26	17	48	9
Role sharers (N = 40)	30	20	43	7

tive construction of the breadwinning boundary (Table 3). Among husbands, those who believe that breadwinning should be a male responsibility, the traditional breadwinners and the reluctant co-providers, are somewhat more likely to have wives who agree with them. Among the wives, it is the employed homemakers and the helpers whose husbands (69 percent of them) are most likely to be in complete or substantial agreement. By contrast, the women whose interpretations of their employment are wholly at odds with their norms, the reluctant providers and the reluctant traditionals, are much less likely to have husbands who agree with them about breadwinning. (Fewer than 40 percent are in agreement.)

What conditions lead a couple to agree about breadwinning? I have used a combination of two-variable and multiple regression analyses to examine the factors that influence agreement. Just as approaches to breadwinning are shaped, in part, by a couple's economic circumstances, so, too, is their level of agreement about breadwinning. It is the ratio of husband's wages to wife's that is critical here (Table 4). Among couples for whom this ratio is either very low (the wife earns as much as or more than her husband) or very high (the husband outearns his wife more than three to one), interpretations are more clearly constrained by circumstances, and the rate of agreement about the use of breadwinning as a gender boundary is more than 60 percent (most often complete agreement). Among couples whose wage ratio falls in the more ambiguous middle range, however, a greater variety of interpretations is possible, and more than 50 percent disagree.

Family circumstances also prove to be important predictors of level of agreement, just as they are of approaches to breadwinning (Appendix B, Table B6). Most important here is the number of years that a couple has been married. The case studies in Chapter 4 demonstrated that the construction of gender in a marriage is an ongoing process of negotiation. Thus, it is not surprising that those in long-term marriages, couples who have been engaged in the negotiation process for a longer time, are more likely to have reached agreement about breadwinning. In addition, it is possible that the marriages of couples who agree about breadwinning are more likely to last; persistent disagreement about the construction of gender may produce strains in the marriage that lead to its breakdown. Number of children also influences agreement about breadwinning, with couples who have fewer children more likely to be in agreement. Larger numbers of children may produce strain in the process of gender construction by simultaneously increasing the need for a wife's income and the salience of her competing domestic responsibilities.

The most important predictors of husband-wife agreement about breadwinning, however, are neither economic nor family circumstances,

TABLE 4

Agreement About Breadwinning by Husband-Wife Wage Ratio

$(X^2 = 16.87, p < .01)$

Level of agreement	Wage ratio low (1.13 or less) (N = 39)	Wage ratio medium (1.14–3.13) (N = 77)	Wage ratio high (3.14 or more) (N = 37)
Complete agreement	44%	17%	49%
Substantial agreement	20	29	13
Substantial disagreement	28	48	30
Complete disagreement	8	6	8

but responses to the gender attitude items, which serve as indicators of overall gender ideology. In general, wives were more likely to express egalitarian views, supporting the blurring or even the elimination of many gender boundaries. Husbands, on the other hand, more often gave responses that called for the continued maintenance of gender boundaries. Therefore, not surprisingly, it is husbands and wives with moderate gender attitudes who were most likely to be in agreement about breadwinning. Strongly feminist attitudes on the part of wives (especially with regard to women's right to paid employment) and strong adherence to conventional gender divisions on the part of husbands (particularly an insistence that the man should be the head of the family) promote disagreement.

Interestingly, even after family circumstances and gender attitudes have been accounted for, the Franco-Americans in the sample are considerably more likely to be in agreement about breadwinning than are couples who are not of French-Canadian extraction. This higher rate of agreement among Franco-Americans may reflect the influence of a common cultural heritage that conditions attitudes about gender. Because of a history of discrimination and financial hardship, the participation of wives and mothers in the paid labor force has long been commonplace and widely accepted among Franco-Americans, as has a sense that marriage is a partnership and that all members of the family must work together for the good of the group. Sharing these assumptions may increase the likelihood that a couple will arrive at a shared construction of breadwinning.

Breadwinning, then, is a contested gender boundary; agreement about it does not just happen, but must be achieved. And some couples are more likely than others to achieve such agreement. Factors that promote agreement include the constraints of very high or very low husband-wife wage ratios, long-standing marriages, relatively small numbers of children, moderate gender attitudes, and the shared culture of Franco-Americans. Do the shared constructions of breadwinning produced by these factors endure over time? This is the issue to which I turn next.

Change over Time in the Deployment of the Breadwinning Boundary

What is most striking about an examination of change in constructions of breadwinning over the five-year period from 1987–88 to 1992–93 is just how common such change seems to be. Among the 50 couples in the follow-up subsample, only 8 (16 percent) reported no change from the breadwinner types constructed in their original interviews. In many cases (38 percent of the couples in the subsample), both husband and wife had changed their constructions of breadwinning by the time of the follow-up survey, and an additional twelve wives and eleven husbands had changed their approaches to breadwinning independent of their spouses. These figures must be interpreted with some caution: It is possible that couples who had experienced changes in their constructions of breadwinning were more likely to respond to the follow-up survey than those who had not. It is also possible that participation in the original study triggered change by making the issue of breadwinning salient. Even taking these possible biases into consideration, however, the prevalence of change in the subsample suggests that change in the construction of breadwinning would be more likely than not in a typical sample of dual-earner couples over a five-year period.

The distribution of breadwinner types in the follow-up subsample in 1992–93 is markedly different from that in the main sample in 1987–88. This difference results from both the process of selection into the subsample and the incidence of change over time in constructions of breadwinning. Table 5 shows the distribution of husbands' and wives' breadwinner types (1) in 1987–88 for the main sample of 153 couples, (2) in 1987–88 for the follow-up subsample of 50 couples, and (3) in 1992–93 for the follow-up subsample. Comparing the first two columns provides some indication of the selection bias in the subsample. Comparing the second and third columns provides a picture of change over time. For example, among husbands, the 1992–93 data show far fewer traditional breadwinners and far more role sharers in the subsample than the 1987–88 data do in the main sample. But, while the first of these differences is due to change over time, the second can be explained primarily by selection bias. Among the wives, we see a sharp reduction in the number of employed homemakers and dramatic increases in the ranks of the co-breadwinners and committed workers in the subsample between 1987–88 and 1992–93, and all of these differences reflect changes over time in wives' constructions of breadwinning.

Moreover, this table underestimates the amount of individual change because it shows only the overall distribution of breadwinner types at the two points in time. You should not assume, for example, that the 14 percent of subsample wives who were classified as helpers in 1987 and the 14 percent who were classified as helpers in 1992 are the same individuals. It is possible that there is no overlap between the two groups at all.

TABLE 5
Breadwinner Types in 1987 and 1992

Type	Pct. in main sample, 1987–88	Pct. in subsample, 1987–88	Pct. in subsample, 1992–93
Husbands			
Traditional breadwinners	36%	34%	22%
Role sharers	26	36	40
Reluctant co-providers	23	16	20
Uncommitted providers	15	14	18
Wives			
Employed homemakers	21	20	12
Co-breadwinners	15	16	28
Helpers	19	14	14
Supplementary providers	12	18	12
Reluctant providers	14	14	10
Reluctant traditionals	12	14	10
Family-centered workers	5	2	2
Committed workers	3	2	12

This is, in fact, the case for the male reluctant co-providers. None of the husbands who were so classified in 1987 were still in that category in 1992; the 20 percent who were classified as reluctant co-providers in the follow-up survey were an entirely different group of men.

As a first step in seeking to understand all this change in husbands' and wives' approaches to breadwinning, I have considered each dimension of breadwinning separately, comparing individuals' 1987 and 1992 ratings (low or high) on each. Surprisingly, although more than 60 percent of the individuals in the subsample exhibited some change in their approaches to breadwinning from 1987 to 1992, stability rather than change was the rule for each dimension. This means that most changes involved only one aspect of breadwinning; it was unusual for a respondent to redefine both behavioral interpretation and norms. Among husbands, it was clearly norms about breadwinning that were most plastic. Almost half of the husbands in the subsample had reconsidered their norms in the five-year period, while only 27 percent had changed their interpretations of their wives' employment. Among wives, no one dimension stood out as particularly prone to redefinition; about one-third of the women in the subsample had changed their position on each.

For the most part, these changes were moves away from using breadwinning as a gender boundary. This was particularly the case for wives; more than 75 percent of their reported changes in the normative and job centrality dimensions were in the direction of shared breadwinning.

So, too, were two-thirds of their changes in the financial support dimension. Husbands' changes were somewhat less consistent, but here, too, the predominant direction of change was away from using breadwinning as a gender boundary. Sixty-two percent of changes both in husbands' norms about breadwinning and in their interpretations of their wives' employment were in this direction. It is important to note, however, that this relaxation of the breadwinning boundary was not a universal trend; a substantial minority of changes (almost 40 percent of husbands' changes and about 25 percent of wives') were moves to strengthen this gender boundary.

In seeking to account for these changes in breadwinning norms and behavioral interpretations, I have turned once again to multiple regression analysis. In doing this analysis, I have begun with the current situation variables that proved so important for understanding respondents' original scores. I have then added the extent of disagreement between husband and wife in the original interviews and their original scores on each dimension of breadwinning, to see if these have any additional explanatory value.

The regression analysis shows that husbands' interpretations of their wives' employment in 1992 can be explained quite well by only a few variables (Appendix B, Table B7). As was true in 1987, situational factors have a strong influence. Men whose wives have high earnings and those whose children are old enough to be leaving home are particularly likely to interpret their wives' employment as shared breadwinning; those whose own earnings are high are less likely to do so. Interestingly, men's interpretations of their wives' employment in 1987 exert an independent influence on their interpretations in 1992. Apparently, once a man has begun to define his wife's employment as shared breadwinning, he is not likely to return to a more conventional interpretation.

For wives, too, interpretations of their employment continue to be influenced by circumstances. Wives' financial support dimension is explained (although weakly) by three such variables. A wife, like her husband, is more likely to regard her employment as something she does for the financial support of her family if she has children (especially children in the nest-leaving stage) and if her earnings are high, and less likely to do so if her husband's earnings are high. Income and family circumstances are even better predictors of wives' job centrality dimension. A woman is more likely to define her job as central in her own and her family's experience if her earnings are high and if she has older children.

For wives, as for husbands, earlier constructions of breadwinning also prove to be important influences. Even after circumstances have been taken into account, a woman's job centrality score in 1987 is a strong predictor of her job centrality score in 1992, indicating that once she has begun to define her job as central, she is likely to continue to do so. A woman is also more likely to rate her job as central in 1992 if she and her husband disagreed about breadwinning in 1987. This is a more difficult finding to interpret. It may be that disagreement leads wives to put more emphasis on their own jobs because they fear divorce, or it may be that the higher job centrality score is an outgrowth of feminist attitudes on the part of the wife, attitudes that were already causing disagreement with her husband five years earlier. (I will defer further consideration of how disagreement about breadwinning influences husbands' and wives' ongoing constructions of gender until Chapter 6, where an in-depth look at particular cases will provide a better understanding of these dynamics.)

In 1992, as in 1987, situational factors are less important for explaining the normative dimensions of breadwinning. For wives, by far the strongest predictor of norms about breadwinning in 1992 is their norms in 1987. In other words, their beliefs about whether breadwinning should be a distinctively male responsibility were very stable over time. The only other variable that emerges as significant for explaining wives' norms in 1992 is their 1987 financial support scores. Women who, in 1987, were already defining their work as something they did primarily to contribute to the financial support of their families were particularly likely to report an ideological commitment to shared breadwinning in 1992.

Husbands' norms about breadwinning were far less stable than those of their wives—more likely to change over time and more responsive to changes in circumstances. Indeed, a man's norms about breadwinning in 1987 do not predict his norms in 1992 at all. To understand his 1992 norms, we do better to look at his family and economic circumstances. If a man has children, particularly adolescents, he is more likely to believe that breadwinning should be a distinctively male responsibility. Interestingly, however, high earnings—either his own or his wife's—decrease his adherence to ideals of male breadwinning.

This analysis confirms the importance of economic and family circumstances in shaping the use of breadwinning as a gender boundary. It suggests that constructions of breadwinning are dynamic because couples' lives are dynamic. But it also indicates that the construction of gender is an ongoing process, one in which norms and behavioral interpretations arrived at earlier continue to have an influence independent of circumstances. For wives, it is norms about breadwinning that are especially likely to be influenced by previous constructions; for husbands, it is behavioral interpretation.

The remainder of this chapter focuses on the 29 couples in the followup subsample who had developed a collaborative construction of breadwinning by the time of the original interviews. Only six of these (21 percent) reported unchanged constructions in 1992–93. In ten cases, both husband and wife had changed breadwinner type, while an additional nine wives and four husbands had changed unilaterally. For the most part, such changes did not disrupt a couple's earlier agreement but represented a refinement of that agreement or the construction of a new one. For 9 of these 23 couples, however, change produced disagreement about the construction of breadwinning in their marriage.

What prompted changes in the use of breadwinning as a gender boundary—particularly changes to disagreement—among couples who had already negotiated a shared construction of breadwinning? The regression analysis suggests that new circumstances are an important catalyst, but, surprisingly, such circumstances played a role in only half (12 of 23) of these cases of change. Moreover, situational variables were least likely to be a factor among the couples who moved toward disagreement (only 44 percent were in new circumstances) and most common among those who refined their previous agreement (71 percent were in new circumstances). Some constructions of breadwinning were more prone to change than others. Among husbands, the reluctant co-providers were most likely to change (all of them did), while the role sharers were least likely to do so (only 27 percent). For the wives, too, the reluctant providers proved to be a particularly unstable group (all of them had changed their constructions of breadwinning by the time of the follow-up study), as, interestingly, were the co-breadwinners (83 percent had redefined at least one dimension of breadwinning by 1992).

A clearer understanding of the processes of collaboration and change in the use of breadwinning as a gender boundary requires a move beyond aggregate data to a detailed examination of individual cases. The six case studies that follow focus on couples who initially agreed about breadwinning and include cases of stable agreement, refined agreement, new agreement, and moves to disagreement. A detailed look at the nature of their initial agreements and what happened to them over time will elucidate the processes of gender construction in marriage.

Agreement and Change: Six Case Studies

Stable Agreement: Jeff and Susan —
Traditional Breadwinner and Helper

The stability of some couples' agreement about the construction of breadwinning in their marriage is facilitated by external factors. Some who begin with conventionally gendered notions of separate spheres for men and women find that those boundaries are supported by their circumstances and experiences. In other cases, strong career commitments and near-equal incomes combine to promote a strategy of role sharing that persists over time. Some couples, however, manage to maintain an agreed-upon construction of the breadwinning boundary, even when it is challenged by their circumstances and experiences, because it is based on strongly held, shared values. Jeff and Susan, a traditional breadwinner and a helper, fall into this last category.

I have pulled up to the curb in front of Jeff and Susan's home in an older residential area on a sunlit July evening in 1987. All over the neighborhood, children have come back outdoors after the family dinner hour, and their shouts reverberate up and down the street. Among them are Jeff and Susan's three children, two boys in their early teens and a nine-year-old daughter. It is Susan who opens the front door in response to my ring and invites me into a living room that is somewhat worn and clearly lived-in, but carefully maintained. I have arranged to interview Susan and Jeff sequentially, and I talk with each in the living room while the other works on cleaning up the dinner dishes in the kitchen.

Jeff and Susan are a deeply religious couple who moved to this community from another state a little more than five years ago to help establish a new branch of their Christian fellowship here. It is a sign of their commitment to their church that Jeff gave up an employment situation that he describes as "the best job I ever had" and took a substantial reduction in pay in order to make the move. Their religious beliefs include a firm attachment to separate spheres for men and women, and this value is reflected in their interviews. Susan not only gives nonegalitarian responses to all six gender attitude items but agrees strongly with three of those items: that "most of the important decisions in the life of the family should be made by the man of the house," that "women should take care of running their homes and leave running the country up to men," and that "a married woman should not work outside the home if her husband can comfortably support her." She gives a similarly gendered response to the hypothetical situation of the dual-earner couple with the high-earning wife and the sick child, insisting, without hesitation, that "the wife should quit working." Jeff's responses to these questions are more often tempered by practical concerns, but he makes it clear that he shares Susan's ideological commitment to gender specialization. He responds to the hypothetical situation by acknowledging that "maybe the husband should stay home since his income is less," but also notes, "My principles say the other way." And these principles very much shape Jeff and Susan's responses to the issue of breadwinning.

For both Susan and Jeff, employment is purely and simply a way of earning the money necessary to get by in life, and both agree that providing that financial support is Jeff's responsibility. Jeff works in the maintenance department of the regional medical center and earns about $17,000 per year. He ranks earning money for basic family needs as his primary reason for employment and says this is the only reason that is very important to him. That Jeff works only for the money becomes particularly clear when he reports that he once moved from a salaried, white-collar, supervisory position to a blue-collar job in the same company because the latter was an hourly wage position that required 30–40 hours per week of overtime and, as a result, yielded a higher income. "The company regarded this as a demotion," he notes, chuckling, "but I considered it a promotion and I asked for it." Jeff expands on this theme when he explains that he would quit his job if he won a $3 million lottery jackpot "because my job isn't very fulfilling to me. I feel I could be more beneficial to my family and to my friends—maybe I should say to mankind in general . . . because I'd get into a lot of volunteer work."

Jeff works in order to provide. He and Susan agree that he is the financial provider for their family, that his job is the important one, that he feels the obligation to provide much more than she does, and that, ideally, he should be the sole provider. They both rank his financial provider role third in importance, just after husband and father, and they both rank the provider role last in importance for Susan.

But Jeff and Susan find that they can't get by on Jeff's earnings. Three children, a commitment to tithing, and the fact that Jeff's annual income is well below the family median for this community all leave them strapped for money. When asked how important it is to earn money for family extras, Jeff laughs and says, "It's always nice, but there are not too many extras coming by." And so, intermittently throughout their marriage, Susan has taken part-time work outside the home to supplement Jeff's earnings. For the past two years, she has been working three or four hours per week as a cashier at a neighborhood store. Her income is small, less than $1,000 a year, but both Susan and Jeff regard it as an important contribution. Susan emphasizes that this money is used for basic family needs and that helping to meet those needs is the only reason she is employed. When I ask her if she expects to be in the labor force continuously until retirement, she responds, "Not necessarily. I'm in it now for financial purposes, and if that were not necessary, I probably wouldn't." For now, though, although Jeff may be the family breadwinner, he needs Susan's help.

When I hear from Susan and Jeff again more than five years later, they are still firmly committed to gender-specialized roles. Jeff's income has gone up very little in the intervening years, barely keeping pace with inflation. Susan has increased her work hours considerably, from four to fifteen hours per week, and now brings in almost $6,000 per year. This expansion of Susan's employment may be a response to growing family expenses as their older children reach college age, or it may reflect fears about how secure Jeff's job is in the depressed local economy. Jeff has responded to Susan's greater financial contribution by giving her financial provider role a slightly higher ranking than he did earlier, fifth on the list of seven roles. But he has also given his own provider role a higher priority and now ranks it first, ahead of husband and father. Despite these changes, Jeff and Susan are still agreed that he is the provider, that his job is the important one, that it is he who feels the obligation to provide, and that, ideally, he should be the sole provider. He is still a traditional breadwinner and she is still helping out.

Refining Agreement: Debbie and Allen— From Supplementary Provider to Co-breadwinner

If some couples develop a shared agreement about breadwinning and maintain it over time, others continue to refine their agreement, bringing their constructions of gender closer and closer together. Debbie, head teller at a downtown bank, and Allen, an auto mechanic with a local car dealership, are such a couple. At the time of the initial interviews, they were in substantial agreement about breadwinning, but by the time of the follow-up survey, they were in complete agreement. To look more closely at the nature and evolution of their agreement, let's go back to my first meeting with them, on a mild, clear August evening in 1987.

I have arranged to interview Debbie and Allen at their home in a quiet residential neighborhood at the confluence of the Androscoggin River and one of its tributaries. This is a popular residence for middle-income Lewiston-Auburn families. It is a convenient location, connected to the central business districts of both cities by bridges, but its relative lack of through streets gives it a sense of seclusion and neighborliness. Most houses, like Debbie and Allen's bungalow, date from the first half of the century. The single-family homes tend to be on narrow lots and close to the streets, but most also have very deep backyards and often boast views down to one of the rivers.

Allen and Debbie are in their mid- to late thirties. They have been married for seventeen years and have three children, two teenagers and a ten-year-old. Although I am meeting them for the first time this evening, I feel as if I already know the whole family. I had several telephone conversations with their sixteen-year-old daughter when I was first trying to reach her busy parents, and several more with both Allen and Debbie in the process of scheduling their interviews. They are open, friendly, and eager to participate in the study; they respond thoughtfully to my questions, and I find them a pleasure to interview.

We agree that I should interview Allen first, while Debbie clears up the dinner dishes. He leads me to a picnic table in the backyard, where we can enjoy the evening air and the view of the river and where he can keep an eye on his younger son and the friends with whom he is playing a game of backyard baseball. The scene is something out of Norman Rockwell: rolling lawns, the river shimmering in the sun, children playing ball, and a family dog racing around and barking excitedly whenever anyone gets a hit. When Allen and I have finished, he goes off to join the baseball players and I head into the kitchen, where Debbie presents me with a tall glass of iced tea and we settle down at the kitchen table for her interview.

The picture that emerges from talking with Debbie and Allen is of a very hardworking couple. Except for one very difficult period in the mid-1970s when the company Allen had been working for went out of business and he was unemployed for a year, both of them have been working continuously, often at jobs requiring long hours, since they finished high school. Both like their jobs and rate the feeling of accomplishment that work gives as a very important reason for being employed. Debbie is eloquent on the subject, saying that her job provides her with a sense of intellectual challenge that she doesn't get at home and that "it gives me a sense of being an individual and not just a cog in the wheel of the world."

Both Debbie and Allen are also clear, however, that family is their first priority. Both rank family roles as most important to them, and both respond to the hypothetical situation of the sick child by considering what would be best for the family. They approach this issue with different emphases, however. Allen focuses on the family's financial welfare and concludes that "the person that should stay home is the one that is . . . least likely to hurt the family's income if it is lost." Debbie is more concerned with balancing the emotional needs of everyone involved. She says that the couple should consider which parent this particular child "tends to lean more toward" and which can be "most efficient at giving them that care," and emphasizes that the solution should have "nothing to do with the importance of either job."

It is hardly surprising, then, that both Debbie and Allen put family first in thinking about why they work. Whatever satisfactions their jobs provide are secondary; both agree that meeting family financial needs is their primary motivation for employment. And, for the most part, they see the responsibility for meeting these needs as something they share.

Allen's answers to my questions about providing place him in the category of role sharer. He says that he and his wife share providing equally, that both jobs are equally important, that he suspects she may feel the obligation to provide somewhat more than he does, and that both incomes are critical for meeting basic family expenses. He can't imagine any situation in which either of them would leave the labor force and be supported by the other. Allen ranks Debbie's provider role only fifth on the list of seven, but this is the same ranking that he gives his own role as provider, placing it after husband, worker, father, and friend. Being the male breadwinner is not central to his sense of self. Rather, he seems committed to breaking down gender boundaries and, like his wife, gives strongly feminist responses to all the gender attitude items (one of only eleven men in the original study to do so). The only exception to all this comes when Allen expresses, as his ideal, a wish that he could provide "a little more" than his wife.

Debbie's responses are similar to Allen's. She also says that they share providing equally and that both incomes are critical for meeting basic family needs. She agrees that she feels the obligation to provide somewhat more than Allen does and provides evidence of this when she reports that she can't imagine any circumstances under which he would be the sole provider for the family, but that she could imagine being the sole provider herself if she could earn enough. She believes that Allen, whom she describes as "very creative," might like to leave his job if he could, to "run the house and handle everything and do his little projects at his own pace." Although she can easily imagine such a scenario, however, it is not her ideal. Ideally, she believes, they should share providing equally.

Where Debbie's responses differ from Allen's is in the matter of job centrality. His job, she says, is definitely more important than hers. She describes a pattern set early in their marriage whereby she dealt with the competing demands of financial support and child care by "aligning" her jobs to fit with her husband's work schedule. "If Allen's shift changed and it was necessary for me to change a shift," she explains, "sometimes it was necessary to leave a job in order to do that." She expects this pattern of adjusting her work to his to continue. "His is always going to be the ongoing important position," she reports, "because he can make more money than I can—because I'm a woman." This last comment is surprising coming from Debbie; although Allen does earn a slightly higher hourly wage than she does, she works longer hours and it is, in fact, she who brings home the larger weekly paycheck. Nevertheless, because she does not consider her job to be central in the life of her family, Debbie falls into the category of supplementary provider, not co-breadwinner.

When I hear from Debbie and Allen five years later, there has been little economic change in their lives. Their combined incomes have gone up only 7 percent during this period, not even keeping pace with inflation. Both are now working only 40 hours per week (probably as a result of the deep regional recession), but Debbie's hourly wage has increased more than Allen's and she continues to earn about $2,000 more per year than he does. Time has brought some changes in their family circumstances; the older children, now in their early twenties, are no longer living at home, and only their younger son, now a high school sophomore, remains.

Their continued near-equal earning power and need for both incomes, the elimination of child care as a primary concern in organizing their lives, and their feminist ideologies have all combined to move Debbie and Allen into closer agreement about breadwinning. Debbie no longer considers Allen's job more important than hers, something she must "align" herself with. Allen now clearly claims shared breadwinning as his ideal; gone is his wish to be "a little more" the family financial provider than his wife. Indeed, on the follow-up questionnaires, they give virtually identical responses to all the questions about breadwinning. If they were in substantial agreement about this gender boundary five years earlier, they are now completely agreed that she is a co-breadwinner and he is a role sharer.

Developing a New Agreement: Jeannette and Roland — From Reluctant Co-providers to Co-breadwinners

While some couples continue to negotiate their substantial agreement about breadwinning into a refined and more complete form of agreement, others develop an entirely new agreement. These people continue to collaborate in the construction of gender but end up in a very different place from where they started. Jeannette and Roland, a pair of older, Franco-American mill workers, provide an interesting example of this phenomenon.

I have arrived at the front door of Jeannette and Roland's modest ranch house just before 9:00 on a cold, rainy October night, feeling both tired and apologetic. I have been out interviewing since 4:00 P.M., and because two of those interviews took considerably longer than antici-pated, I am now running almost an hour behind schedule. I have tele-phoned ahead to let Jeannette and Roland know that I'll be delayed, but I am uncomfortably aware that I will not be out of their house until well after 10:00, a very late hour for people whose workday begins at 7:00 A.M. Jeannette and Roland are gracious and welcoming, however, and they quickly put me at ease. They are a lively, fun-loving couple, both with twinkles in their eyes and irrepressible senses of humor, and their interaction includes a great deal of playful banter. We spend a lot of our time laughing, and by the time I leave them, I am feeling far more alert and energetic than I did when I arrived.

This couple's love of fun is not a consequence of easy lives. At ages 48 and 50, they have been married for 27 years and working in the mills for far longer than that. Like many Franco-Americans of their generation, they both left school to go to work as soon as they were legally able to do so, and neither of them got past the ninth grade. Their employment his-tories are a saga of hard work and struggling to get ahead in two declin-ing industries, shoes and textiles. Over and over, they tell of layoffs and of mills closing, of trying to gauge when work in a mill was getting slow and trying to get out before disaster struck. Jeannette notes with pride that "the only time I've ever quit a job is for better money or because the mill closed." They both talk with animation about one particularly bad time, early in their marriage, when Roland worked at five different jobs in one year. "There was no work around," he explains. "There was nothing; I was bouncing around like a yo-yo." "I was pregnant," his wife adds, "so he had to find work." They have only the one child, a daugh-ter, now grown and married, whose birth kept Jeannette out of work for three months. For the most part they handled child care in the same way that Debbie and Allen did, by working different shifts.

In the context of their experiences, Jeannette and Roland's current work situations are notably stable. For the past fifteen years, Jeannette has been fairly steadily employed with one of the last remaining textile mills in the area. Now an experienced and highly skilled weaver, she is able to do better than most of her co-workers at the company's piece-work rates and, in a typical 48-hour week, she earns $300. Roland is now in his tenth year of working as a custodian in an athletic shoe factory. He earns less than Jeannette, only $240 for a 40-hour week, but his current job carries something that is unusual in their work experience, the possibility of a pension. For even as their combined incomes of $28,000 allow them to live in some comfort, they are worrying about the future. "We have to think about what we're going to do when it's time to retire," Jeannette reports. They talk about it a lot, she says, both about the possibilities and about what they will do "if something goes wrong." As insurance against the latter, Roland is trying to stick it out at the physically demanding custodial work that he is finding more and more difficult. "I think he's trying to survive to get to our retirement," his wife explains, "so we can have a pension."

Jeannette and Roland struggle together to improve their lives, and one of the most striking things about their relationship is their strong sense of togetherness and teamwork. This marriage is very much a partnership. They insist on sitting in on one another's interviews because to go off and answer my questions in secrecy would violate the spirit of their marriage. They repeatedly emphasize their compatibility and the ways in which they think alike. "We've always been close," Jeannette says, "and we've always had pretty much the same dreams and the same ideas." "We're really compatible," her husband adds, and then he jokes, "We can tell what each other will want for lunch!"

One of the ways in which they "think alike" is about breadwinning. They are completely agreed about the status of this gender boundary in their marriage. Financial providing, like everything else in their lives, is a joint venture. They both report that they share providing equally, that both jobs are equally important ("We need them both to survive," Jeannette explains), that they both feel the sense of obligation to provide, and that both incomes are critical for meeting basic family expenses. Jeannette ranks both her provider role and her husband's as among their three most important social roles.

Roland, however, gives a somewhat different ranking, placing his own provider role in the top three, but ranking Jeannette's only fifth. This discrepancy reflects Roland's sense that, as a man, he ought to be the family breadwinner. Indeed, this belief is something else that Roland and Jeannette share: They both report that their ideal would be for Roland to be the sole provider. This is not a goal that they expect to attain, however; neither of them can imagine it happening. After all, they have no hopes of advancement, they don't expect their earning power to improve, and the fact is that they need both incomes to get by. They are not bitter or resentful about this necessity; they don't expect life to be ideal. Roland does not feel that Jeannette has intruded on his masculine prerogatives; on the contrary, he deeply appreciates the alacrity with which she has shared the burden. (When asked about her motivations for working, he quips, "To make me happy.")

But it is a *burden* that they share. This becomes most clear when I ask them what they would do if they won a $3 million lottery jackpot. It is immediately apparent that they have indulged in this fantasy many times. Both are incredulous that I even have to ask if they would quit their jobs; of course they would. "We'd have what we want without having to kill ourselves and scrounge," Jeannette says. She dreams of going back to school, and Roland would like to travel. In many ways, the possibility of winning the lottery seems less remote to them than the possibility that Roland might ever earn enough to be sole provider, and they discuss it more seriously and completely. This animated discussion contrasts with Jeannette's perfunctory response to the question about who, ideally, should be the family financial provider. "The man," she replies, "sure, if it would be possible." Roland finds it hard to approach this question with any seriousness. Even as he reports that being sole provider is his ideal, he can't resist adding jokingly and with a teasing glance at his wife, "Then I could have her shine my shoes every night; I wouldn't have to do it myself."

Five years later, a perusal of Jeannette and Roland's follow-up questionnaires suggests that little has changed for them. They still exhibit the same unanimity of opinion that they did in the original interviews, and it is easy to imagine them with their heads together over the kitchen table, filling out their questionnaires and discussing their responses. Their incomes have gone up a little, keeping pace with inflation. Jeannette still earns a few thousand dollars more per year than Roland does, and he is still sticking it out in his custodian's job, five years closer to qualifying for the pension that could make the difference between relative security and relative poverty in their retirement. They are still completely agreed that they share providing equally, that both jobs are equally important, that they both feel the obligation to provide, that both incomes are critical for meeting their basic needs, and that they work primarily for the money.

But when I look more closely, I see that something important has changed here. Jeannette and Roland no longer profess male breadwinning as their ideal; instead, they say that their ideal is just what they are doing, sharing providing equally. Thus, in a deft ideological move, Jeannette and Roland have transformed themselves from a couple who have had to sacrifice their ideals in order to meet the grim demands of financial necessity to pioneers in the vanguard of social change—from reluctant co-providers to co-breadwinners.

How can we make sense of this transformation? First of all, a construction of gender in which norms are completely at odds with behavior is a difficult one to maintain. Of the eight men and seven women in the follow-up subsample who had originally fallen into the categories of reluctant co-provider or reluctant provider, none of the men and only two of the women were still in these categories five years later. The tension between norms and behavioral interpretation that is embodied in such an approach to breadwinning can be resolved only by rethinking one or the other.

But Jeannette and Roland had presumably lived with this tension for 27 years before participating in the study; what prompted them to change their ideals at this late date? One possibility is that their initial interviews with me (and the discussions of those interviews that I'm sure they had after I left) brought what had been a well-buried tension to the surface and, by making it salient, acted to catalyze change. Another possibility is that both their experiences and changing gender ideologies in the world around them had already been moving them to blur gender boundaries (both, for example, gave predominantly egalitarian responses to the gender attitude questions in their original interviews) and that giving up the ideal of male breadwinning was a logical and relatively easy next step. It is conceivable that each of them had been clinging to this ideal only because they thought it was important to the other, that discussion revealed that this was not the case, and that they were then happy to relinquish it. Whatever the explanation, this case highlights the dynamism of the breadwinning boundary; even complete agreement and stable circumstances may not protect it from dramatic reconstruction.

Adjusting to Changing Circumstances: Fred and Peggy— Negotiating a Gendered Construction of Breadwinning

In many cases, the most important inducement for negotiating a new agreement about breadwinning is not tension between norms and behavioral interpretation, but a change in circumstances. This was the case for Fred, an uncommitted provider, and Peggy, a supplementary provider.

On a Friday afternoon in August 1987, when I pull into the driveway of their split-level house in a suburban neighborhood near the edge of the metropolitan area, Fred is standing in the front yard talking with a neighbor. He is a very outgoing person and a great storyteller, and it takes him a few minutes to extricate himself from his conversation and invite me inside to begin the interview. We have arranged for Fred to be interviewed first, while Peggy is still at work, and for her interview to follow immediately afterward. I find, however, that my interview questions act as a spur to Fred's story-telling propensities and that I often have to recall him to the matter at hand. His interview consequently takes much longer than anticipated, and Peggy arrives home long before we are finished.

My interviews with Fred and Peggy reveal that they were childhood sweethearts who married while they were still in high school and had two children before they were out of their teens. Now in their late forties, they have been married for over 30 years. They are at an age when many couples are facing the financial and psychological challenges of raising adolescents, but their nest is just about empty, with two of their three children already grown and gone and the youngest engaged to be married within the month.

It is clear from their interviews that Fred and Peggy's early years as teenage parents were a struggle. Fred enlisted in the navy about a year after their marriage and stayed in it until he was eligible for retirement twenty years later. Since the pay of a low-rank sailor was hardly sufficient to support a family, however, Peggy soon found herself looking for ways to supplement his income with part-time jobs and schemes for earning money at home. She has worked at an amazing variety of jobs—factory work, domestic work, child care, hairdressing, and clerical work, among others. Indeed, except for two years when they were living overseas, she has earned money in one way or another throughout their marriage.

Peggy now works full time as a clerk in a retail store that is known locally for its high pay scale and generous benefits package, and she earns an annual income of $16,500. Fred combines his military pension with a full-time job as a clerk at the local Social Security office and brings in a total income from both sources of $32,000. Both Peggy and Fred identify him as the primary provider for their family, although Peggy ranks earning money for basic family needs as her most important motivation for working and reports that her income, like her husband's, is used mostly for paying monthly bills. At the same time, though, when Peggy is asked whose job is considered more important in the family, she answers instantly, "His, because he is the breadwinner."

Interestingly, however, both report shared breadwinning as their ideal. "If I could change the world," Peggy says, "I think we should be equal or fairly close. I don't think it's fair to [put the burden on] one person or the other." Fred describes himself as a fairly recent convert to this way of thinking. "I wanted for a while for her to stay home," he says. But then, he explains, he began to see his wife as a talented woman who needed a wider sphere of accomplishment than the home, and, as the children grew older, his beliefs evolved so that "it's more a together thing now."

It is not clear how firmly attached either Fred or Peggy is to the ideal of shared providing. Peggy makes it clear that she is willing to defer to her husband on this point. When I ask if she can imagine any circumstances under which she would leave the labor force and he would be sole provider, she responds, "If the house were paid, we had no outstanding bills, and he wanted me to be at home." Moreover, Fred and Peggy's expressed ideal of shared breadwinning is not part of a more general belief in role sharing. Rather, their responses to the gender attitude items indicate that both see some gender specialization as appropriate. Both, for example, disagree with the statement that "if a wife works on the job as many hours as her husband, he should spend as much time in housework and child care as she does."

Perhaps it is not surprising, then, that five years later, Fred and Peggy's norms about breadwinning have changed. The impetus for their reconsideration seems to have been a change in Peggy's work situation that has tipped their wage ratio further in Fred's direction. During the deep New England recession of the early 1990s, Peggy was laid off from her plum job at the retail store. She quickly found another full-time job, but at reduced wages, and she now earns only $12,000 per year. Although Fred's wage increases have not kept pace with inflation, he now outearns his wife almost three to one. This change in circumstances has led to a reinterpretation of Peggy's employment. She no longer says that she works primarily to meet basic family expenses. Instead, she ranks independence, a feeling of accomplishment, and contact with other people as her most important motivations for paid employment. She ranks her former top two choices, earning money for basic family needs and earning money for family extras, fifth and sixth on her current list. Fred, who formerly said that his wife's job was just as important as his, now says that his is more important. And Fred and Peggy are now agreed that, ideally, he should be the primary provider. They have become a traditional breadwinner and an employed homemaker.

New Circumstances and New Strains: Joan and Hal—
The Rise of Disagreement

Changed circumstances do not necessarily lead a couple to negotiate a new agreement about breadwinning. Some couples find that they can incorporate their new circumstances into their existing construction of the breadwinning boundary. For others, changed circumstances introduce new strains and create disagreement about that boundary. We can see an example of the latter in the case of Joan and Hal.

When I first met this couple in 1987, they had been married 30 years and had two grown children. Hal had been working for a large regional heating oil company for more than 25 years, had worked his way up through the ranks, and was now a midlevel manager earning a salary of $38,000. After years of part-time employment, Joan had recently gone into business for herself, opening a knitting shop that specialized in premium yarns and designer patterns and catered to an affluent clientele. For the time being, she was not taking any income from the business but was instead building up her equity. As I first encountered them, Hal and Joan were hard workers who thoroughly enjoyed their work and were in happy accord about the meaning of their jobs in their lives. By the time of the follow-up survey, however, both their circumstances and their agreement had deteriorated. Let's begin with the picture of agreement that they presented when I first interviewed them, on a weekday afternoon in late July.

I have arrived at Joan's yarn shop in the late afternoon. I find that Joan is a forthright, no-nonsense person, cheerfully efficient and energetic. She takes me into her office at the back of the store and deftly juggles the interview with periodic instructions to her assistant and occasional interruptions from suppliers. When we have finished, I get into my car and drive out to Joan and Hal's house, where I am to interview Hal at the end of his workday. Their spacious farmhouse sits atop an east-facing ridge, nestled between a ski area to the north and orchards to the south. Hal, a thoughtful, gentle-spoken man with a broad smile and a tendency to poke fun at himself, invites me to sit out on the broad, covered porch that wraps around the house on three sides, and there we begin the interview.

Joan and Hal's interviews reveal that they are in complete agreement about breadwinning. Not surprisingly, since Hal's salary is relatively high and Joan is not taking any income from her business, they both name Hal as the family financial provider. They also agree, although with some hesitation, that Hal's job is considered more important in the family.

"Everyday, I would probably put equally," he explains, "but if it really came down to which had to be done first, it probably would be mine—for the simple reason that, at the present time, I think we would have a hard time to live on . . . what she could do." Joan approaches the issue somewhat differently but comes to the same conclusion: "Well, financially, if I didn't have him to support me, I wouldn't have been able to do this . . . so I would say it would have to be his." They also agree that it is he who feels the obligation to provide, that it is his income that is used to meet their basic family needs, and that earning money for those needs is a very important motivation for his employment but not at all an important one for hers. Finally, they agree that all this is as it should be—that, ideally, Hal ought to be the primary provider.

A closer look, however, reveals that their similar constructions of breadwinning, particularly their norms of male providing, are based on some differing assumptions. For Joan, the important considerations are practical ones. In explaining why she and Hal have never used her earnings for day-to-day expenses, she points to the flexibility that is needed for raising children: "We've been adamant about that because I'm the one who's had to be flexible. If a child needed me, I had to be able to [stop working]. . . . I think that's a trap that a lot of couples get into these days; they live on both incomes and then, when something happens to one, they're in trouble." She does not insist, however, that it must be the woman whose job is flexible, and when she is presented with the hypothetical situation about the dual-earner couple with the sick child, she does not automatically assume that the mother should stay home. She can imagine the man being the flexible nonprovider, and she can imagine circumstances in which a husband and wife might take turns being the provider. Indeed, she envisions a version of this latter scenario in her own marriage: Neither she nor Hal has any pension coverage beyond Social Security, and she sees her business as a nest egg that will provide for them in their retirement.

For Hal, however, the idea that he should be the primary provider is rooted in an ideological attachment to breadwinning as a manly responsibility. Describing his norms about breadwinning, he says, "I'm still old-fashioned enough to believe that the man or the husband should provide the majority." He does not mention the possibility of Joan's business providing support in their retirement and, although he says that he would have "no objection" to other couples' allocating breadwinning responsibility differently, he responds to the hypothetical situation of the sick child by assuming that the wife should defer to the husband:

Of course, I'm still basically a little old-fashioned and figure that it basically would be the woman [who would stay home]; but under certain circumstances, as long as they're both agreeable. . . . In some cases, it could cause a lot of friction in a marriage, a lot more than it would be worth the extra few hundred dollars or few thousand dollars. It wouldn't be worth it for the husband to do it just for the money . . . if the wife would do it.

Five years later, these different assumptions have introduced a note of discord into Joan and Hal's construction of breadwinning. Their circumstances have changed dramatically since I first interviewed them. The local recession, combined with the national trend for corporations to downsize and reduce managerial "fat," resulted in the elimination of Hal's position. He quickly found another job, but his lack of a college education kept him from getting one with comparable responsibility and pay. Indeed, his income is now less than half what it was in 1987. In their original interviews, both Hal and Joan insisted that many things in life were more important than money, and Hal argued, "We could live on a lot less money than I'm making and probably be just as happy as we are now." But when it came to the reality of reducing their income and their standard of living by more than half, Hal and Joan decided that, while they could do it if they had to, they didn't have to. Joan's business, they decided, was now sufficiently well established to afford an income, and she started drawing a salary of $12,000 per year. This, combined with Hal's earnings, brought their income up to $30,000, of which Joan contributes 40 percent.

In 1992–93, Joan and Hal are agreed that Joan's contribution is critical. They now report that they share providing equally, that both jobs are equally important, that they both feel the obligation to provide, and that her income is just as important as his for meeting their basic family expenses. Where Joan and Hal disagree is about the desirability of this change in their lives. With the children grown and gone, Joan no longer sees a practical need to keep one income "flexible." She has reconsidered her norms about breadwinning and now describes her ideal as one in which she and her husband would share providing equally. Hal, however, cannot so easily adapt to their new situation; he still feels that being a breadwinner is part of what it means to be a man, and his ideal is still to be the primary provider for his family. It is hard to know how Hal and Joan will resolve this tension. Perhaps Hal will gradually adapt his norms to the reality of his situation. It is also possible that he and his wife will simply agree to disagree, with Hal acknowledging the justice of Joan's position but explaining apologetically that he is just too "old-fashioned" to adopt it.

Resistance and Compensation: Keith and Roseanne— From Co-breadwinner to Family-Centered Worker

More often than not, a move from husband-wife agreement to contention about the use of breadwinning as a gender boundary is not triggered by changing circumstances. What accounts for these changes, then? Sometimes, one or both partners attempt to renegotiate the breadwinning boundary as a way of dealing with a tension or strain in their relationship. The case of Keith and Roseanne provides an example.

Keith and Roseanne have a house out in the country, on a dirt road that winds deep into the woods, and I have driven out there on a frosty, starlit evening in October. Keith and Roseanne have bought this house, a weathered ski chalet on several acres of wooded land, within the past year and are still working on remodeling it. It combines the virtues of being only ten miles from the middle school where Roseanne teaches and of having a large, detached garage, which they are converting into a studio for Keith, a potter. The house itself is of a simple design, with an open-plan country kitchen / living room downstairs, dominated by a large fieldstone fireplace, and an upstairs loft with two bedrooms. The house is warm and welcoming, with a fire burning in the fireplace, thick braided rugs on tile floors, and stoneware bowls and vases in rich earth tones, evidence of Keith's craft, sitting here and there. It is in this comfortable setting that I interview first Roseanne and then Keith.

Keith and Roseanne are both in their fifties, have been married for thirteen years, and have no children. For Roseanne this is a first marriage. Keith was married before, for nineteen years, and has three grown children from his first marriage. Given that they married late in life, that they have no dependent children, that each of them was self-supporting and living independently before they married, and that both are dedicated to work they love, it is perhaps to be expected that Keith and Roseanne would regard breadwinning as a shared responsibility. And, indeed, they do. After fifteen years of teaching in the same school system, Roseanne's income is slightly more than $26,000 per year. Keith, whose income declined when he left a management position in the textile industry to turn his amateur potting into an artistic career, earns considerably less, $17,500 during 1987. They report that they share providing equally, that both jobs are considered equally important, and that neither feels the obligation to provide more than the other. Both rank earning money for basic family needs very high among their reasons for working; Roseanne puts it first, and Keith ranks it second, right after the feeling of accomplishment that his craft provides. They also agree that their shared participation in breadwinning is appropriate. Roseanne states unequivocally that fully shared responsibility for financial providing is her ideal. Keith hedges a bit. Although being a breadwinner is not a strong component of his sense of self (he ranks it fourth on the list of seven social roles), he says that, nevertheless, his ideal would be to provide somewhat more than his wife.

But neither Keith nor Roseanne embraces shared breadwinning as part of a larger commitment to eliminating gender boundaries. In explaining why she feels the obligation to provide as much as her husband does, Roseanne emphasizes their particular situation, saying, "I may not be typical because I got married quite late and never had children. . . . I've always worked . . . and I don't see Keith in a position to just give me money." It's easy for her to imagine a different scenario. In responding to the hypothetical situation about the dual-earner couple with the sick child, for example, she focuses on the mother's responsibility to care for the child: "If it were possible for her to work lesser hours . . . and if she could cut her job to a half-time job and provide care for the child half-time—because I think it's very important, with an ill child especially, that they have the contact." She never considers the possibility that the father might cut back on his work hours. For Roseanne, mothering is a woman's responsibility, and mothering and breadwinning are complementary gender boundaries. It is because mothering is not a factor in their situation that she and her husband have no need to deploy the breadwinning boundary.

Keith, however, reveals some attachment to breadwinning as a gender boundary, regardless of circumstances. His responses suggest some discomfort with his wife's higher earnings. I have already noted that he would like, ideally, to provide somewhat more than she does. When I ask whose job is considered more important, he answers that both are considered equally important and then adds, "I would honestly say so; I'd have to at this point. I mean, dollar-wise, she's still ahead of me. I'm catching up a little, but . . ." He seems to hope that his lower earnings are temporary. When he reports that both he and his wife feel the obligation to provide, he qualifies his response by noting, "That might change in the future." He says that he can imagine her leaving the labor force if his income improves: "I wouldn't need Roseanne working," he explains. "She might go into a substituting or part-time thing, or something like that."

Perhaps the most telling sign of Keith's attachment to the breadwinning boundary, however, is his description of his family financial arrangements. Keith and Roseanne do not pool their incomes; instead, each takes responsibility for certain expenses. According to Roseanne, this arrangement yields a roughly equal sharing of their normal, everyday, basic living expenses, although she notes that "it's not really fifty-fifty" because Keith takes responsibility for extraordinary expenditures, such as a new car or the remodeling of the house. Keith, however, presents a quite different picture of how expenses are divided. He claims that he provides for almost all of their basic expenses and that Roseanne pays only for groceries.

Clearly, Keith feels some resistance to the elimination of breadwinning as a gender boundary, and we might expect such resistance and the strains associated with it to lead to continued negotiation about breadwinning. So I am not surprised to find that, five years later, Keith and Roseanne's constructions of breadwinning have changed. What is surprising is the direction those changes have taken. The gap between their incomes has grown as Roseanne's salary has continued to rise and Keith's has not. The result is that Roseanne now outearns Keith almost two to one. But, as each has moved to ease the strains produced by this continued income gap, their responses have brought them into greater disagreement, rather than agreement, about breadwinning.

Keith has responded to his circumstances by relinquishing his attachment to breadwinning as a gender boundary. Now nearing the age when most men think about retirement and married for almost twenty years to a woman who earns more than he does, he has become more comfortable with an ideal of shared responsibility for providing. Roseanne, however, has moved in a very different direction, recasting both her norms about breadwinning and her interpretation of her own employment in a more conventionally gendered mold. Although she continues to maintain that her job is just as important as her husband's, she now defines him as the primary provider and says that this is her ideal. Roseanne, it would appear, has been aware of Keith's resistance to shared breadwinning. She is compensating for her own high earnings by downplaying the importance of her income and emphasizing his role as provider. She has apparently accomplished this redefinition in the face of her own much greater income by reconfiguring how their incomes are used. In an interpretation reminiscent of Charlene's in Chapter 3, she now says that her income is earmarked primarily for family extras and that it is her husband's earnings that are used for basic family expenses. Even as her own relative contribution to the family income has increased, Roseanne has redefined herself from co-breadwinner to family-centered worker.

Agreement and Continued Negotiation—Forces for Change

This chapter has documented the remarkable dynamism of the breadwinning boundary and confirmed that the construction of gender is a dynamic, ongoing process. The use of breadwinning as a gender boundary is often contested. Moreover, constructions of breadwinning are not simply negotiated once and then maintained. Rather, even among couples, like those in this chapter, who have negotiated a collaborative construction of breadwinning, renegotiation and reconstruction are the rule rather than the exception.

Changing circumstances are clearly one important factor promoting such renegotiation. Because the use of breadwinning as a gender boundary is very much shaped by adult experiences and circumstances, new experiences and circumstances can be expected to act as strong catalysts for change. And, indeed, of the couples in this chapter who continued to negotiate and redefine their construction of breadwinning despite having reached agreement, slightly more than half (12 of 23) had experienced substantial change in economic or family circumstances between the time of the initial interviews and the follow-up survey.

A substantial change in one or both partners' incomes is an obvious impetus for renegotiating the breadwinning boundary, and such economic changes played a prominent role in the case studies in this chapter. For Fred and Peggy and Joan and Hal, reconstructions of breadwinning seemed to be both triggered and shaped by changing economic circumstances. Changes in family circumstances, such as the arrival of a new baby, may also lead a couple to reconsider the construction of gender in their marriage. Remember Elise, the surgical nurse from Chapter 3 who earned more than her automobile-salesman husband, but who was determined that they not rely on her income for basics because she wanted to reserve the right to cut back on her employment when they had children? By the time I hear from Elise and Gerard again in 1992, they have two children and Elise has, indeed, reduced her hours of work, from full time to sixteen hours per week. Gerard, in the meantime, has changed jobs and almost doubled his income. This confluence of events has allowed

Elise and Gerard to establish a gendered division of responsibility in their marriage, one in which he is a traditional breadwinner and she is an employed homemaker. A new baby and a new job have also led David, our role sharer from Chapter 4, and his wife, Molly, to renegotiate their construction of breadwinning. Although Molly continues to work three days per week and has, in fact, increased her income by several thousand dollars, David has finished his degree and moved into a white-collar job, and he now earns $15,000 more than he did five years earlier. Although David and Molly have not given up their ideal of shared breadwinning, Molly's increased responsibilities at home and the growing gap between their incomes have led them to redefine their situation, at least for now, as one in which David is the primary provider.

What about the eleven couples whose redefinitions of breadwinning were not a response to changed circumstances? For some, such redefinition is not so much a reconstruction of this gender boundary as a process of continued construction. These are couples like Debbie and Allen who, already in substantial agreement, continue to modify and refine that agreement, coming closer and closer to complete accord.

For others, however, reconstruction of the breadwinning boundary is a response to tension, often tension between behavioral interpretation and norms about breadwinning. The constructions of reluctant provider and reluctant co-provider, which involve daily violation of one's own norms, are particularly unstable; the tension inherent in these approaches to breadwinning cries out for resolution. Sometimes, as in the case of Elise and Gerard, new circumstances provide an opportunity to resolve this tension by reinterpreting the wife's employment behavior to bring it into line with norms. More often, as in the case of Jeannette and Roland, it is the norms that are adjusted to coincide with behavior. Indeed, one thing this analysis has made clear is that norms and attitudes about gender are much more plastic and liable to change than has been generally believed.

But tension between norms and behavioral interpretation is not the only kind of strain that may act as an impetus for change in the use of breadwinning as a gender boundary. In some marriages, agreement about this boundary conceals underlying tensions about the construction of gender. This was the case for Rod and Anita in Chapter 4 and for Roseanne and Keith in this chapter. In such cases, one or both partners may attempt to redefine the breadwinning boundary to reduce this tension. If, as in Roseanne and Keith's case, the tension is exacerbated by circumstances, redefinition may be designed to offset or compensate for those circumstances. Thus, Roseanne can't change the fact that she earns more than her husband, but she can and does move to ease the tension created by her substantially higher earnings by downplaying the importance of those earnings and by redefining Keith as the real provider.

It is clear, then, that a number of factors can prompt couples who are in agreement about the use of breadwinning as a gender boundary to renegotiate and redefine that boundary. What about couples who disagree? I will focus on such couples in Chapter 6.

6

Contested Constructions of Gender
Couples Who Disagree About the Breadwinning Boundary

In many dual-earner marriages, the use of breadwinning as a gender boundary is not something that has been collaboratively constructed, but something that is contested. This was the case for almost half (46 percent) of the 153 couples that I interviewed in 1987–88. For some of these couples, disagreement is total, encompassing both normative and interpretive dimensions of breadwinning. Thus, some co-breadwinners may be married to traditional breadwinners. The wives insist that breadwinning should not and does not distinguish their employment from that of their husbands, while the husbands say that breadwinning is and ought to be a male responsibility in their families. It is also possible to find employed homemakers, women who report that their employment does not and should not constitute a sharing of responsibility for breadwinning, married to role sharers, men who reject the use of breadwinning as a gender boundary. Similarly, some reluctant providers (women who say that they share providing, but shouldn't have to) may be married to uncommitted providers (men who claim that their wives don't share providing, but ideally should), and women who are reluctant traditionals are sometimes married to men who are reluctant co-providers.

It would seem difficult to maintain a marriage in which partners are so completely at odds about a central feature of their lives together, and, in fact, such complete disagreement was relatively rare in this study, accounting for only 7 percent of the couples in the original sample. However, 39 percent of the couples in that sample were in what I have defined as substantial disagreement: either their norms about breadwinning or their interpretations of the wife's employment were at odds. For example, a female co-breadwinner would be in substantial disagreement with her husband if he were either a reluctant co-provider (whose norms about breadwinning differ from her own) or an uncommitted provider (who interprets her employment differently than she does). Once again, wives' more complex constructions of breadwinning (encompassing two behavioral interpretation dimensions, rather than just one) can create anomalous situations of spouses who disagree partially about interpretations of the wife's employment. These couples would be categorized as in substantial disagreement only if they also disagreed on the normative dimension. (As discussed in Chapter 5, couples who agree only partially on the behavioral interpretation dimension but agree on the normative dimension are classified as being in substantial agreement.)

For the couples studied here, disagreement about the breadwinning boundary was most frequently normative. Eighty-four percent of the couples who were in disagreement about breadwinning reported conflicting norms. In 34 percent of the cases of disagreement, it was norms alone that were contested. In the remaining 50 percent, there was also at least partial disagreement about interpretation of the wife's employment. Only 16 percent of the couples with contested constructions of breadwinning confined their disagreement to the behavioral interpretation dimensions. In total, almost two-thirds of the couples who disagreed had some disagreement about behavioral interpretation, but this was usually combined with disagreement about norms. Disagreement about whether the wife's employment actually constitutes breadwinning was, therefore, less common than disagreement about whether she should be a breadwinner. Apparently, situational factors (e.g., the husband/wife wage ratio) constrain behavioral interpretation more than they constrain norms, thereby making disagreement about the former somewhat less likely.

What characterizes couples who disagree about breadwinning? You will remember that some approaches to breadwinning seem more likely than others to be part of a contested construction of gender (Table 3, Chapter 5). This is particularly true among the wives; more than 60 percent of the reluctant providers and the reluctant traditionals were in disagreement with their husbands about breadwinning at the time of the original interviews. The effect of breadwinner type is less clear among husbands, but those who reported a normative commitment to shared breadwinning (the uncommitted providers and the role sharers) were somewhat more likely to have wives who disagreed with them than were those who embraced norms of male breadwinning. Another way to examine who disagrees is to look at variables that predict disagreement. As we saw in Chapter 5 (Table 4 and Appendix B, Table B6), these variables include a wage ratio in which the wife contributes more than one-fourth but less than half of the family income, recent marriage, large number of children, feminist attitudes among wives, and strong attachment to conventional gender divisions among husbands. These predictors of disagreement once again highlight the importance of adult experiences and circumstances in the construction of the breadwinning boundary.

However, if I have argued throughout this book that the construction of gender in marriage is influenced by circumstances and experiences, I have also argued that it is an ongoing process. What, then, happens to these disagreements about breadwinning over time? To address this question, I will turn once again to the subsample of 50 dual-earner couples whose constructions of breadwinning were assessed in 1992–93.

Disagreement and Change in the Construction of Breadwinning

The data from the follow-up subsample confront us once again with the ubiquity of change. If change over time in constructions of breadwinning was widespread among those who agreed about this gender boundary at the time of the original interviews, it was virtually universal among those who disagreed. Of 21 couples in the subsample who disagreed about the breadwinning boundary when they were interviewed in 1987–88, all but two made some kind of change in their constructions of that boundary in the subsequent five years (see Table 6).

These changes were overwhelmingly in the direction of agreement. Among couples who disagreed in 1987, more than 75 percent (16 of 21) had negotiated an agreement by the time of the follow-up survey. Of the five couples who had not reached agreement, two had not changed their construction of breadwinning during the five-year period. In the remaining three couples, husband, wife, or both did alter their construction of the breadwinning boundary, but these reconfigurations did not result in agreement.

Interestingly, it was husbands who were more likely to change their constructions of breadwinning in response to disagreement about it. It is not that wives were unlikely to change; more than half (57 percent) of those who disagreed with their husbands at the time of the initial interviews did so. But more than three-quarters (76 percent) of the husbands made such changes (Table 6).

These changes in couples' constructions of breadwinning cannot be explained simply as responses to disagreement, however. After all, as

TABLE 6

*Change in Breadwinner Types Between 1987–88 and 1992–93
by Agreement in 1987–88*

	Pct. of those who agreed in 1987–88 (N = 29)	Pct. of those who disagreed in 1987–88 (N = 21)
Type of change		
No change	21%	10%
Change resulting in agreement	48	76
Change resulting in disagreement	31	14
Who changed		
No change	21%	10%
Wife only changed	31	14
Husband only changed	14	33
Both wife and husband changed	34	43

demonstrated in Chapter 5, couples who agreed often changed their constructions too. Another important contributor to reconfiguration of the breadwinning boundary (even more so among couples who disagreed than among those who agreed) was changing circumstances. Of the nineteen couples who responded to disagreement by revising their constructions of breadwinning between 1987 and 1992, thirteen (68 percent) had experienced changed circumstances. Thus, this longitudinal analysis reminds us of something that is often obscured by studies done at one point in time: People's lives are not static. New babies are born; pre-school-age children get older; older children leave home. Spouses' economic circumstances change as hours of employment increase or decrease, people change jobs, incomes change, and the husband/wife wage ratio shifts. And, since use of breadwinning as a gender boundary depends very much on circumstances, it is not surprising that as these circumstances change, so too do couples' constructions of breadwinning.

Interestingly, patterns of response to disagreement and new circumstances were distinctly different for husbands and wives. For husbands, change was predominantly a reconsideration of norms about breadwinning. Of the sixteen men in the subsample who changed their constructions of breadwinning in response to disagreement, all but one changed their norms. Nine of them changed only their norms, and six others changed both norms and behavioral interpretation, completely reconceiving their approaches to breadwinning.

Wives were much less likely to respond to disagreement by reconsidering their norms about breadwinning. Instead, they more often changed their interpretations of their employment. Of twelve wives who reconfigured their approaches to breadwinning between the initial interviews and the follow-up survey, ten changed their interpretations of their employment, and eight of those ten changed only those interpretations. Most of these changes represented fine-tuning, with the women altering only one of their behavioral interpretation dimensions; only three women reconfigured both. Moreover, unlike their husbands, the women seldom modified their constructions of breadwinning unilaterally or solely as responses to conflict. In almost all cases, wives' reconstructions were triggered by new circumstances as well as by disagreement and were accompanied by corresponding changes in their husbands' approaches to breadwinning.

Only two women responded to disagreement like the majority of husbands, by changing only their norms, and the profile they present is dramatically different from that of the other wives. For both these women, change in norms was unilateral; their circumstances had not changed substantially and their husbands had not altered their constructions of breadwinning. Moreover, both women were reluctant providers who moved to adopt their husbands' norms of shared breadwinning, thus coming into agreement with their husbands that breadwinning would not be used as a gender boundary in their marriages.

How typical was such a move away from the use of breadwinning as a gender boundary as couples transformed disagreement into agreement? A scant majority (52 percent) of the 21 subsample couples who disagreed at the time of the original study had moved to relax the breadwinning boundary by the time of the follow-up survey. In only five cases, however, did these changes result in complete elimination of breadwinning as a gender boundary. Two of these were the cases discussed above of reluctant provider wives who moved to adopt their husbands' ideals of shared breadwinning. In another two cases, the husbands adjusted their constructions to join their wives in relinquishing breadwinning as a gender boundary, and in the remaining case, both husband and wife reconfigured their approaches to breadwinning. Two couples, however, made clear moves in the opposite direction, resolving their conflict about breadwinning by affirming its importance as a gender boundary, and another six couples made changes that were mixed or ambiguous in their direction.

Fuller understanding of how and why couples disagree about the use of breadwinning as a gender boundary and of the consequences and resolution of those disagreements requires a more detailed analysis of representative cases. I turn now to six case studies of couples for whom breadwinning was a contested gender boundary when they were interviewed in 1987–88. Some disagreed about breadwinning norms, some about their interpretation of the wife's employment, and some about both. Their responses to disagreement varied, but most changed their constructions of breadwinning in some way. And most, but not all, resolved their disagreement.

Contested Constructions of Breadwinning: Six Case Studies

Unresolved Disagreement: Patricia and Denis — Contested Norms

Disagreement about the breadwinning boundary usually involves disagreement about norms. Indeed, for one-third of the couples in this study who disagreed about breadwinning at the time of the 1987–88 interviews, only norms were contested. You may picture such disputes as involving a man who clings to the ideals and prerogatives of male breadwinning while his wife works toward a blurring of gender boundaries, but as the case of Patricia and Denis will show, this is not necessarily so.

I have met Patricia and Denis for the first time on a mild, sunny Saturday in late summer. They rent an apartment in a quiet residential neighborhood of tree-lined streets and mixed single-family and multifamily residences. Their four-unit building is attractive and well maintained, and their first-floor apartment is spacious and pleasant. I interview Denis first, on a small patio reached via a sliding glass door from the dining area. When we have finished, I join Patricia in the living room.

Denis and Patricia both grew up in the community and knew one another as children. They fell in love when they were in their teens, married when they were both twenty, and had three children well before they reached their thirties. Now in their late forties, they have been married for almost 30 years, and all their children are grown and gone. The children live nearby, however, and it is clear from my conversations with Patricia and Denis that connection with their children and a strong sense of family are important in their lives.

Patricia has suffered for her family, and her story is one of those mythic tales of struggle and success that continue to be compelling no matter how often you hear them. During the first eleven years of her marriage, she worked off and on as a textile-mill operative, alternating this work with periods of being at home with the children. "I'd work for three or four months, maybe five," she explains, "and then I'd quit because I would become physically ill. I really would. I hated it so bad, and the money was so bad, that I would become physically ill and I had to quit." Why did she keep going back to work that literally made her sick? Because they needed the money. Even today, twenty years later, she cannot think about this period of her life without bitterness: "When I felt we needed money, then I'd go to work for a while. And then, as soon as the pressure was off, I would stop. It was awful. That's a terrible job and a terrible way for people to have to earn a living!" Finally, when her youngest child was four and Patricia was in her early thirties, she landed a clerical job in the mill office. She found this work somewhat more tolerable and was able to stick with it longer. It wasn't that she liked it, though; she just hated it less.

And so, when her youngest child entered first grade, Patricia did something she had been dreaming about for a long time: She enrolled in college. This was a momentous and frightening move for her. She had always loved school as a child and had been an *A* student through high school, but college, she knew, was much more difficult than high school. She didn't know anyone who had actually been to college. In fact, high school graduation was relatively rare among her peers, and her husband had only an eighth-grade education. But this was the early 1970s, when women were being encouraged to expand their horizons, and her husband, far from seeming threatened by her dream of college, was urging her to take the plunge.

So Patricia enrolled for two night courses at the university extension. But this first experience of college confirmed all her worst fears. She had forgotten how to study and had trouble following what was going on in class. "I would spend my time making lists of the words the professors used that I didn't know," she recalls, "so that I could look them up when I got home." At the end of the semester, she had barely squeaked by with a *C* and a *D*. She was discouraged, humiliated, ready to give up. Maybe she had been a good student in high school, but she obviously wasn't college material.

But Denis urged her to stick it out, to try one more semester before she made a decision. And so, with much trepidation, she enrolled for two more courses. This time her experience was very different. Her study skills improved, the work seemed easier, she did well, and by the end of the semester, she had decided to matriculate. Once Patricia saw a college degree as a reasonable goal, there was no stopping her. She began commuting to the main university campus, 40 miles away, so that she could take courses during the day when the children were in school. She took on a heavy course load, including summer sessions, and three years after she had enrolled in her first college course, Patricia was the proud holder of a bachelor's degree in social work. Two years later, she started a full-time job as a social worker with the state Department of Public Welfare.

After ten years of work for the welfare department, Patricia is still in the same job and loving it. Her official workweek is 40 hours, but she usually brings paperwork home with her and actually works an average of 50 hours. She finds the work challenging and rewarding and feels that her awful years in the mills help her to understand her clients. She has no plans for leaving this work and even thinks about making a further commitment to it by earning a master's degree in social work. In response to my question about what she would do if she won a $3 million lottery jackpot, Patricia waxes enthusiastic about her job and finally concludes, "I'd never quit."

Patricia is still amazed at the good fortune that enabled her to become a college-educated professional earning $17,000 per year, and she is particularly grateful to her husband for having provided the support and encouragement that made it possible for her to pursue her dream. Such strong encouragement for pursuing a college degree may seem surprising from a man with an eighth-grade education, but Denis is also a man who believes strongly that people should do what makes them happy. If getting a college degree and becoming a professional would bring his wife happiness, Denis was more than pleased to encourage her. Besides, Patricia's new career and relatively high pay have made it possible for Denis to do what makes *him* happy—cut back on work and spend more time being outdoors, fishing and hunting, and socializing with friends and family.

Like his wife, Denis found his early years of work difficult ones, and he left several jobs (some of them fairly high-paying and secure union jobs) because they interfered with his ability to enjoy life. Whereas Patricia dealt with the problem of work she hated by training for a professional career, Denis adopted a very different strategy. He decided to work for himself, and using his knowledge of basic carpentry, electrical work, and plumbing, he became a kind of odd-jobs man—someone who could be called on to do light carpentry or simple electrical and plumbing repairs or to open and close summer cabins. Sometimes he hired himself out as a maintenance subcontractor to big companies. When he did that, he often worked long hours, but the important thing was that he had control of when those hours would be. "I make my own hours," he explains; "if I go in at 2:00, I might work until 10:00 at night—or, if the weather's real good, I might not work at all."

It is that ability to control his hours, to take the day off if the weather is fine, that is most important to Denis. He finds it difficult to be indoors on a sunny day, and his choice to be interviewed on the patio reflects this. Although he and his wife have never owned a home, they do own a summer cabin on a lake about twenty minutes north of the city and often spend weeks at a time there during the summer months. Even so, Denis would be happy to increase his time at the lake.

Three years ago, Denis made a decision to pursue his own happiness. With his youngest child leaving home and his wife secure in her job, he decided to cut back to part-time work. He now puts in an average of 30 hours per week and expects to earn only about $10,000 this year. Denis greets an interview question about how important job advancement is to him with a hoot of laughter, and he explains his philosophy about work this way: "If we're at the [cabin] and the weather's good and I'm supposed to go to work today—or if my kids are there and we're having a barbecue, whoever wants me to work is going to either take it somewhere else or—I'm not showing up." He does not want to stop working altogether because he does not want to be financially dependent on his wife and he likes the contact with people that work provides, but he doesn't want his life to be controlled by work. He considers his current arrangement perfect. If he won a $3 million lottery jackpot, he explains, "I'd stay the way I am . . . because I'm doing what I want to do."

Denis and Patricia might seem like a perfect match. She loves her work and can't imagine ever leaving it. He considers work something that adds spice to life, not the main course, and he is happy to have a professional wife whose relatively high earnings make it possible for him to give work a low priority. And, indeed, when they are asked about how responsibility for breadwinning is allocated in their family, they agree that they share providing equally, that Patricia's job is more important (because it is more structured than Denis's), and that both incomes are used to meet basic family expenses. Denis, they both agree, does not regard breadwinning as a core element of manhood. He ranks financial provider sixth on the list of seven roles (only houseworker is a lower priority for him), and when asked who he thinks should, ideally, be the family breadwinner, he responds, "I don't think it matters who does. Whatever time tells you at the moment; whoever is the most qualified." Sharing responsibility for breadwinning suits Denis just fine.

Nevertheless, there is a problem here: Patricia is strongly attached to the idea of breadwinning as a gender boundary. It is not that she wants to quit her job; what she wants is to work just for the joy of it. When asked to respond to the statement that "a married woman should not work outside the home if her husband can comfortably support her," she explains, "I'd have to disagree with that, because she might want to." "But," she adds, "it would be nice not to have to." A married woman should have the right to work outside the home, but not a duty to do so.

Thus, despite her commitment to her work, Patricia believes that, ideally, Denis should be the sole provider for their family, and she resents his lackadaisical attitude toward work. She feels that she can't depend on him and says that her most important reason for working is to be independent. When asked if she can imagine any circumstances under which she would become sole provider for the family, she responds, with barely concealed anger, "If he just decided he wasn't going to go to work any more." She reports that she feels the obligation to provide much more than he does. But it is an obligation that she does not want. When asked how important it is to her to be a good provider, she replies, "It's not important; it's necessary." In fact, she gives her role as financial provider the same low ranking that her husband gives his—sixth, just ahead of houseworker. But she says that his role as financial provider is very important to her, second only to his role as husband.

Denis is certainly aware of how Patricia feels. He reports accurately that being independent is her most important reason for employment and explains that need for independence by saying, "I'm unstable; sometimes I scare her." But, for the most part, Denis tries to avoid conflict with Patricia by avoiding the issue. Where most participants in the study emphasize how well they understand and can speak for their partners, Denis repeatedly argues that he cannot predict how his wife would respond. At one point, he says bluntly, "I don't know how she thinks." Patricia seems more inclined to try to get Denis to take responsibility for breadwinning by forcing him to confront the issue. Indeed, participating in the study (which seems to be something that she wanted to do and that he deferred to her wishes on) is probably an attempt to do just that.

If Patricia hoped that participation in this study would make breadwinning a salient issue in her marriage and thereby bring Denis to take more responsibility for providing, she has been disappointed. When I hear from them again five years later, little has changed and their disagreement about breadwinning is unresolved. The gap between their incomes has widened; Denis's earnings have remained the same, while Patricia has added a master's degree to her educational credentials and moved into a higher-paying job in the welfare department's protective services division. Patricia now earns more than two and one-half times what Denis does, and they both now name her as primary provider. Denis continues to report that it doesn't matter to him who the financial provider is. Patricia has made some ideological adjustment to the reality of her situation; she no longer wishes that her husband would be sole financial provider, just primary provider. But she is still a reluctant provider, outearning her husband and wishing that he would act like a man and take responsibility for breadwinning.

Change Without Agreement: Wayne and Linda — New Circumstances, Continuing Strain

Patricia and Denis are, in a number of ways, atypical of couples for whom the breadwinning boundary is contested. The first characteristic that distinguishes them is the length of their marriage; disagreement about breadwinning is more common among couples in relatively recent marriages. The ratio of Denis's income to Patricia's also makes them stand out; disagreement more often occurs when the wife earns more than one-fourth but less than half the family income. Finally, Patricia and Denis are notable for the stability of both their circumstances and their disagreement; it is unusual to find so little change in these over time. Wayne and Linda provide a more typical case of disagreement about breadwinning. When I met them in 1987, their marriage was recent and Linda earned 33 percent of their total family income. Over the next five years, both their circumstances and their constructions of breadwinning would change.

My research assistant, Lisa, and I have climbed the stairs to Wayne and Linda's second-floor apartment on a Friday afternoon in July. We have arranged to interview them simultaneously, at the end of their workday but before they go out for pizza and a movie with friends. After introductions, Lisa and Wayne go off to the living room for his interview, while Linda and I settle down to talk in the kitchen. During the pauses in my interview with Linda, I can hear not only the sounds of traffic and children's play that drift up from the street, but also the faint murmur of Wayne and Lisa's voices from the other room.

Wayne and Linda are a young couple who have been married for less than a year and have no children. At age 24, Linda has been working as a fourth-grade teacher in the local school system for two years. Wayne, three years older than his wife and with only a high school education, has been in the labor force longer and is employed at a nearby paper mill. There are a number of ways in which Linda reminds me of Patricia. She is a committed professional who loves her job and can't imagine ever giving it up, even if she won the state lottery. Her husband, who has considerably less education than she, is a blue-collar worker who doesn't particularly enjoy his job. Linda regards her income as critical to her family's survival; although she names Wayne as the primary provider, she says that her job is more important in the family than his, that she works primarily to earn money for basic family needs, and that she and her husband equally feel the obligation to provide. But she wishes that this weren't the case, that she could work just for the enjoyment of it. Linda expresses her ambivalence about work and breadwinning most clearly when she is asked if she can imagine any circumstances under which she would leave the labor force and her husband would be sole provider. "I've always liked the traditional roles," she muses, "but I'd miss my job too much."

Linda, like Patricia, is committed to her career but also attached to conventional gender boundaries. She agrees that "there is some work that is men's and some that is women's and they shouldn't be doing each other's," and she makes it clear throughout the interview that breadwinning is one of the gender boundaries that she would like to keep in place. Thus, Linda ranks Wayne's provider role high in importance to her, second only to husband, while she gives her own role as provider a low priority. Ideally, she says, her husband should bear sole responsibility for financial providing.

But if Linda is like Patricia in being a career-committed reluctant provider, she is also different from her in important ways. First of all, Linda does not feel as though her husband has left her holding the bag financially. Wayne is a very hard worker who puts in long hours of overtime and earns twice as much as his wife. Moreover, Wayne shares Linda's commitment to conventional gender boundaries. He, too, agrees that "there is some work that is men's and some that is women's and they shouldn't be doing each other's." He believes that male responsibility for breadwinning is the complement of female responsibility for home and family. He does not think that mothers should be employed full time, and he agrees strongly that "a married woman should not work outside the home if her husband can comfortably support her." Like his wife, he ranks her role as financial provider very low in importance and ranks his own provider role in the top three. And like his wife, he believes that, as a man, he should ideally bear primary responsibility for breadwinning.

Where Wayne differs from his wife is not in norms about breadwinning, but in his interpretation of her employment. Linda defines herself as sharing the responsibility for providing, but Wayne disagrees. Although he reports, when asked, that they share providing equally, he means by this only that she contributes a significant proportion of the total family income; otherwise, he distinguishes his employment from hers. Wayne says that his job is more important in the family than his wife's and that he, more than she, feels the obligation to provide. While she reports that earning money for basic family needs is her primary reason for working, he says that she works primarily to keep busy and that meeting basic family expenses is only somewhat important as a motivation for her employment. Their descriptions of their financial arrangements also differ. He reports that it is, in fact, his income that supports them. "What I do," he explains, "is that I pay all the bills and she is supposed to throw all her money in the bank." The only reason not all of her income is put into savings, in Wayne's view, is that "she has a few bills that she wants to take care of herself, like her student loans and stuff like that." According to Linda, however, Wayne's income is used to pay most of their monthly bills (but not groceries, which she pays for) only because they are saving most of her income for a down payment on a house.

Five years later, both Wayne and Linda's circumstances and their constructions of gender have changed. They've bought the house they were saving for and started a family, and they now have a preschooler at home. What's more, their relative incomes have shifted dramatically. As she has gained experience and seniority as a teacher, Linda's income has risen steadily, and she now earns $25,000, almost twice as much as she did in 1987. Meanwhile, the recession of the early 1990s has meant cutbacks in the paper industry, and Wayne is no longer getting the long hours of overtime that he once did. Consequently, even though his hourly wage has continued to rise, keeping pace with inflation, his actual income has gone down and he now earns about $1,500 less per year than his wife.

How have Linda and Wayne responded to these changes in their situation? For the most part, Linda has not changed her construction of breadwinning. She says that they share providing equally, that she works primarily to earn money for basic family needs, and that her income is critical in meeting those basic expenses. Her major adjustment is that while she still maintains that breadwinning should be a male responsibility, she now says that her ideal is for her husband to be primary provider, not sole provider.

Wayne, however, has made dramatic changes both in his interpretation of his wife's employment and in his norms about breadwinning. Although he continues to insist that Linda's earnings are set aside primarily for extras, he reports that he and his wife share providing equally, that both jobs are equally important, and that, in fact, she now feels the obligation to provide somewhat more than he does. He still ranks her role as financial provider near the bottom of the list of seven roles, but he also ranks his own role as provider lower than he did five years ago.

What is most interesting about Wayne's transformation, however, is that, like most men in this study, he has responded to disagreement about breadwinning by also adjusting his norms—even though this was not where his disagreement with his wife lay. He now says that, ideally, he and Linda should share providing equally. The result is that, although Wayne has adjusted his construction of breadwinning in response to both disagreement with his wife and his changing circumstances, he and Linda have not managed to reach agreement about the use of breadwinning as a gender boundary. What has changed, instead, is the nature of their disagreement; whereas they used to disagree about whether she was a breadwinner, they now disagree about whether she should be a breadwinner.

Developing a Shared Construction of Breadwinning: Mark and Gail — From Complete Disagreement to Complete Agreement

Unlike Patricia and Denis or Linda and Wayne, most of the couples in the 50-couple subsample who disagreed about breadwinning in 1987– 88 had forged some kind of agreement by the time of the follow-up survey. These new agreements were usually developed in response to new circumstances, and they often involved adjustments in both spouses' constructions of gender. The case of Mark and Gail illustrates how such mutual adjustments can turn total disagreement about the breadwinning boundary into a shared construction of breadwinning.

I have arrived to interview Mark and Gail on a snowy evening in February. They live in an upper-middle-class residential development with few through streets and many cul-de-sacs. I am worried about being late because I have been slowed down by slippery roads and it has taken me a while to find my way through the maze to Mark and Gail's address. But, as I pull into the driveway of their spacious L-shaped ranch house, it is just 7:00 and I can pause a moment to observe the scene around me. Gail and Mark's house, as is typical in this neighborhood, is set on a large, beautifully landscaped lot. A fenced-in backyard play area, also typical, holds a snow-covered swing set and jungle gym, suggesting that there are small children in the household. And, indeed, when Gail opens the door to invite me in, the children, ages five and three, are right behind her, curious and excited about the arrival of company.

Mark and Gail are a professional couple in their mid-thirties, with a combined annual income of more than $65,000. Gail, a registered nurse, works the day shift and has been home several hours by the time she opens the door to me. She settles the children in the playroom and then takes me into the living room to begin her interview. Mark, an accountant who commutes to the state's major city, 40 miles to the south, has not arrived home yet but is expected soon. Indeed, he comes in not long after we begin, is greeted with cries of excitement by the children, and stops to introduce himself before going off to join their play. Except for a brief moment when he pokes his head in to ask if either of us would like something to drink, I don't see Mark again until Gail and I have finished her interview and it is time for him to come into the living room for his.

The children, on the other hand, wander through the room periodically throughout both interviews, curious about what is going on. Sometimes, they watch silently for a moment; at other times, they demand attention. The five-year-old sings a song into my tape recorder. The three-year-old carries around a sheaf of discarded envelopes that she variously describes as "mail" or "bills." At one point, she spreads them out on a table in a corner of the room and, in response to an inquiry from her accountant father, explains solemnly, "I'm doing my taxes." It is a pleasant family scene, full of warmth, comfort, affection, and cooperation. Given this sense of togetherness, I find the responses that Gail and Mark give to my questions surprising. The pictures they paint could not be more different.

The image Mark presents is of a couple committed to role sharing and the elimination of gender boundaries. His ideological commitment to such a position seems strong. He describes himself as the son of a path-breaking feminist mother, and he is one of the few men in the study to give strongly feminist responses to all the gender attitude items. He responds to the hypothetical situation of the dual-earner couple with the sick child by saying that the best solution would be for both parents to adjust their work hours and schedules so that they could share the child's care, and he has no trouble imagining situations in which either he or his wife might be supported temporarily by the other. Although Mark says that his most important reason for working is to earn money for basic family needs, he is not committed to gender-specialized family roles or to breadwinning as a peculiarly male prerogative. Thus, he ranks his role as financial provider for the family sixth in importance on the list of seven roles, ahead only of houseworker. His norms about breadwinning reflect this sense; ideally, he says, he and his wife should share providing equally.

Mark's interpretation of Gail's employment is consonant with these norms. He reports that they do indeed share providing equally, that they both feel the obligation to provide, and that both jobs are equally important. When asked about family financial arrangements, he says that both incomes are used to meet basic family needs and that for his wife, as for himself, meeting these expenses is the single most important motivation for working.

Gail, however, interprets her employment very differently. Although she agrees that both incomes are used for basic family needs, she emphasizes the $15,000 gap between her earnings and her husband's, and she reports that he is the primary provider, that his job is considered more important in the family than hers, and that he feels a much greater obligation to provide than she does. Whereas Mark described earning money for basic family needs as Gail's primary motivation for employment, she says that this is not at all important to her and that her most important reasons for working are earning money for family extras, having contact with other people, and getting the feeling of accomplishment that work provides.

Gail seems more than a little ambivalent about her work. She says she enjoys working, but when asked how many hours she works in her current job, she prefaces her answer of 43 by saying, "More than I care to admit." When asked if she expects to be employed continuously until retirement, she replies, "I hope not, but it doesn't look too promising not to. . . . Until they're through college, at least, I would say I'll be working . . . unless Mark were to get a really good promotion." She can't imagine any circumstances under which Mark would leave the labor force and she would be sole provider, but she can imagine the reverse if she suffered from "burnout." She would only stay out of the labor force temporarily, she says, but she wouldn't go back to nursing; she would do "something fun" or "work with my husband in our own business." And she has no trouble deciding that she would quit her job if she won a lottery jackpot. "I'd volunteer my time once a week for them," she says; "I always think I'd like to just pick my hours." Given these responses, I am not surprised when Gail says that her ideal is that Mark should be family breadwinner.

The source of Gail's ambivalence about her employment seems to be the enormous tension she feels between the demands of a paid job and her responsibilities to her family. Gail does not share her husband's commitment to eliminating gender boundaries. In particular, she feels that mothers have a special responsibility for their children. Thus, when she is presented with the hypothetical situation about the dual-earner couple with the sick child, she responds, "I just feel like the mother should be the one. I mean, that would be a decision that we'd have to really make, but, I don't know, I just think they can get more from their mother. It's a different kind of care than they get from their dad." Despite her professional career, Gail is oriented primarily to being a mother and a homemaker. She works to provide the good life—and college educations—for her children, but she does not want that work to take her away from them.

When I hear from Mark and Gail again five years later, they have negotiated an agreement about the use of breadwinning as a gender boundary. Their road to agreement has been smoothed somewhat by circumstances. The children are now older and in school, easing some of the work-family tension that Gail felt earlier. She has also cut back on her hours and now works a more manageable 36 hours per week. Nevertheless, Gail is still employed full time and still brings in more than one-third of the family income.

For the most part, Mark and Gail have come to agreement not by responding to changed circumstances, but by making adjustments in their constructions of breadwinning that are characteristic of their gender groups. Mark, as is typical of men in this study, has responded to disagreement by rethinking his norms. He still says that he and Gail share providing equally, that both jobs are equally important, and that they both feel the obligation to provide, but he has raised his role as financial provider to a higher priority in his life and he has embraced his wife's ideal that he should be the primary provider. Gail has met this move by reinterpreting the meaning of her employment. Although she works fewer hours and brings in a smaller portion of the total income than she did five years earlier, she now interprets that employment very differently, agreeing that she and Mark share providing equally, that her job is just as important to the family as his, and that she works primarily to earn money for basic family needs. Mark and Gail have moved from the opposing constructions of role sharer and employed homemaker to complete agreement that they are reluctant co-providers.

New Circumstances and New Definitions: Todd and Christina —
A Husband's Transformation

In many cases, it was husbands alone who changed their constructions of breadwinning to transform disagreement with their wives into agreement. Some reconfigured both their norms and their interpretations of their wives' employment, and, quite frequently, changing circumstances provided a catalyst for these reconstructions. The case of Todd, a welder, and Christina, a supermarket deli worker, provides an example.

I have scheduled interviews with Todd and Christina for a balmy afternoon in May. It is spring in Maine and signs of it are everywhere: The grass has turned suddenly and intensely green, daffodils are in bloom, trees are lacy with new foliage, and bird songs fill the air. It is a beautiful day for a drive out to the western edge of the city, where I find Todd and Christina's older single-family house on a short, unpaved street that is barely within the city limits. As I pull my car into the driveway, I notice a ladder propped against the house and some new shingles piled on the roof. Apparently, repairs are under way, and such activity seems somehow in keeping with the spirit of the season. I walk past the ladder and ring the doorbell at a screened-in porch on the side of the house. It is Christina who comes to the door and invites me in. The arrangement we have made is that I will interview her before she leaves for her evening work shift at a nearby supermarket. By the time we finish, Todd should be home from his job at a large shipyard about thirty miles to the east and available for his interview.

Christina and Todd are in their early thirties and about to celebrate their second wedding anniversary. This is a second marriage for each of them, and Christina's two children from her first marriage, ages eleven and fourteen, live with them. Christina makes it clear that life is better for her now than it has been in a long time. She spent most of the eleven years of her first marriage as a full-time homemaker. "He had a job that took a lot of time," she explains, "and we had an agreement that I would stay home with the children, and then, when the youngest one was in school full time, I would go to school. Only we broke up at that point." As Christina struggled to support herself and her children after the divorce, she was forced to give up her dream of going back to school and instead take on long hours of work outside the home. When she met Todd, she was working at two different part-time jobs, each demanding 25–30 hours per week. She happily gave up one of these when they married and is grateful to be working only 25–30 hours per week now, an arrangement that leaves her more time to attend to her husband and children. Because the supermarket job is unionized and pays well, the move to part-time work has not come at great financial cost. Christina has earned $10,000 there during the past year, more than a full-time job at minimum wage would pay.

Todd, too, is pleased with his current situation. After graduating from high school, he worked for many years at a series of unskilled and semi-skilled blue-collar jobs, mostly in the shoe industry. It was a work situation characterized by low pay, frequent layoffs, and prolonged periods of unemployment. Then, three years ago, when the nearby shipyard won a big navy contract and began hiring new workers, Todd applied for and received on-the-job training and a job as a welder. His position at the shipyard is the highest-paying and most secure job he has ever held. With an average of ten hours per week of overtime on top of his base pay, he will earn $24,000 this year.

Todd and Christina have no trouble agreeing about the facts of their work lives, but, like Gail and Mark, they have completely different interpretations of those facts. Their disagreement about the meaning of Christina's employment could be described as the mirror image of Gail and Mark's: It is Christina who claims status as a co-breadwinner and Todd who says that breadwinning is and should be his responsibility.

Christina feels that the economic contributions she brings to the family—both her $10,000 in wages and the child support from her first husband—are significant. Her earnings alone account for 30 percent of the family budget. Moreover, she does not consider their current wage ratio a permanent feature of their marriage. "Sometimes in our married life and when we've lived together," she notes, "he's been out of work and I've been helping him . . . now I make less than he does." So, Christina says that she and Todd share providing equally, that both jobs are equally important in the family, and that both she and her husband work primarily to earn money for basic family needs. She does acknowledge some inequality in their current contributions, however. She reports that, at least for the time being, Todd feels somewhat more of an obligation to provide than she does and that, although her earnings, like his, are used primarily for basic family needs, his greater income is more critical in meeting those expenses.

Christina's interpretation of her employment as breadwinning is based, in part, on her firm attachment to the labor force. Although she admits that she sometimes misses staying home, she has no real desire to go back to full-time homemaking. It is not just that she doesn't want to give up the independence and sense of self that employment provides; she also appreciates the corollary independence and sense of responsibility that her working promotes in her husband and children. When you're employed, she explains, "the family expects less of you; they know you have to go to work. I think a [full-time] mother can be stepped on." Christina expects to remain in the labor force until retirement. If she won a big jackpot in the state lottery, she would quit her current job, but she would not stop working; instead, she would use the opportunity to train for a job that she could really enjoy. She can imagine being supported by her husband very briefly, "during a job change," but she would also expect to provide the same support to him.

But Christina's definition of herself as a co-breadwinner is not only a matter of labor force attachment. She combines her commitment to working outside the home with feminist sensibilities, giving strongly feminist responses to all the gender attitude items. Moreover, in explaining why she left a full-time job as secretary to the president of a small business, even though she desperately needed the money, she provides evidence that she is willing to act on her feminist principles. Her eyes flash with anger as she tells the story: "There were a lot of things he wanted me to do that weren't in the job description when I began," she recounts, "[like] entertaining his children . . . while my children were at the baby-sitter—I really resented that—[and] washing his Porsche!" Christina's feminism is not limited to the workplace; she is also interested in eliminating gender boundaries in the family. Thus, she thinks it would be fine for the father of the hypothetical sick child to quit his job to provide child care, and her ideal of family financial support is that she and her husband would share providing equally.

Todd, however, sees all of this differently. Whereas Christina stresses their joint responsibility for breadwinning, he emphasizes the sizable differences in their economic contributions to the family and, especially, in the number of hours that they devote to paid employment. His job, he feels, is at the center of his life, while Christina's is something she does on the side. When he is asked who the financial provider for the family is, he responds, "The way our bills are structured, I pay the bills, and she has a part-time job; she pays the grocery bill." He says that his job is more important in the family and that, while his income is committed to paying the family's bills, "I only ask her to pay for groceries; whatever's left over, that's hers to do what she wants."

Todd is quite willing to acknowledge that, right now, both incomes are necessary for meeting the family's expenses, but he hopes that this won't always be the case. Thus, he says that both he and Christina work primarily to earn money for basic family needs, and that both feel the obligation to provide. "We both feel like we have to do what we're doing," he explains, "in order to keep at the level we're at." But he also imagines being sole provider at some time in the future "when we get out of debt and don't have so many bills."

Todd—like Patricia, the social worker we met earlier in this chapter—believes that women should have the right, but not the obligation, to work outside the home. He would never ask his wife to stop working, he explains, but she shouldn't *have* to work "if she wanted to stay home to do the house, or beautify the yard, or whatever." Todd takes it for granted that work is a central component of a man's identity and that breadwinning is, ultimately, a male responsibility. Thus, he ranks his financial provider role very high on the list of seven roles, second in importance only to being a husband, and he believes that, ideally, being the provider for his family should be part of his responsibilities as a man, saying, "I'd rather have her be able to make the choice to do what she wants."

Five years later, however, circumstances and Christina's stronger commitment to her construction of breadwinning have conspired to bring Todd to rethink his position. When defense spending was cut back in the early 1990s, Todd was lucky not to be affected by layoffs at the shipyard, but he did lose his overtime. Although his hourly wage has gone up to keep pace with inflation, his total income is about $2,000 less than it was five years earlier. Meanwhile, Christina's children have gotten older; the younger one is in high school and the older one is enrolled at the local branch of the state university. Christina has responded to these changes in her circumstances by leaving her part-time job at the supermarket and taking a full-time clerical job. The hourly wage is not as high, but she now earns about $2,000 more per year than she did earlier. All of this means that Christina is now committing as much of her time to work as Todd is and is bringing home more than 35 percent of the family income.

Todd has adjusted his interpretation of Christina's employment to take account of these changes. Although he still considers his higher-paying job the more important of the two, he now says that they share providing equally and that her income is just as important as his for meeting basic family expenses. While he still gives a high ranking to his role as financial provider for the family, he now also ranks his wife's provider role high in importance, just after wife and mother. But Todd has gone even further in his reconstruction of the breadwinning boundary. He says not only that he and his wife now share responsibility for providing, but that this is his ideal. Todd has transformed both his norms about breadwinning and his interpretation of his wife's employment, and he and Christina now agree that they are co-breadwinners.

Adjusting Norms About Breadwinning: Helene and Norman — A Husband's Unilateral Response

When men in this study disagreed with their wives about gender issues, one of their most common responses was to adjust their expressed norms and attitudes about gender, bringing them into harmony with those of their wives. Of the 21 couples in the subsample who disagreed about breadwinning at the time of the initial interviews, 15 husbands (71 percent) responded by rethinking their breadwinning norms—and the majority of these changed only their norms. Responding to disagreement about breadwinning by adjusting only norms was particularly characteristic of husbands whose reconstructions of breadwinning were unilateral. We have already seen that some of these husbands adopted egalitarian norms and attitudes as a way of meeting their wives' demands for greater gender equality. In other cases, however, like that of Helene and Norman, husbands created agreement by moving to embrace their wives' more conventionally gendered approaches to breadwinning.

When I first meet Helene and Norman in 1987, they are around thirty, have been married for thirteen years, and are the parents of four children, ages seven to twelve. They married when Helene was only 16, and she had borne all four children by the time she was 22. Helene first went back to work when her second child was a year old and did intermittent and part-time clerical work until the birth of her youngest child. When that child was six months old, she began working 55 hours per week as a day-care provider in her own home. She did this for over six years. When her youngest child began school, however, Helene gave up her day-care business and took a part-time job outside the home as a typist, at which she is now earning about $6,000 per year. Unlike Helene, Norman continued his education after high school. He has earned an associate's degree in business and works for a large, regional supermarket chain. It is his recent promotion from assistant manager to produce manager and a pay raise to $27,000 that has made it possible for Helene to reduce her work hours and for them to buy a larger house than they had previously owned.

I have agreed to meet Helene and Norman at their new house on a Saturday morning in August. I have been hesitant about this arrangement because they have just moved into the house this week and it seems a very inconvenient time to be interviewed. Helene and Norman have insisted, however, explaining that they will be leaving for their annual summer camping trip when the unpacking is completed and that they will be very busy getting the children ready for the opening of school when they return. Besides, they have reassured me, being interviewed will provide a welcome respite from the hassles of moving.

The scene I enter as I walk through the front door could best be described as cheerfully chaotic. Helene and Norman, all four children, Norman's parents, and Helene's sister are all involved in a final push to finish the unpacking. There are boxes everywhere, some still unopened, some partly empty, and some already folded flat and stacked neatly in a corner. Norman and his father are busy installing drapery rods at the living-room windows while Helene irons the draperies in preparation for their being hung. Helene's sister and Norman's mother are working in the kitchen, washing and putting away newly unpacked dishes. The children are helping them, working in teams—two children unpacking boxes of dishes and two breaking down the empty boxes. It is clear that such cooperative effort is an expected part of family life in this household.

Given this ethos of cooperation, we might expect to find Helene and Norman among the couples who agree about breadwinning. And, to some extent, they do agree. They are largely in agreement about the interpretation of Helene's employment; Norman is the breadwinner, and Helene works to help out. They both report that Norman is the financial provider for the family, that his job is the more important of the two, that he feels much more of an obligation to provide than Helene does, and that the financial provider role is the least important of the roles she plays.

Helene and Norman also agree that family comes first. They both respond to the hypothetical situation about the dual-earner couple with the sick child by saying that one of the parents should certainly stay home with the child and that they should decide which one by thinking not about individuals' wants, but about the family's needs, particularly the need for good health care benefits. Norman ranks his father role as most important on the list of seven roles, and Helene notes that she seldom experiences any conflict between her mother and work roles because she gives mothering such a high priority. "If my family needs me more," she explains, "it's just an automatic 'no' to outside things."

There are also areas of disagreement, however. Helene and Norman give somewhat different accounts, for example, of why Helene works and of how her earnings are used. Helene says that she works primarily for family extras, and her account of family financial arrangements confirms this. Norman, she says, "covers the basics." Her income is set aside for "extras," a category that turns out to cover a wide range of expenses, from medical bills and children's clothing to birthday gifts and vacation expenses. Helene explains that this arrangement is not a rigid one, however; sometimes her husband asks for a portion of her income to cover the monthly bills, and if any of her income is left over after she takes care of the "extra" expenses, it is added to his pay in the joint checking account.

It is this pooling of incomes that Norman's account emphasizes. He says that Helene works primarily to contribute to basic family expenses and that her income is pooled with his in a joint checking account to meet those needs. He does acknowledge that some of her income is sometimes withheld from this joint pool, noting, "Before she puts money into the checking account or whatever, if she feels she needs $10 or would like $10, she takes whatever she wants and she puts the rest in." Norman de-emphasizes this separation of money, however, and describes the small amounts that Helene keeps out of the joint financial pot as personal discretionary money, not family funds (a description with which Helene disagrees).

There is also some confusion and disagreement here about whether or not Helene would prefer to be a full-time housewife. Norman says that she would. When asked if he can imagine any circumstances under which Helene would leave the labor force, he responds, "Yes, at any point in time where we feel we can just strive on my own income." "Do you mean that if you were earning enough to support the family at the level you'd like, she'd be free to stay home?" I ask. "That's correct," he responds, "and she'd be more than happy to." But this is not the impression that I get from Helene. She says that she likes to work outside the home. "I'm not in the position where I *have* to work," she notes. "I work because I want to; I want to help him." When asked if she plans to work outside the home continuously until retirement, she responds, "Yes, if everything goes right."

These are, however, only minor disjunctures in Helene and Norman's overall consensus that he is the family breadwinner. Their major point of disagreement is in their norms about breadwinning. Helene considers their current situation ideal; she feels it is appropriate that Norman should be the primary provider and that she should help him with these efforts. But Norman dreams of a world where responsibility for breadwinning would not be allocated on the basis of gender. One of the themes that emerges in his interview is how often he feels torn between the need to give his time and attention to his children and the competing demands of providing for them financially. His ideal world is one in which he could resolve this tension by choosing to stay home with the children. He begins jokingly as he describes this vision, but he soon turns serious:

Well, I guess a lot of times we joke around, but I said if I could have it any way that I could, since I'm not a male chauvinist—and if she could go to work, earn all the money she wanted—I'd be more than happy to stay home, take care of the kids, and do the things around the house that need to be done. And I think, basically, that it would work out because she's the one that likes to be outside the house and I enjoy being home.

Norman does not expect this vision to be realized. But, although he accepts his duty to provide for his family, he does not have a strong personal stake in using breadwinning as a gender boundary. He is an uncommitted provider.

Five years later, Norman has reconsidered his norms about breadwinning. Helene is still working at her part-time typing job and is still earning about $6,000 per year. Norman, however, has been promoted again, to general store manager, and now has a salary of $45,000 per year—almost $20,000 more than he was earning five years earlier. Given the growing gap between their earnings, it is probably not surprising that Helene and Norman still agree that he is the primary provider, that his job is the more important one in the family, and that it is he who feels the obligation to provide. But they now also agree that this is the ideal. Like many men in this study, Norman has adjusted his norms to fit his circumstances and to bring them into agreement with his wife's. Whereas he earlier ranked his financial provider role fifth of seven, he now names it as one of the most important roles he plays, just behind husband and father. Perhaps he has come to see his dream of nongendered breadwinning as a childish fantasy. Perhaps he has found that he can ease his work-family role conflicts by emphasizing providing as a family role. For whatever reason, Norman and Helene are now in agreement about the use of breadwinning as a gender boundary, and he is now a traditional breadwinner married to an employed homemaker.

Agreeing to Relinquish the Breadwinning Boundary: Chuck and Valerie—A Wife's Unilateral Adjustment

Wives in this study were much less likely than husbands to respond to disagreements about breadwinning as Norman did, by making unilateral adjustments to their constructions of this gender boundary. On the contrary, when wives changed their constructions of breadwinning, it was usually in response to corresponding changes by their husbands or to changed circumstances. In the few cases where wives did make unilateral adjustments, however, they did so by moving to adopt their husbands' more egalitarian norms. It was just such a move that resolved the disagreement between Chuck and Valerie.

I have made the five-minute drive from my office to Chuck and Valerie's house on a Monday morning in June. Valerie and Chuck are in their late thirties, have been married sixteen years, have two school-age children, and are both teachers in the local public school system. She is a middle-school music teacher, and he is a history teacher and basketball coach at the high school. They are meeting with me on the first day of their summer vacation, and with the summer months stretched out luxuriously before them, they are both feeling carefree and relaxed. It is fitting, then, that we sit out on their deck to do the interviews, sipping morning coffee and basking in the warmth of the early summer sun.

Like Helene and Norman, Chuck and Valerie agree about the extent to which breadwinning is shared in their marriage but disagree about the extent to which it should be shared. But the parallel to Helene and Norman ends there. Unlike the latter couple, Chuck and Valerie have similar credentials, similar jobs, and similar incomes. Both work full time, both have earned their master's degrees, and both earn between $30,000 and $35,000 per year. Chuck's income is several thousand dollars higher than Valerie's only because he earns extra money by coaching.

Chuck and Valerie respond to these similarities by concluding that financial providing is shared in their marriage. They agree that they share providing equally, that both jobs are equally important in the family, that they both work primarily to earn money for basic family needs, and that their incomes are pooled to meet those needs. They also agree that Chuck feels a little more of an obligation to provide than Valerie does.

Nevertheless, disagreement emerges when we turn to norms. Chuck shows little attachment to breadwinning as a gender boundary. He gives the provider role a low priority, fifth out of seven roles, and he notes that he pays little attention to how family finances are arranged because "my wife is the banker." His response to the hypothetical situation of the dual-earner couple with the sick child does not assume that the man should be the breadwinner. "I don't have any set feeling that it should automatically be the man to work . . . [and] the wife to be back home, or vice versa," he says. "There'd be a lot of things to consider." Valerie, on the other hand, expresses attachment to breadwinning as a gender boundary. Male responsibility for breadwinning is, in her view, the complement of female responsibility for mothering. And responsibility for mothering is an issue for Valerie, who feels a lot of conflict between her work and family responsibilities and wishes that she could stay home "to spend more time with my children because they're young." In her ideal world, her husband would make this possible by being the primary financial provider.

Although their responses to interview questions classify Chuck as a role sharer and Valerie as a reluctant provider, a closer look reveals that their constructions of breadwinning are not really very far apart. Chuck has some sympathy with Valerie's ideals and admits to feeling sometimes that he should provide more than she does. That's "probably why I'm always running around looking for different ways to make money," he explains, referring to his coaching and to the summer jobs that he has sometimes taken on. For her part, Valerie is tentative about her ideal that Chuck should be primary provider. In fact, she expects to work continuously until retirement, and she responds to the hypothetical situation, as her husband does, by saying, "I don't think it's necessarily that the woman should take off, or the man; it's whoever can get the leave [from their job]." Moreover, Valerie's ideal of male breadwinning seems at odds with the strongly feminist responses she gives to all the gender attitude items.

Perhaps it is to be expected, then, that when I hear from Valerie and Chuck five years later, they have negotiated an agreement to relinquish breadwinning as a gender boundary in their marriage. It is not that their circumstances have changed substantially; they are both still at their teaching jobs, and Chuck continues to coach basketball and therefore to earn a few thousand dollars more per year than Valerie. Their children, of course, are older and are now both in high school. Chuck and Valerie continue to report that they share providing equally, that both jobs are equally important, and that both incomes are critical for meeting basic family needs. In addition, Chuck has solidified his rejection of breadwinning as a gender boundary. He no longer expresses any feeling that he should provide more than his wife. He now says that she feels the obligation to provide as much as he does, and he now gives both their provider roles fairly high rankings, third of seven. It is Valerie, however, who has made the biggest change in her construction of breadwinning. She has transformed her norms so that, like Chuck, she now claims shared responsibility for providing as her ideal.

Why is it the wife who has adjusted her norms in this case and not, as is more typical, the husband? One explanation is that this particular reconfiguration not only has brought Valerie into agreement with her husband, but has also made her own norms consonant with her interpretation of her employment. By contrast, if Chuck had adopted Valerie's normative position, the strain between these two basic components of breadwinning would have been increased. It is also possible that Valerie's feminist attitudes predisposed her to adopt her husband's egalitarian norms. Finally, it is important to remember that Valerie's attachment to ideals of male breadwinning was a corollary of her felt responsibility for mothering and her concerns about work-family conflicts. As her children have grown older and more independent, those conflicts have lessened. It is hard to feel that the children need her at home when they are hardly ever there themselves. Moreover, as her children begin to plan for college, it is clear to Valerie that they need her in a new way; the income she earns will be important in financing their educations. Thus, a combination of adult experiences, circumstances, and negotiation have brought Chuck and Valerie to a consensus that breadwinning is and should be something they share.

Conclusions

The extent to which disagreement leads to change in couples' constructions of breadwinning is striking. Of the 21 couples in the subsample who disagreed in 1987, all but two had changed their constructions of breadwinning by 1992. Most of these changes produced collaborative constructions of breadwinning. And, more often than not, agreement was reached by moving toward shared responsibility for financial providing.

It would be premature, however, to conclude from this analysis that dual-earner couples in the study community are well on their way to eliminating breadwinning as a gender boundary. First of all, we cannot assume that the follow-up subsample is generally representative of couples who disagree. Remember that such couples were somewhat less likely to respond to the follow-up survey than were those who agreed. Couples who resolved their disagreement into agreement are also more likely to be included in the subsample than those who did not. Consider some of the other possible outcomes of disagreement. Unresolved contention about such an important issue as breadwinning might put considerable strain on a marriage, eventually leading to its dissolution. Only three couples responded to the follow-up survey by reporting that they had divorced, but this is almost surely an undercount, and it is suggestive that these three had all disagreed about breadwinning at the time of the original interviews. Such disagreement was probably more likely among couples who later divorced, and these couples were probably also less likely to respond to the follow-up survey (or even to receive the mailing) than those in intact marriages. In any event, divorced couples, even those who did respond to the survey, did not qualify for inclusion in the subsample.

Even if disagreement about breadwinning does not lead to divorce, it may remain unresolved. If conflict about a central issue cannot be resolved, a couple may reduce the threat to their marriage by making a tacit agreement to ignore the issue. Thus, if disagreement about breadwinning were a buried source of strain in a marriage, the couple would be more likely to avoid conflict by ignoring the follow-up survey. One clue that this may have occurred can be found by looking at couples in which the wife earned considerably more than her husband at the time of the original interviews, a situation that often causes strain in a marriage and that cannot easily be resolved. There were eleven such couples in the original study, and nine of them (including the six with the highest-earning wives) did not respond to the follow-up survey. In the two couples who did respond, the wives continued to earn much more than their husbands. One of these wives was Patricia, whose unresolved conflict with her husband about breadwinning we have already examined in this chapter. The other was Roseanne, the wife from Chapter 5 who tried to ease the strain created by her much greater earning power by declaring her husband the breadwinner and downplaying her own contributions.

It is also possible that couples in this subsample are unlike the general population of dual-earner couples because they have been affected by their participation in the original study. As I noted in the case of Jeannette and Roland in Chapter 5, the interviews sometimes brought buried tensions about the construction of breadwinning to the surface, making them the subject of negotiation and attempts at resolution. Thus, such couples were probably more likely to reach agreement over the five-year period between the initial interviews and the follow-up than similar dual-earner couples who had not been interviewed.

The subsample couples are also older, on average, than the general population of dual-earner couples, and their age increases the probability of agreement. We know that the longer a couple has been married, the more likely they are to have negotiated a shared construction of breadwinning. Since all the couples in the subsample have, by definition, been married more than five years, they can be expected to have a higher rate of agreement about breadwinning than would a sample that included more recent marriages. Older couples also tend to have older children. Very few of the couples in the subsample had new babies in the five years between the initial interviews and the follow-up survey. This means that preschool children are now in school and that school-age children are now adolescents—changes that this analysis indicates may influence how their parents approach responsibility for breadwinning.

Even if the couples in the subsample were reasonably representative of dual-earner couples in the general population who disagree about bread-winning, however, it would not be reasonable to assume that their reso-lutions of that disagreement are permanent. After all, one of the most im-portant lessons of this analysis is that constructions of breadwinning are highly dynamic. Even among couples who agreed about the use of bread-winning at the time of the initial interviews, changes were widespread, and approximately one-third of them resulted in disagreement. We can expect that couples' circumstances will continue to change and that they will continue to negotiate the construction of gender in their marriages.

Note, also, that the changes that transformed husband-wife disagree-ment into agreement about the breadwinning boundary were more of-ten changes in norms than changes in behavioral interpretation. Such changes in attitudes have often been assumed to be momentous, leading in time to corresponding changes in behavior. But the gender construc-tion model and the analysis presented in this book caution us against such assumptions. There is no evidence here that changes in norms are stable or that they lead to changes in behavior. Remember that it was hus-bands, in particular, who responded to disagreement by adjusting their norms about breadwinning—and we have already seen that husbands' norms about breadwinning are remarkably plastic. There is no reason to believe that husbands who have adopted norms of shared breadwinning will not replace them with norms of male breadwinning at a later date. Indeed, the husbands who changed their norms between 1987 and 1992 were just as likely to adopt their wives' norms of male breadwinning (as Mark and Norman did) as to move in the direction of eliminating bread-winning as a gender boundary (as Wayne and Todd did).

Changes in breadwinning norms are often part of an ongoing negotia-tion about gender issues rather than the endpoint of negotiation. Thus, spouses may use changes in norms as a kind of peace offering to ease ten-sions about gender issues. Adopting the position of uncommitted provider, as Rod did in Chapter 4, may be a relatively painless way for a man to express sympathy with his wife's egalitarian ideals. Roseanne's move, in Chapter 5, to compensate for the growing gap between her income and her husband's by embracing ideals of male breadwinning can probably also be understood as such a peace offering, and I think that this is the most plausible explanation for Mark's transformation, in this chapter, from role sharer to reluctant co-provider.

In other cases, changes in norms may result from the discovery that such a peace offering is unnecessary. Thus, a wife who works full time, likes being employed, and earns a considerable portion of the family income may declare herself a reluctant provider in deference to her husband, as a way of avoiding injury to his masculine pride. When she discovers that he is not at all reluctant to share responsibility for breadwinning, that he in fact considers such sharing ideal, she feels that she now has his permission to give up breadwinning as a gender boundary. I think this dynamic probably provides part of the explanation for the transformation of Jeannette's norms in Chapter 5 and may have also played a role in Valerie's adoption of egalitarian norms in this chapter. Similarly, an uncommitted provider may declare ideals of shared breadwinning as an expression of sympathy with the gender equality that he believes is important to his wife, but when he finds out she is happy to have him bear primary responsibility for providing, he feels he has permission to become a traditional breadwinner. This dynamic probably operated in the case of Fred and Peggy in Chapter 5 and may also have been a factor in Norman's transformation from uncommitted provider to traditional breadwinner in this chapter.

Finally, changes in norms are often a response to changes in circumstances. Most of the couples in the subsample had experienced substantial changes in their economic, employment, or family circumstances between 1987 and 1992, and their reconstructions of breadwinning are as much a response to these situational changes as to disagreement between wife and husband. Thus, Norman's promotion and increased income have exerted some pressure on him to give up his dream of staying home and to embrace breadwinning as a responsibility of manhood. Todd's rethinking of his norms about breadwinning has probably been triggered at least as much by Christina's move to a full-time job and by his own reduced income as by her ideals of shared breadwinning. Wayne's reconstruction of the breadwinning boundary, too, has been a response to changed circumstances, particularly his wife's increased earnings.

These couples will probably continue to change their constructions of breadwinning. Both Patricia and Denis and Wayne and Linda are still in disagreement, a condition that exerts its own pressure for change. Patricia and Denis, however, do not seem to be good candidates for resolving their disagreement. If, as I suspect, Patricia is holding on to norms of male breadwinning as a way of protecting her prerogatives in the existing gender system and trying to get her husband back into line, she will relinquish these norms only when he demonstrates a serious commitment to work. He has resisted this pressure for more than eight years now, and it is hard to imagine the circumstances that would induce him to change. Wayne and Linda seem like much better candidates for reaching agreement. They now disagree only about norms, and that disagreement would be eliminated if Wayne reembraced the norms of male breadwinning that he held in 1987. Although that change would bring Wayne and Linda into agreement, however, it would be the unstable agreement of reluctant co-providers, a construction that is especially likely to be temporary. It is precisely this unstable position that Mark and Gail now find themselves in, and so they, too, are likely to experience further change in their constructions of breadwinning. Todd and Christina are in a more stable form of agreement, that of co-breadwinners, but it is not clear how firm Todd's commitment to shared breadwinning is. If the gap between his earnings and his wife's were to widen again, he might reassert his status as breadwinner. The stability of Helene and Norman's agreement may also depend on circumstances; as the children get older and need her presence less, Helene may increase her hours of work and her earnings and reconfigure her approach to breadwinning. Chuck and Valerie, on the other hand, are probably not very likely to change. Not only are they now in complete agreement, but wives do not usually revert to norms of male breadwinning once they have relinquished them. It would take a dramatic change in circumstances, probably one that involved her family's needing her at home, to lead Valerie in this direction.

The case studies in this chapter also demonstrate that breadwinning is part of an interconnected system of gender boundaries. The changing circumstances that strongly influence constructions and reconstructions of breadwinning sometimes do so indirectly, through their effects on other gender boundaries in the web. In particular, constructions of breadwinning are often linked to constructions of mothering. Thus, for Valerie, having adolescents who need her financial support more than her physical care has meant that mothering and breadwinning no longer seem to conflict with one another, and this has led her to embrace shared bread-winning as her ideal. Similarly, Gail became willing to accept her economic role in the family as critical only after her children entered school. Though Linda sees herself as sharing breadwinning in practice, she is reluctant to embrace this as an ideal, because she wants to reserve the right to stay home with her children. Helene, too, insists on putting mothering first. The next chapter of this book explores the relationship of the gender boundaries of breadwinning and mothering.

7

Breadwinning and Mothering
The Relationship of Gender Boundaries

In Chapter 2, I suggested that we think of gender as a complex web of interconnected boundaries—a dynamic web that is continually being breached and reinforced, torn and repaired, constructed and reconstructed. This book has focused on one strand in that web, the breadwinning boundary. But a complete understanding of breadwinning as a gender boundary must also include its relationship to other boundaries in the web. How is the construction of one boundary affected by the construction of others? Which boundaries are parallel and mutually reinforcing, and which are in tension? How do negotiations about various boundaries influence one another?

At a time when the gender system is a site of challenge and change, it seems particularly important to consider the implications of change in one gender boundary for the gender system as a whole. The analysis presented thus far in this book suggests that the breadwinning boundary is being relaxed in the late-twentieth-century United States, but what does this tell us about change in other gender boundaries? Is it reasonable to conclude that what is happening with breadwinning indicates a weakening of the entire system of gender difference? Or is the breaching of this particular boundary being compensated for elsewhere in the system by the shoring up of other boundaries or the construction of new ones?

In this chapter, I will begin to explore these issues by focusing on the relationship of breadwinning with one other gender boundary, mothering. When I talk about mothering, I am referring not to the process of giving birth, but to the routine, day-to-day care of children; mothering is being used as a gender boundary if and when such routine care is used to differentiate "real women" from "real men." I have chosen to focus on the relationship between these particular boundaries for two reasons. First, mothering, like breadwinning, seems central to the construction of gender in the family. As it developed in the nineteenth century, male responsibility for breadwinning was the complement of female responsibility for homemaking. But in the late twentieth century, as the employment of married women has become more widespread and widely accepted, and as the importance attached to housework has declined, "homemaking" has come more and more to mean "mothering"—making a stable home and providing day-to-day care for children. Second, the case studies presented thus far in this book have repeatedly suggested that constructions of breadwinning are intertwined with those of mothering. Rod's surprising construction of breadwinning makes sense only in the light of his conflict with his wife about parenting. Brad's desire to earn enough so that Michelle could be a full-time mother is another example of the interconnection of these boundaries, as is the way that women like Marie, Elise, Linda and Gail resist being defined as breadwinners so that they can reserve the right to stay home with their children. All of this indicates that the breadwinning/mothering relationship is an important one and a fruitful site for investigation.

A word of caution is in order here. This study of dual-earner couples was designed specifically to examine the issue of breadwinning. It was not designed to investigate mothering, and it provides only crude measures of that gender boundary. Thus, while data from this study can be used to explore the relationship of the breadwinning and mothering boundaries, the resulting analysis should be treated as just that, an exploration—a source not of definitive answers, but of intriguing suggestions and directions for further research.

Mothering as a Gender Boundary

Like breadwinning, the mothering boundary can have a number of dimensions, including both norms about who should care for children and the actual behavior of caring for children. Thus, mothering is being used as a gender boundary if women provide most of the child care, or if they are considered the appropriate providers of such care (whether they are providing it or not). The use of mothering as a gender boundary may also involve attaching different meanings to the same caretaking behavior, as in the example I noted earlier, in which a mother bathing her child is regarded as engaged in routine and appropriate parenting behavior, but a father bathing his child is considered to be "babysitting."

To evaluate the extent to which mothering is used as a gender boundary, I turn back to data from the 1987–88 interviews with the main sample of 153 couples. These interviews included a number of items that could be used as measures of the mothering boundary.

Respondents' randings of the roles that they and their spouses performed can provide some clues about the use of mothering as a gender boundary. Women's ranking of their own, and men's ranking of their wives', roles as mothers might seem an obvious indicator of the importance placed on female mothering. There are two problems with this measure, however. First, high rankings for the mother role do not necessarily indicate that women's responsibility for mothering is distinctive. Such rankings may mark a child-centered family in which parenting is considered of the first importance and in which the father role, too, is given high rankings. A second, more practical problem is that almost everyone gave the mother role a very high ranking; 91 percent of wives and 84 percent of husbands ranked it either first or second. This tells us that almost everyone considers mothering very important, but it doesn't help us differentiate those who emphasize women's distinctive responsibility for mothering from those who emphasize both men's and women's parenting roles. Ranking of the mother role is not a sufficiently discriminating measure.

Rankings of the father role do not present either of these problems; they have more variation than rankings of the mother role, and a high ranking of the father role clearly indicates that parenting is not considered an exclusively female responsibility. Therefore, I use ranking of the father role as one indicator of the extent to which mothering is used as a gender boundary. If the father role is ranked as one of the two most important roles a man plays, I regard this as evidence that mothering is not being used as a gender boundary. If, on the other hand, the father role is ranked third or lower, I regard this as an indication that mothering is being used as such a boundary.

Ranking of the father role, however, is not by itself an adequate indicator of the use of mothering as a gender boundary. While a high ranking of the father role indicates that parenting is not gendered female, a low ranking does not necessarily mean that it is. A low ranking may mean that children are grown and on their own and that parenting is no longer considered a very high priority for either husband or wife. Under these circumstances, both the mother and father roles would be ranked low. Therefore, I have computed a second measure of the mothering boundary, the difference between the rank assigned to the father role and the rank assigned to the mother role by each respondent. If mothering is given a higher rank than fathering, I regard this as an indication that mothering is being used as a gender boundary.

A third indicator of the use of mothering as a gender boundary is based on responses to the hypothetical situation about the dual-earner couple with the sick child. Interviewees were left free to answer this question in any way that they chose. Responses ranged from statements that the mother should stay home with the child to statements that the lower-earning parent, the father, should stay home. Some respondents suggested that both parents reduce or rearrange their work hours so they could share the child's care or that both parents remain at their jobs and hire someone to care for the child. I have regarded any response that the mother is the appropriate parent to care for a sick child, whether it is an insistence that the mother should leave her job and stay home with the child or a more tentative suggestion that the mother would be the best person to provide care if it could possibly be arranged, as evidence that mothering is being used as a gender boundary.

Each of these indicators—the ranking of the father role, the difference between the rankings of the mother and father roles, and the response to the hypothetical situation—taps a somewhat different aspect of mothering. Another way to measure the extent to which respondents use mothering as a gender boundary is to combine this information and consider how consistently they invoke women's special responsibility for mothering. Thus, a final measure used in this analysis counts whether an individual emphasizes women's special responsibility for mothering on none, one, two, or all three of these indicators. Respondents who do not make a distinction between women's and men's parenting on any of the indicators are regarded as not using mothering as a gender boundary, while those who distinguish women's mothering on all three indicators are considered committed to that boundary. Overall, I regard an individual as using mothering as a gender boundary if she or he invokes a special responsibility for mothers on at least two of the three indicators.

These measures are not available, however, for all 153 couples in the main sample. Because respondents were asked to rank only those roles that they actually filled, rankings of the mother and father roles are available only for those who are parents. Thus, the analysis presented here is limited to the 123 wives and 124 husbands who were parents at the time of their interviews. As Table 7 shows, most of these respondents do not consistently use mothering as a gender boundary. Only 11 percent of wives and 10 percent of husbands can be classified here as demonstrating

TABLE 7

Percentage of Respondents Invoking Mothering as a
Gender Boundary on the Aggregate Measure

Number of indicators	Wives (N = 123)	Husbands (N = 124)
0	34%	36%
1	36	31
2	19	23
3	11	10

a clear commitment to such a boundary, and only 30 percent of wives and 33 percent of husbands invoke special responsibility for mothers on at least two of the three indicators. By contrast, slightly more than one-third of husbands and wives do not distinguish women's mothering on any of these three indicators, and another third invoke mothering as a gender boundary on only one measure.

These figures must, however, be interpreted cautiously. The available indicators primarily tap the normative dimension of mothering. As a result, it is very likely that they underestimate the use of mothering as a gender boundary. As is true with breadwinning, some probably relinquish the mothering boundary ideologically even as they deploy it in practice. Thus, data on actual parenting behavior and on gendered interpretations of that behavior would most likely reveal a more complex picture and considerably greater use of mothering as a gender boundary.

Although the available measures provide only a partial view of the mothering boundary, they nevertheless yield some interesting results. Men and women tend to use mothering as a gender boundary on different indicators (see Table 8). Women are somewhat more likely than men to invoke mothering as a gender boundary on only one indicator, and this is usually the hypothetical situation. Forty-three percent express a preference that the mother care for the sick child, while only about one-third invoke mothering as a gender boundary on each of the other two indicators. Men, on the other hand, are somewhat more likely to invoke mothering as a gender boundary on two indicators—and, almost always, these two are the role rankings. They are particularly likely to invoke the relative importance of the mother role more generally.

These differences suggest that respondents distinguish women's distinctive responsibility for mothering under unusual circumstances from that responsibility under ordinary conditions. In effect, the women who invoked mothering as a gender boundary only in the hypothetical situa-

TABLE 8

Frequency Distributions for Three Indicators of Mothering

	Pct. of wives (N = 123)	Pct. of husbands (N = 124)
Importance of father role		
Not used as gender boundary	70%	65%
Ranked most important	(23)	(22)
Ranked second most important	(47)	(43)
Used as gender boundary		
(ranked third or lower in importance)	30	35
Relative importance of mother role		
Not used as gender boundary		
(mother role not ranked higher)	66	60
Used as gender boundary	34	40
Mother role ranked somewhat higher	(19)	(27)
Mother role ranked much higher	(15)	(13)
Hypothetical situation		
Used as gender boundary	43	32
Mother should definitely stay home	(32)	(23)
Mother should stay home if possible	(11)	(9)
Not used as gender boundary	57	68
Hire someone to care for child	(6)	(17)
Share care of child	(16)	(10)
Father should stay home	(11)	(13)
Other responses	(24)	(28)

tion were saying, "Under ordinary circumstances, mothers and fathers should be equally involved in the care of their children, but when a child needs special care, mothers are better equipped to provide it." In contrast, the men who invoked mothering as a gender boundary only on the role rankings were saying, in effect, "Under ordinary circumstances, women bear a special responsibility for mothering, but in an emergency, gender boundaries can be relaxed temporarily while everyone pitches in to help." These results suggest a gender difference in the salience of mothering as a gender boundary. In general, circumstances requiring extraordinary care of children increase the salience of that boundary for these mothers, but decrease it for the fathers. These are only general tendencies, however, and there are important exceptions. As Table 9 shows, male role sharers display the pattern of salience more generally typical of mothers, and female co-breadwinners and supplementary providers give responses more like those of fathers.

This analysis indicates that mothering is used as a gender boundary by at least a substantial minority of these dual-earner couples. Moreover, the limited evidence available here suggests that the use of mothering as a

TABLE 9

Percentage of Respondents Invoking Mothering as a Gender Boundary by Breadwinner Type

	Rank of father role	Importance of mother role	Hypothetical situation	Aggregate measure
Wives' types				
Employed homemakers (N = 30)	43%	47%	50%	40%
Co-breadwinners (N = 14)	29	21	14	21
Helpers (N = 25)	24	32	52	28
Supplementary providers (N = 14)	29	50	21	36
Reluctant providers (N = 15)	20	27	67	27
Reluctant traditionals (N = 18)	22	11	22	11
Family-centered workers (N = 5)	40	60	100	60
Committed workers (N = 2)	50	50	50	50
Husbands' types				
Traditional breadwinners (N = 49)	45	45	39	41
Role sharers (N = 27)	15	11	18	11
Reluctant co-providers (N = 27)	44	59	44	44
Uncommitted providers (N = 21)	29	38	19	29

gender boundary is, like the use of breadwinning, complex, with patterns that differ by gender. How, then, are the constructions of these two gender boundaries related?

The Relationship of Mothering and Breadwinning

If we think of the gender system as a web of gender boundaries, there are two basic forms of relationship that any two boundaries may have to one another. The first is complementary. That is, boundaries may be parallel strands in the web, reinforcing one another and changing in ways that mirror one another. Thus, if the relationship between breadwinning and mothering is complementary, a breaching or relaxation of the breadwinning boundary should be accompanied by a similar breaching or relaxation of the mothering boundary. Alternatively, the relationship between two boundaries may be compensatory; these strands of the gender web may run in different directions and be in tension with one another, so that a breaching or relaxation of one boundary is compensated for by a shoring up or strengthening of the other. If the relationship between breadwinning and mothering is compensatory, it is likely that those who have relaxed the breadwinning boundary emphasize mothering as a gender boundary and that those who have relaxed the mothering boundary emphasize breadwinning as a gender boundary.

Classifying individuals' use of mothering as a gender boundary by their constructions of breadwinning suggests that the relationship is primarily complementary (Table 9). On every measure of mothering and among both husbands and wives, those who most clearly embrace breadwinning as a gender boundary (the traditional breadwinners and the employed homemakers) are more likely to use mothering as a gender boundary than are those who have relinquished the breadwinning boundary (the role sharers and the co-breadwinners). Among husbands, the most striking difference is in the relative importance of the mother and father roles. Forty-five percent of the traditional breadwinners rank the mother role as more important than the father role, but only 11 percent of the role sharers do so. For wives, it is the hypothetical situation that yields the most dramatically different responses. Fully half (50 percent) of the employed homemakers, but only 14 percent of the co-breadwinners, say that the mother in this situation should, if possible, stay home with the sick child. Although responses on the other indicators of mothering do not provide such striking results, they tend in the same direction. Overall, 41 percent of the traditional breadwinners and 40 percent of the employed homemakers invoke mothering as a gender boundary on at least two of these indicators, compared with only 11 percent of the role sharers and 21 percent of the co-breadwinners. Indeed, 12 percent of the traditional breadwinners and 27 percent of the employed homemakers invoke mothering as a gender boundary on all three indicators, whereas none of the role sharers or co-breadwinners does so.

A closer look at this complementary relationship between breadwinning and mothering reveals that it is shaped primarily by norms about breadwinning.* The relationship is most apparent for the men in the sample; husbands' norms about breadwinning are related to every measure of mothering as a gender boundary, whereas their interpretations of their wives' employment are not. Thus, reluctant co-providers' construc-

---

* This may be, in part, an artifact of the indicators of the mothering boundary available here, which are primarily measures of norms about mothering.

tions of the mothering boundary are much more like those of the traditional breadwinners (whose norms they share) than like those of the role sharers (whose interpretations of their wives' employment are similar). The patterns are less clear for the wives; norms of male breadwinning predict the use of mothering as a gender boundary only for the hypothetical situation. There is some tendency toward a similar relationship for the aggregate measure, but no clear pattern emerges for the role rankings (Table 9). For the most part, the relationship between the use of mothering as a gender boundary and the behavioral interpretation dimensions of breadwinning is more complex than its relationship with the normative dimension. Unlike breadwinning norms, which are consistently in a complementary relationship with mothering, the behavioral interpretation dimensions show some signs of a compensatory relationship. Specifically, those whose interpretations of husband's and wife's employment disagree with their norms seem to compensate for this contradiction by taking particularly strong positions on the use of mothering as a gender boundary.

Among the husbands, the reluctant co-providers most clearly demonstrate this compensatory use of mothering as a gender boundary. On almost every measure, they are the category of husbands most likely (even more likely than the traditional breadwinners) to invoke mothering as a gender boundary. More than a quarter of them (26 percent) do so on all three indicators of mothering. It is as though they are compensating for their inability to effectively maintain breadwinning as a clear gender boundary by putting extra emphasis on other forms of male/female difference—in this case, women's distinctive responsibility for mothering. Note that these are the same men who cling most strongly to norms of male breadwinning; they are more likely than any other group of husbands in the study to say that they should be the sole breadwinners for their families.

Among the wives, the compensatory relationship is most clearly apparent among the reluctant traditionals, those who believe in eliminating the breadwinning boundary but have not succeeded in doing so. The reluctant traditionals resemble the reluctant co-providers in that their lived experience of breadwinning violates their norms, and in that they seem to be compensating for those violations in their responses to questions about mothering. More than any other group of wives, the reluctant traditionals reject the use of mothering as a gender boundary. This is especially true in their role rankings; they emphasize the relative importance of their husbands' roles as fathers and de-emphasize any distinctive responsibility for parenting on their own part. Overall, only 11 percent of these wives can be counted as deploying the mothering boundary, and none of them embraces that boundary by invoking it on all three indicators.

The issue of whether the relationship between the breadwinning and mothering boundaries is complementary or compensatory becomes even more complex if we consider yet another aspect of that relationship— how contested constructions of one boundary may affect constructions of the other. Just as husbands and wives do not always agree about breadwinning, they do not always agree about mothering. Although the mothering boundary (at least as measured by these admittedly limited indicators) seems to be somewhat less subject to disagreement than the breadwinning boundary, more than one-third of these couples (36 percent) are in substantial disagreement about the use of mothering as a gender boundary. Moreover, for almost two-thirds (65 percent) of the 122 couples with children, at least one of these gender boundaries is contested (Table 10).

Disputes about gender boundaries, like the boundaries themselves, may be in either complementary or compensatory relationship to one another. A complementary relationship here means that an individual involved in a disagreement tries to construct the two boundaries so that they reinforce one another and thereby strengthen the individual's contested position. Patricia, in Chapter 6, provides an example. She reinforces her position that her husband should be the breadwinner by emphasizing her own complementary responsibilities as a mother. She gives his role as father a relatively low ranking, ranks her own mother role as her most important, and says that the high-earning mother in the hypothetical situation should stay home to take care of her child. If both partners reinforce their positions in this way, both boundaries will be contested, with the spouses taking consistent, but opposed, positions.

TABLE 10

Percentage of Respondents Contesting Mothering and Breadwinning Boundaries

Level of contention	Pct. (N = 122)
Neither boundary contested	35%
Breadwinning boundary only contested	29
Mothering boundary only contested	22
Both boundaries contested	14

But there is another possibility. Individuals may try to compensate for their intransigence in the construction of one contested boundary by taking a conciliatory position on a related boundary. We see a hint of this strategy in the case of Rod, the uncommitted provider in Chapter 4. You will recall that Rod's conflict with his wife, Anita, about the construction of gender in their marriage seemed to revolve primarily around his role as a parent. Rod worked long hours in his construction business and had little time or attention to spare for his children. Anita wanted Rod to be a more involved parent. He acknowledged this as a worthwhile goal but was unwilling or unable to make the changes in his life that becoming a truly active parent would require. Instead, he expressed sympathy with his wife's ideals by adopting egalitarian norms about breadwinning. Rod compensated for his dispute with his wife on one gender boundary (mothering) by yielding to her on another (breadwinning).

My exploratory analysis suggests that when two boundaries are contested, a spouse is much more likely to develop a conciliatory construction of one boundary as a compensatory peace offering than to develop a construction of that boundary that will shore up his or her position on the other. Only about 10 percent of couples with contested constructions of gender are dug into consistently opposing positions in their constructions of the breadwinning and mothering boundaries. Another small group of couples are in substantial disagreement about both boundaries, but not in a consistent way. It's as though each partner in these marriages is willing to yield to egalitarian trends on only one of these boundaries, and husband and wife make different choices. The vast majority of couples who disagree about the construction of gender, however, only contest one of these two boundaries. This suggests that, while one partner maintains a consistent position on the two boundaries, the other eases the disagreement by yielding on one of them.

Who does the yielding? There is no simple answer to this question; each boundary seems to have a distinctive pattern. When the breadwinning boundary is in dispute, the partner who advocates shared breadwinning seems to be in the stronger position. Eighty-four percent of the wives and 77 percent of the husbands who use the mothering boundary to compensate for a dispute about the breadwinning boundary have adopted a nongendered construction of mothering to match their spouses' nongendered positions on both boundaries. When it is the mothering boundary that is contested, however, the partner who wants to maintain this boundary usually prevails. Eighty-five percent of the wives and 73 percent of the husbands who used breadwinning to compensate for a dispute about the mothering boundary yielded to their spouses' gendered constructions and adopted breadwinning as a gender boundary.

This exploration suggests, then, that the relationship of the breadwinning and mothering boundaries is a complex one, involving both complementary and compensatory elements. Individuals tend to construct the two boundaries as complements to one another, particularly on the normative dimension, but they also use constructions of mothering to compensate for difficulties in effecting their desired constructions of breadwinning. When constructions of gender are contested within a marriage, a more complex dynamic of compensation comes into play. One partner usually moves to keep the conflict within bounds, limiting it to only one of these boundaries and yielding to the spouse's construction of the other. To gain a better understanding of this complex relationship between breadwinning and mothering, I turn now to case studies of five representative couples.

Complementary and Compensatory Relationships: Five Case Studies

Complementary Constructions of Breadwinning and Mothering: Ellen and Bob — Removing Gender Boundaries

For more than one-third of the couples in this study, neither the breadwinning boundary nor the mothering boundary was contested at the time of the original interviews. These couples had usually developed constructions of gender in which these two boundaries paralleled and reinforced one another, and most often, those complementary constructions minimized the use of both boundaries. Sometimes, as in the case of Ellen and Bob, such couples replaced conventional gender boundaries with an active commitment to role sharing.

Ellen and Bob are a professional couple who were in their mid-thirties when I first interviewed them. They met in law school and married at the end of their second year. When they completed their degrees, they were pleased to obtain positions with different large law firms in the same city. Although the work was sometimes grueling and the hours were long, both found that they truly enjoyed practicing law. The future seemed golden as Ellen began to specialize in family law, Bob focused on labor law and discrimination cases, and, after two years at their respective firms, they began a family.

Ellen and Bob soon found that the tensions between the demands of two high-powered careers and those of parenting were overwhelming.

No child-care provider was willing to cover the 80–90 hours per week that they were used to putting in at their law firms. They had to arrange their schedules so that at least one of them was home by 7:00 every evening. To make up the lost work time, they started spending more time in the office on weekends, one on Saturday and one on Sunday, and they brought more work home with them. They couldn't decide whether they wanted their baby to be awake during the hours they were at home, so that they could spend time with her, or whether they wanted her to be asleep so that they could have some time with one another, get some work done, and get some sleep themselves.

By the time their daughter was two, these difficulties had reached crisis proportions. Ellen and Bob found themselves increasingly impatient with one another and with their child. Once they had spent long hours discussing legal issues; now they felt like strangers. More and more, the child resisted going to bed at night and begged to be allowed to stay up a little longer with her largely absent parents. Worse, when she got upset, she pushed them away and sobbed the name of her full-time nanny. The situation was wretched; Ellen and Bob were unhappy and their child was unhappy. Clearly, something had to give. But what?

It was not hard for Ellen and Bob to see that they simply could not combine two absorptive careers with their idea of adequate parenting. One solution would be to cut back to one career, but whose? Neither of them wanted to give up the practice of law, and both wanted to devote more time and energy to their daughter. In other words, both Ellen and Bob wanted to be practicing lawyers who worked reasonable hours and were also active, involved parents. The answer, they decided, was to share one position in a law firm.

Eagerly, they approached the senior partners of their respective firms with the job-sharing proposal, and both firms promptly turned the idea down as unthinkable and unworkable. Discouraged, but determined, Ellen and Bob decided that, as an interim measure, one of them should leave his or her current job to spend time on child care and to take on the task of finding a law firm willing to consider a job-sharing arrangement. Since it was more difficult for Ellen to extricate herself from her current cases and because, as Bob explains it, "she has a dread of being stuck at home," he submitted his resignation. Within a year, they had convinced a medium-sized firm in the study community to try the experiment and had moved there to take up their new life.

Several years later, everyone is pleased with the way the arrangement has worked out, and Bob and Ellen have every expectation of being offered a shared partnership in their firm. They have bought a house on a quiet residential street within walking distance of the law office and have had a second child, a son, who is now three. Their move to a smaller, less prestigious firm meant a reduction in salary, but although they are earning a combined income of only $38,000—far, far less than they would have been bringing in by now if they had stayed with their old firms—they have no doubts that their much saner life-style is well worth the cost.

Since law positions typically demand long hours, sharing a job means that Ellen and Bob each put in about 35–40 hours per week. To the extent possible, they try to keep their schedules flexible, with each putting in two full days, one or two half days, and some evenings at the office, and also bringing some work home. Their daughter, now in second grade, finds one or the other of her parents at home when she returns from school in the afternoon. Their three-year-old attends a local day-care center part time and is cared for at home by his parents the rest of the time.

Bob and Ellen have suggested that we schedule the interviews at their office, and I have arrived there, as arranged, on a Friday noon in early September to interview them sequentially. Ellen meets me in the reception area and invites me into her office, a very pleasant space on the second floor of an old Victorian house that has been converted to commercial use. The office has deep plush carpeting, oak furniture, original prints by local artists on the walls, and family pictures on the desk. Ellen suggests that we make ourselves comfortable in two wing chairs that flank an oak coffee table on one side of the office, and there we begin the interview.

At 12:45, just as we are finishing, Bob arrives with his son in tow. It is clear that the child visits his parents' office frequently and is at home here. He ignores me and rushes over to look at his favorite piece of office artwork as Ellen introduces me to her husband. This is both a work shift change and a child-care shift change for Ellen and Bob. Bob has already fed his son lunch, and as Ellen gets ready to walk back home with the child, I hear her suggesting a detour through a nearby park with a duck pond, a favorite attraction of local children. As Ellen and her son leave the building and Bob and I begin his interview, I can hear a piping voice talking excitedly about ducks and goldfish.

In their interviews, Ellen and Bob minimize gender boundaries and emphasize the extent to which they share both work and parenting. They have no trouble identifying breadwinning as a shared responsibility in their marriage. Both report that they share providing equally and that both jobs are equally important. ("Well," Bob explains, laughing, "it's the same job!") They also agree that earning money for basic family needs is a very important reason for each of them to be employed. Bob says that they also feel an equal obligation to provide, although Ellen thinks that she may feel it slightly more. Finally, they are fully agreed that they *ought* to share providing equally.

Interestingly, however, although Ellen and Bob fully share the responsibility for providing, it is not at the center of either of their lives. Both give their own and their spouses' provider roles low rankings. It's not that providing is unimportant; it's just an accepted part of the background of their lives. Ellen explains it this way:

> I don't think either of us thinks about it very much because we've never been in a situation where we've been unemployed, and we're doing what we want to do. . . . It sounds awfully overprivileged to say that earning money for basic family needs is an incidental thing. I mean, if we had to do it, it wouldn't be incidental, but given that basic family needs are covered, neither of us really thinks about it.

Bob comments that he finds it difficult to rank the provider role because, as he puts it, "financial provider is very hard to put in with these [other] things which are all personal."

It is not the work that is taken for granted here, but the providing. Indeed, both emphasize the importance of their roles as professionals. Bob ranks this role third in importance, just after husband and father. Ellen refuses to differentiate professional, wife and mother, arguing that they are all equally and vitally important. Not surprisingly, neither of them would quit working if they won a lottery jackpot, and when asked why not, they both reply in the same words: "I like my job." Indeed, Ellen can't imagine any circumstances under which either of them would leave the labor force and be supported by the other, and Bob can imagine it only if one or the other of them wanted to take some time off to do legal work for which he or she wouldn't be paid.

If breadwinning is a shared responsibility in the background of Ellen and Bob's lives as lawyers, however, shared parenting is very much in the foreground. After all, in leaving their big-name, big-city law firms for a shared position in an unremarkable firm in a relatively obscure community, they made an active commitment to shared parenting, and this commitment is reinforced daily as they juggle their work schedules to take account of the needs of their children. Both Ellen and Bob rank their roles as parents at or near the top of the list of social roles, and neither of them sees one parent as more important to the children than the other. When presented with the hypothetical situation of the dual-earner parents with the sick child, both of them draw on their own experience and suggest that the best solution would be some kind of part-time or flexible work scheduling that would allow the parents to share the child's care.

This is not just a matter of practicality for Ellen and Bob; it is a matter of principle. Together, they have embraced a feminist ideology of shared roles and minimal gender differentiation. By the time we get to the gender attitude items at the end of the interview, both feel they have expounded this ideology so firmly and consistently that their attitudes must be obvious. When I read Ellen the first item, "There is some work that is men's and some that is women's and they shouldn't be doing each other's," she playfully responds, "I strongly agree," and then laughs as I struggle not to react. Bob waits until I get to the statement that "women should take care of running their homes and leave running the country up to men," and then laughs and says, "Go ahead. Put what you think down."

In Ellen and Bob's construction of gender, the breadwinning and mothering boundaries are complementary, a relationship that has been reinforced by their experiences. They left law school committed only to dual careers, but they soon learned that they could not eliminate breadwinning as a gender boundary without also confronting the mothering boundary. This realization led them to rethink their goals and life-styles and to commit themselves to active role sharing and a total reconsideration of the gender system.

Complementary Constructions, Contested Boundaries: Gilbert and Yvonne — Conflicting Constructions of Gender

In some marriages, individual spouses develop constructions of breadwinning and mothering that are complementary but that conflict with their partners' constructions of those same boundaries. In other words, although husband and wife agree that breadwinning and mothering are parallel gender boundaries, they disagree about the extent to which these boundaries are or should be deployed in their marriage. We have already seen an example of this in the case of Patricia and Denis from Chapter 6. Patricia maintains that her husband should bear primary responsibility for breadwinning, and, as reinforcement for her position, she also emphasizes the gender-specialized role of women as mothers. Denis, on the other hand, would like to eliminate these gender boundaries and takes a position in favor of both shared breadwinning and shared parenting. In

Denis and Patricia's case, the lines of disagreement are starkly drawn. More often, however, such disagreement is more tentative; as in the case of Gilbert and Yvonne, it is combined with overlapping constructions and with room for negotiation.

Yvonne and Gilbert were high-school sweethearts who married when they were seventeen and eighteen, respectively. They were 39 and 40 when I met them, had been married for 22 years, had three children, ranging in age from eleven to nineteen, and were both employed full time. As soon as he graduated from high school, Gilbert took a job as an hourly wage employee with a manufacturer of dental equipment. After several years, he was accepted into a management training program and began to work his way up into salaried positions. Since then, he had worked for several dental equipment suppliers, most of them small companies, and was now a district sales manager with a salary of $28,000. Yvonne, too, made a career in the dental field. During the past decade, she had worked in a series of dental offices as receptionist, office manager, and sometimes dental assistant. She was currently paid an hourly wage and was earning about $16,000 per year.

When I first spoke with Gilbert and Yvonne on the telephone about the possibility of participating in the study, they were interested but not sure when and how they could fit the interviews into their busy lives. It was the beginning of August, their nineteen-year-old daughter was getting married at the end of the month, and they were very much caught up in preparations for the wedding. After much discussion, however, Yvonne found a small opening in her schedule and we arranged her interview for a late afternoon about two weeks before the wedding. I have arrived at their modest two-story house to keep this appointment and have found a strong sense of excitement in the air and signs of the impending festivities everywhere: Yvonne is sitting at the kitchen table, opening wedding invitation responses that have arrived in today's mail; gifts from a recent bridal shower are piled on the dining-room table; and a bridal gown is hanging on a closet door beside the stairs awaiting alterations.

Yvonne is at the center of this whirlwind of activity and seems harried. The interview does not begin well; she is impatient with my questions and balks at the task of reconstructing her complicated work history. I am beginning to think that I should have waited to schedule the interview after the wedding when it takes a turn that makes me realize I have misjudged the source of Yvonne's irritation. I ask her how important a sense of accomplishment is as a reason for her to be employed, and she responds, "I don't feel like I get much accomplishment from my job." She explains that she is working for a semiretired dentist who still wants to keep his office open but sees patients only irregularly. Although Yvonne must be on the job 45 hours per week, there is little to do and no one to talk to, and it is driving her crazy. "I'm like a bear when I come home," she notes apologetically; "I'm not in a good mood. And, you know, I've only been there a little over two months and I'm already looking for work."

Why doesn't Yvonne just quit this job? She wouldn't do so without first finding another one because she considers working one of her responsibilities as an adult. She has been employed throughout most of her adult life, expects to be employed continuously until retirement, and can't imagine any circumstances under which she would leave the labor force and her husband would be sole provider for the family. Although Yvonne thinks of her work as a career and expects it to be satisfying, she is clear that her primary motivation for employment is to provide financially for her family. "I think the most important thing is to get the money to pay the bills and to eat," she says, "and see that my kids have clothes." She acknowledges that Gilbert's higher earnings make his job more important in the family, and she thinks that he may feel a little more of an obligation to provide than she does, but she stresses the similarity in their situations and reports that they share providing equally. She also says that such shared responsibility for providing is her ideal.

Yvonne's current construction of breadwinning has developed over time. After she reports that she and her husband ought, ideally, to share the responsibility for providing, she adds that she has not always thought this way. "Years ago," she explains, "I would have said strictly him." There is still some hint of this former construction in her responses. She gives her provider role a low priority, ranking it sixth out of seven, while she ranks her husband's financial provider role third in importance. Moreover, when she is asked whether she agrees that "a married woman should not work outside the home if her husband can comfortably support her," she seems to forget about shared responsibility for breadwinning and responds, "Not unless she wants to."

Nevertheless, Yvonne has moved in the direction of relaxing gender boundaries, a tendency that is even clearer when she talks about parenting. Yvonne ranks her role as mother as the most important one she plays, but she also gives top billing to her husband's role as father, arguing, in effect, that parenting should be at the center of both parents' lives. When she is presented with the gender attitude items, she rejects the idea that mothers have a special responsibility for parenting. She strongly agrees that "a woman who works full time can establish just as warm and secure a relationship with her children as a mother who does not work" and that the husband of such a working mother "should spend as much time in housework and child care as she does." She does not even grant mothers special abilities or responsibilities in caring for a sick child; she responds to the hypothetical situation by saying, "If they could afford it, I think probably they should hire someone."

I have almost forgotten Yvonne's responses by the time I catch up with her husband three weeks later. Gilbert is one of those people who can never seem to find enough time, but it is two days after his daughter's wedding, and the sudden completion of all the wedding preparations have left him feeling relatively relaxed. He answers my questions thoughtfully and often expands on his responses, and as he does so, it becomes clear that his construction of gender is different from his wife's.

As far as Gilbert is concerned, he is the family breadwinner. He says that he is the financial provider, that his job is more important than his wife's "because of the pay scale," and that he feels much more of an obligation to provide than she does. When I ask about his motivations for paid employment, he responds, "It's basically to provide for my family." He says that his wife, by contrast, works primarily for her own independence and for family extras, that providing basics is not a very important reason for her employment.

Gilbert, like many men in this study, feels that a married woman should be free to work outside the home if she wants to, but that she shouldn't have to. It's not that he expects Yvonne to stay home, but he does feel that she should have the option. When I ask him if he can imagine any circumstances under which Yvonne would leave the labor force and he would be the sole support of the family, he replies,

Say I got a job where I was making another $20,000 a year, or even $10,000 a year. Then, and only then, she would probably drop out of the work force and say, "Okay, now I can take it easy." . . . I think she would probably only do it for a short period of time and then go to work part time. She's not the type of person who would stay home.

Even though Yvonne isn't "the type of person who would stay home," however, Gilbert does not feel that they should depend on her earnings. "I've always . . . tried to do things," he explains, "to where I would be 'the provider,' in case something happened to her or she couldn't work, we could still afford the bills."

Gilbert says that he learned his strong commitment to male breadwinning from his parents. His mother "didn't work for pay" but worked "very hard . . . to provide a home." His father had a very strong work ethic and instilled this in his son. Gilbert tells the following story by way of illustration: "I was thirteen. I asked my father for some money and he told me to go get a job. He said, 'I'm all done dishing out money to you. . . . You're thirteen years old. . . . I went to work when I was ten, and you're going when you're thirteen. . . . I'll give you three years.'" Gilbert was not the only Franco-American man in the study to tell such a story, but where some expressed resentment against fathers whom they considered harsh and oppressive, Gilbert expresses gratitude: "I can thank the man," he concludes; "he showed me how to work." He embraces his parents' model by ranking his financial provider role as the most important one he plays.

Gilbert has also adopted a conventional construction of mothering, regarding it, like breadwinning, as appropriately gender-specialized. He is one of the minority of fathers in this study who rank their role as father third or lower in importance. He emphasizes his wife's special responsibility for parenting, ranking her role as mother higher in importance than his role as father and expressing concern that her employment may interfere with this special responsibility. He disagrees with the statement that "a woman who works full time can establish just as warm and secure a relationship with her children as a mother who does not work."

But Gilbert's construction of gender, like Yvonne's, is still developing. Although he admires his parents' example, he thinks that family life requires more flexibility today than it once did. He is willing to relax the breadwinning boundary somewhat because "it takes both to live," and he is also willing to relax the mothering boundary in unusual circumstances. Thus, when he is presented with the hypothetical situation of the dual-earner family with the sick child, Gilbert does not focus on women's special responsibility for mothering, but on the practical need of a family under stress to use its economic resources most efficiently. He looks for the solution that will leave the family with the highest possible income, whether it be working separate shifts and sharing care of the child, hiring someone to care for the child, or having the person with the lower income (the husband) leave the labor force.

But practical considerations are not the only catalyst for Gilbert to rethink his construction of gender. He combines his commitment to gender specialization with an equally strong commitment to marriage as a partnership of equals. Thus, when I ask him who, ideally, should be the financial provider for his family, he surprises me by responding, "Well, I think it should be an equal thing." As he expands on his answer, however, it becomes clear that he is not talking so much about equal responsibility for providing as equal say in family financial matters. He describes the process of financial decision making in his marriage as one based on regular discussions: "We'll discuss what we want to do, or if we can do this next week, or three months down the road, what do we want to plan for. . . . If we can't come to an agreement, then we won't discuss it; we'll shelf it and then discuss it at another time. . . . That's the way it should be handled; we should share. . . . I don't think one person should be better than the other." Thus, Gilbert's commitment to complementary role specialization is tempered by his belief that husbands and wives should be equals.

Both Yvonne and Gilbert assume the complementarity of breadwinning and mothering. As they negotiate their constructions of gender, each of them reconstructs these two boundaries so that they remain parallel. But their current constructions are out of sync; Yvonne has committed herself to breaching both boundaries, while Gilbert wants to keep them intact. Nevertheless, there is overlap in their divergent constructions, and it does not seem likely that this couple will dig into their opposed positions as Patricia and Denis have done. More likely, Gilbert and Yvonne will move to resolve, or at least to compensate for, their disagreement.

Compensating for Violated Norms: Peter and Catherine — Reluctant Co-providers

The relationship between the breadwinning and mothering boundaries is not always so clearly complementary; at times, particularly when the normative and interpretive dimensions of breadwinning do not coincide, there are signs of a compensatory dynamic. Thus, the reluctant co-providers, men whose interpretation of their wives' employment violates their own norms, often compensate for this violation by emphasizing the importance of female mothering. Peter, a fifth-grade teacher, and his wife, Catherine, a pediatric nurse, provide an example of this form of compensation.

I have arrived at Peter and Catherine's older single-family house in mid-afternoon on a Tuesday in early August. Theirs is one of a row of similar houses huddled together on the edge of a busy state highway. When the houses were built, this was a sleepy rural road; but it now serves as the main access route for a nearby paper mill, and the houses are repeatedly shaken by the rumble of heavy logging trucks. Indeed, the heavy truck traffic makes it very difficult to slow down and look at house numbers, and I am grateful that Catherine's detailed directions have made their house so easy to find. Since there is no place to park on the street, I pull into the driveway and make my way to the back door.

It is Peter, a tall, broad-shouldered man with graying hair and a shy manner, who answers my knock at the door. As he invites me into the kitchen, I am greeted by the aroma of a blueberry pie that Catherine, who is in the first week of a three-week vacation, is just taking out of the oven. After introductions have been completed, Peter and I go off to the living room for his interview while Catherine finishes up in the kitchen. When we are finished, I join her there and happily accept a slice of the fresh-baked pie.

Peter and Catherine are about fifty years old, have been married for 23 years, and have two daughters, one in high school and one in college. Except for a brief stint as an elementary school principal, Peter has been working as a teacher since he graduated from college 28 years ago. Catherine stayed home for about two years after the birth of each child, the first time as a full-time housewife and the second time providing day care for other people's children in her home, but she, too, has been working at her chosen profession for most of her adult life.

Peter and Catherine are in professions of similar status, work similar hours, and have almost equal yearly incomes, so it is not surprising that they describe breadwinning as a shared responsibility. Both report that they share providing equally, that their jobs are equally important in their family ("I don't see a bit of difference," Peter says), that they both work primarily to earn money for basic family needs, and that their incomes are pooled to meet those basic expenses. Peter also reports that they feel about equal obligations to provide, although Catherine suspects that he may feel a somewhat greater obligation than she does.

But such shared responsibility is not necessarily their ideal. Peter entered their marriage with a firm belief that breadwinning should be a male responsibility. "When I started out," he explains, "my wife wasn't going to work. Period. There's no way in the world. But life has changed. . . . She got terribly bored when she stayed home with the kids, and she needs her independence." As inflation outstripped raises in the mid-1970s, the extra income was nice, too. So, Peter accepted his wife as a co-provider—but reluctantly. Today, he still ranks his role as financial provider for the family as the most important role he plays, while he ranks Catherine's provider role sixth out of seven, more important only than houseworker. His current ideal is not the equal sharing that is his reality, but a situation in which he would be primary provider and his wife would supplement his efforts.

For despite having rethought his earlier beliefs about breadwinning, Peter is still very much committed to the importance of gender boundaries. He particularly emphasizes mothering as a gender boundary. Peter downplays his wife's provider role, but he ranks her role of mother as her most important one, while ranking his own father role only third in importance. When he is asked to react to the statement that "a woman who works full time can establish just as warm and secure a relationship with her children as a mother who does not work," he struggles with the tension between his emphasis on the importance of female mothering and his own wife's employment. "See," he says, "if it's young children, I almost feel that the mother should be home for a while, and if it were older children, I don't think it affects them anywhere near as much." He asks me to read him the statement again, decides that he "strongly agrees" with it, and then immediately qualifies his agreement by saying, "I'd disagree if they were young children." From Peter's point of view, it's fine for a mother to work only as long as her children don't need her at home. Thus, he has no difficulty at all with the hypothetical situation that most respondents found so troubling. He listens to the scenario and then, without a moment's hesitation, declares, "She should stay home with the child."

How does Catherine feel about all this? She, too, thinks that it is the mother in the hypothetical situation who should stay home to care for the sick child, but she does not share her husband's more general attachment to conventional gender boundaries. Whereas he strongly agrees that "there is some work that is men's and some that is women's and they shouldn't be doing each other's," she strongly disagrees, noting, "I think, nowadays, they do each other's." When she is asked whether "a woman who works full time can establish just as warm and secure a relationship with her children as a mother who does not work," she responds instantly, "I agree with that—strongly agree." Although Catherine may think that a sick child needs special care that only a mother can provide, she believes that day-to-day parenting should be a shared responsibility. She strongly agrees that the husband of a working wife should share fully in housework and child care, and she ranks her husband's role as father at the top of the list, equal in importance to her own role as mother.

Catherine does not put as much emphasis on shared breadwinning as she does on shared parenting. When she is asked who should be financial provider for her family, she responds by shrugging and saying, "Oh, probably the male, you know." "Him only?" I ask. "No," she replies, "just maybe him more than me." I am left with the impression that

Catherine is not so much expressing her own beliefs here as deferring to her husband's, perhaps because she realizes that the idea of role sharing is difficult for him.

Peter and Catherine have met one another halfway in their constructions of the breadwinning boundary, agreeing to maintain it as an ideal even as they relinquish it in practice. Why, then, does Peter contest his wife's construction of mothering, putting a strong emphasis on mothering as a gender boundary despite Catherine's very different ideals? Like many reluctant co-providers, Peter is in a bind. His ideological attachment to a gendered division of labor in the family has been challenged by his own experience. His early vision of marriage was that he would devote his time and energy to breadwinning, and Catherine would devote hers to making a home and raising a family. But being at home full time left Catherine miserable, bored, and depressed; it was only when she returned to nursing that she became once again the vivacious, fun-loving person that he had fallen in love with. Seeing what a difference practicing her profession has made to Catherine's happiness has led Peter to rethink his attitudes about married women's work—but not his commitment to gender difference. So, he maintains a modified version of the breadwinning boundary, and he compensates for his own breaching of even this modified boundary by shoring up the mothering boundary, emphasizing women's special abilities and responsibilities in this sphere.

Meanwhile, Catherine is involved in her own form of compensation. She does not share Peter's deep attachment to the principle of gender difference and, indeed, feels that children are generally better off with two active parents rather than just one. But she knows how difficult all this has been for Peter, she appreciates his efforts to change, and, using a pattern that I will explore more fully below, she compensates by deferring to him on norms about breadwinning.

Compensating for Violated Norms and Contested Boundaries: Nancy and Mike—Reluctant Traditional and Traditional Breadwinner

The male reluctant co-providers are not the only ones who use their constructions of the mothering boundary to compensate for violating their own norms about breadwinning. This pattern is also evident in the responses of the female reluctant traditionals. But, since the norms that the reluctant traditionals are violating are norms of shared breadwinning, they compensate for their violation by de-emphasizing the mothering boundary, not by shoring it up. How do the husbands of these reluctant traditionals deal with this tension in the construction of gender? Sometimes they agree with their wives' constructions of both breadwinning and mothering. More often, however, they disagree with their wives about breadwinning but compensate by concurring in the relaxation of the mothering boundary. Nancy and Mike fit this latter pattern.

I have driven out to meet Nancy and Mike after dinner on the same Tuesday in August that I interviewed Peter and Catherine. If the day is the same, however, the scene is very different. Nancy and Mike live not in an older house on the edge of a busy highway, but in a newly constructed colonial tucked away in the woods. Indeed, their house is still under construction. Nancy and Mike have kept the cost of their new home within their means by doing much of the finish work themselves, and although they have already moved in, they are still installing baseboard and painting trim in their spare time. As Nancy opens the front door and invites me in, I can hear the sound of hammering elsewhere in the house.

Nancy and Mike are in their late thirties, have been married for eighteen years, and have one child, a delightful and curious three-year-old. Their son wanders in and out of the room where I am interviewing his parents, carrying his own plastic toolbox of construction tools, stopping here and there to "work on the house," and occasionally offering commentary on the interview proceedings. He has recently mastered his colors and becomes so excited by the color-coded cards that I hand to respondents at various points during the interview that I give him a spare set so he can play "interview" himself—a gift that gives him great pleasure.

Nancy, whom I interview first, is a part-time secretary at the local junior high school. She has done various kinds of clerical work throughout her adult life, working full time until her son was born. At that point, she left the labor force to stay home with the baby, but she went back to part-time work shortly after his first birthday. She currently works twenty hours per week during the school year, has summers off, and earns $4,500 per year. Nancy is not particularly excited by her job, but she likes the part-time hours and feels that the summers off will be important when her son begins school in a few years.

Unlike Nancy, Mike, a detective with the city police department, enjoys his work and talks about it with animation. He likes the camaraderie of the police force and finds the nitty-gritty of crime investigations intellectually challenging. With almost nineteen years of seniority, he is also satisfied with his pay and now earns an annual income of $22,000.

Given the gaps in their earnings, hours of work, and commitment to their jobs, it seems likely that Nancy and Mike will name Mike as the family breadwinner, and indeed they do. They both report that Mike is the financial provider for the family, that his job is the important one in the life of the family, that earning money for basic family needs is the most important motivation for his employment and the least important for Nancy's, and that it is his income that is critical for meeting those basic expenses. Mike explains that, although some of Nancy's income is deposited in the various bank accounts from which they pay their weekly, monthly, and occasional bills, most of the money in those accounts comes from his paychecks. Nancy says simply, "I take care of child care, and, basically, he takes care of the rest."

While Nancy and Mike agree that he is the breadwinner, however, they disagree about the desirability of this state of affairs. For Mike, breadwinning is part of what defines him as a man. Although he is happy to have his wife earning and contributing something to the family pot, his ideal is that he should be the primary provider. He ranks his financial provider role as his most important and says that it is he who feels the obligation to provide for the family. Moreover, this emphasis on breadwinning as a manly responsibility is part of a larger set of attitudes that endorse gender boundaries. Mike gives conventionally gendered responses to most of the gender attitude items, agreeing that "there is some work that is men's and some that is women's and they shouldn't be doing each other's" and that "women should take care of running their homes and leave running the country up to men," and disagreeing that "a woman who works full time can establish just as warm and secure a relationship with her children as a mother who does not work."

Nancy is much less concerned with constructing boundaries that define gender difference, and she gives feminist responses to four of the six gender attitude items. (Indeed, she snorts with laughter at the idea that women should leave running the country up to men—a statement with which her husband agrees.) Her norms about breadwinning also deemphasize gender boundaries. She says that breadwinning should, ideally, have nothing to do with gender, that it shouldn't matter whether the financial provider is the husband or the wife, and that she feels as much of an obligation to provide as Mike does. As far as she is concerned, that Mike is the breadwinner right now does not reflect her womanly prerogative to be supported or his manly responsibility to provide, but the exigencies of their situation—their child's need for parental care, the fact that Mike finds his work more fulfilling than she finds hers, and the reality that she has never been able to earn anywhere near as much money as he does.

Nancy's responses to questions about mothering make it even clearer that the conventionally gendered life she is leading is not an endorsement of conventional gender boundaries. Although she wants to be at home with her son part time and ranks mother as the most important role she is playing at this point in her life, she does not focus on mothering as a distinctive responsibility of women. On the contrary, in apparent compensation for her own violation of her nongendered norms about breadwinning, she puts a particularly strong emphasis on shared responsibility for parenting. Just as she ranks her role as mother as her most important, she ranks Mike's role as father as his most important. When presented with the hypothetical situation of the dual-earner couple with the sick child, she once again de-emphasizes gender. Although she thinks one of the parents should take primary responsibility for the child's care, which one would depend on criteria other than gender. I am left with the impression that when Nancy "somewhat disagrees" that a mother's working full time won't interfere with her relationship with her children, she is thinking about parents and that she would give the same answer if the question asked about working fathers.

How does Mike respond to Nancy's construction of mothering? This is not a critical issue for him. Breadwinning is central to his sense of himself as a man, but the mothering boundary does not have the same resonance. So, he takes advantage of this opportunity to compensate for the contention about breadwinning in his marriage. Like Nancy, he gives a high ranking to his role as father (second only to financial provider) and considers it just as important as her mother role. Like Nancy, he agrees that husbands of working mothers should share equally in housework and child care. And, like his wife, he gives a nongendered response to the hypothetical situation, saying, "I think it should be a parent . . . [but] I guess it would depend on what their careers are . . . not so much the income as the career." In other words, he defers to Nancy's construction of mothering.

Once again, then, we see that the relationship of the breadwinning and mothering boundaries is both complementary and compensatory. Nancy's norms about the two are complementary, but in her construction of the mothering boundary, she compensates for her violation of her own breadwinning norms by emphasizing shared responsibility for parenting. Mike's constructions of these two boundaries are in tension, but he is not shoring up the breadwinning boundary to offset a breaching of the mothering boundary. Rather, Mike's nongendered construction of mothering is a gift to Nancy, a way to compensate for his disagreement with her about breadwinning.

Contesting Gendered Parenting: Andrea and Bernard — Using Breadwinning as Compensation

Nancy and Mike's constructions of breadwinning and mothering are not unusual. When the breadwinning boundary is contested, the partner who advocates its relaxation typically receives some form of compensation from the resistant spouse. In many cases, that spouse compensates by agreeing to relax the mothering boundary. When it is the mothering boundary that is contested, however, it seems that the partner who wants to maintain it is in the more compelling position. The other spouse is likely to compensate by deferring to the partner's wish to use breadwinning as a gender boundary. Andrea and Bernard provide an example.

I have driven out to Andrea and Bernard's house, in a small subdivision on the outskirts of the city, one weekday evening in mid-December. The drive has been a pleasant one; it is one of those crisp, clear nights when the sky seems wondrously full of stars and the feel of winter is in the air. It is the Christmas season in Maine, and although there has not been a significant snowfall yet and the ground is bare, the ski areas have been making artificial snow every night, and the television meteorologists have begun to introduce the possibility of snowstorms with the words, "There is good news in the weather forecast tonight." Andrea and Bernard's house, like many, is dressed up for the holidays, and both the roofline and a spruce tree in the front yard are strung with brightly colored lights.

Bernard, a city fire fighter, and Andrea, who works as a part-time secretary at the local college, are 38 and 30, respectively, and have just celebrated their tenth anniversary. Their household includes their four-year-old son and nine-year-old daughter, Bernard's sixteen-year-old daughter from an earlier marriage, and assorted pets. As Andrea opens the front door and invites me into the foyer of their raised ranch-style house, I catch a glimpse of the sixteen-year-old in a classic teen pose—slumped against a wall with the telephone cradled against her neck. The four-year-old, whose naturally high energy level has been cranked up still more by the excitement of the holiday season, is running back and forth in pursuit of the family cat.

Andrea takes my coat and shows me into the living room, where I meet Bernard, and we agree that he will be interviewed first. Before we begin, however, the four-year-old questions me closely about who I am, what I am doing at his house, what all the stuff is that I'm carrying, and so on. As I interview his father, he comes in frequently to check up on us. His presence is sufficiently obtrusive that when Andrea pokes her head in to say that she is going out to pick the nine-year-old up from her weekly dancing class, Bernard suggests jokingly, "Why don't you bring Brian with you for a ride? I think he wants to get out and get some air."

Bernard's interview, which proceeds more smoothly once his son has left, reveals that he is committed to conventional gender boundaries. He gives conventionally gendered responses to several of the attitude items, agreeing, for example, that "there is some work that is men's and some that is women's and they shouldn't be doing each other's." Indeed, as far as Bernard is concerned, breadwinning is one of the ways that men's work differs from women's. He names himself as the financial provider for his family and says his job is regarded as the more important one. He acknowledges that, for the time being, Andrea, too, works primarily to earn money for basic family needs, and he says that she feels just as much of an obligation to provide as he does, but he also makes it clear that this is not the way he wants it to be. Bernard's ideal is that he should be sole provider for the family. He ranks his financial provider role as the single most important one he plays, and when asked if he can imagine any circumstances under which his wife would leave the labor force and he would become the sole provider, he replies, "Yup, if I made enough money to do it on my own. . . . I'd like to have her do that now."

From Bernard's point of view, men's responsibility for breadwinning is only part of the story. Its complement is women's responsibility for making a home, and particularly for mothering. He ranks Andrea's role as mother as one of the most important ones she fills, second only to that of wife, but he gives his own father role a lower ranking. As far as he is concerned, being a good father revolves primarily around financial providing, but being a good mother requires being at home with the children. This becomes particularly clear when he is presented with the hypothetical situation of the couple with the sick child. His response is firm: "I know what I would do. My wife would stop working; I'd continue working. I feel that it's more the responsibility of the husband as the breadwinner than it is the wife—and, plus, I think that she'd be able to better care for [the child]."

Does Andrea share her husband's construction of mothering as a gender boundary? Hardly. While he disagrees that "a woman who works full time can establish just as warm and secure a relationship with her children as a mother who does not work," she agrees, and she also agrees that the husband of such a mother should share fully in housework and child care. She wants her husband to be just as actively involved with the children as she is. She ranks both their parenting roles equally high in importance, and her response to the hypothetical situation is quite different from her husband's: "All I can think of is they'd have to take turns. . . . It'd be one who stayed home for six months, and the other one stay home for another six months, and—I don't know, it depends on how much time they have coming. I think it should be a shared responsibility."

Andrea doesn't just wish Bernard would play an active role in parenting; her behavior during the interviews suggests that she pushes him to do so. She doesn't interfere with Brian's disruptive presence at his father's interview until she is specifically asked to do so (the half-joking request that she take Brian out with her). Moreover, by volunteering to be interviewed after her husband, she has arranged it so that Bernard will be the parent available to take charge of Brian's bedtime. As Andrea and I sit down to begin her interview, Bernard leads his son off for his evening bath. Part of the backdrop for my interview with Andrea is the chatter of Brian's voice, as he tells his father some complicated story about the events of his day. Later, it is Bernard's deeper voice, as he reads Brian a bedtime story.

Andrea is not willing to give in on the importance of shared parenting, but she compensates for contesting Bernard's construction of mothering by yielding to his views on a boundary she cares far less about, breadwinning. Although she brings in almost one-third of the total family income, she downplays the importance of her contribution. Like Bernard, she names him as the financial provider for the family and says that his job is more important than hers. She also says that he feels more of an obligation to provide than she does, and she de-emphasizes economic reasons for her own employment, choosing instead to highlight the contact with other people and the feelings of accomplishment and independence that work provides.

Although Andrea defers to her husband's construction of breadwinning, she does not support it wholeheartedly. For example, she does not go so far as to adopt Bernard's norms that he should be sole provider; her work is important to her and she can't imagine any circumstances under which she would leave the labor force. She also attaches less importance to his financial provider role than he does, ranking it only fourth on the list of seven roles. Moreover, she shows that she is aware of breadwinning as a potential area of disagreement when I ask what she would do if she won a \$3 million lottery jackpot. "He would want me to quit my job," she sighs. "I don't know. I don't know if I would quit. . . . I'd be home all the time with the kids and I wouldn't be out and seeing other people. I don't know. . . . I spend a lot of time home when I'm not working, and I can't imagine being here all the time." As long as they need her income, however, this is a moot issue. She can continue to have a paid job, she can push Bernard to take an active role in parenting, and, by endorsing the ideal of the man as primary financial provider, she can compensate for that pushing by deferring to her husband's construction of breadwinning as a gender boundary.

The Relationship of Breadwinning and Mothering

We have seen that when couples disagree about the construction of the breadwinning or mothering boundary, one partner usually compensates for that disagreement by deferring to the spouse's construction of the other boundary. Which partner in a marriage is more likely to yield, at least partially, to a spouse's construction of gender? Various possibilities present themselves. Wives might be more likely to yield because they have less power in the relationship, or husbands might be more likely to do so because they consider the family their wives' sphere of expertise. The spouse who invokes the gender boundary may be in the more powerful position because the weight of tradition is on his or her side, or the spouse who wants to relinquish the boundary may be more likely to prevail because this is the direction of social change.

The analysis presented here indicates that this kind of compensation does not depend on gender, on convention, or on trends, but on which boundary is at the heart of the couple's contested construction of gender. If the breadwinning boundary is the source of contention, then, as in the case of Mike and Nancy, the balance of power is likely to be with the partner who advocates relaxing that boundary. The resisting spouse is likely to compensate by yielding to a nongendered construction of parenting. If, on the other hand, disagreement centers on the mothering boundary, the spouse who wants to maintain that boundary is in a stronger position. As in the cases of Peter and Catherine and Andrea and Bernard, marital partners who insist on trying to relax the mothering boundary in the face of opposition usually compensate for their contentiousness by deferring to their spouses' deployment of the breadwinning boundary.

Why is it that the relaxation of gender boundaries seems more compelling in one situation, while the maintenance of those boundaries holds sway in the other? Perhaps it is behavior that tips the scales. Given that all the women in these dual-earner families are in the paid labor force and that most are contributing income to the family coffers, a partner who wishes to relax the use of breadwinning as a gender boundary may be able to point to this behavior as support for that position. On the other hand, research has repeatedly shown that women who are employed retain most of the responsibility for housework and child care. A spouse who wishes to eliminate the use of mothering as a gender boundary, then, has less behavioral corroboration for such a position.

It is important to note that these compensatory constructions of gender boundaries seem to be largely symbolic. We saw this in the case of Rod in Chapter 4. In a gesture that runs counter to the usual pattern, Rod compensated for resisting his wife's push for shared parenting by adopting her egalitarian norms about breadwinning. But Rod's gesture of conciliation is just that, a gesture. Given that he outearns his wife more than ten to one, there is little chance that he will actually be called on to share breadwinning. A similar pattern emerges in the case studies in this chapter. Andrea can magnanimously grant Bernard breadwinner status because she knows that the family needs her income. Similarly, Catherine yields to her husband's ideals of male breadwinning because she knows that he won't actually ask her to quit her job. And Mike can afford to adopt Nancy's norms of nongendered parenting because, as long as she is working part time at a job that gives her little satisfaction and is thus heavily invested in parenting, he won't be expected to fully enact his expressed norms of shared child care.

The analysis in this chapter suggests that the intricate connections of mothering and breadwinning multiply the dynamism of the gender system, as challenges to and negotiations about one boundary are played out in reconstructions of the other. I must emphasize again, however, that this examination of breadwinning and mothering has been an exploratory one. Confirming, contesting, or developing its insights would require better measures of mothering as a gender boundary. In addition, it would require an enhanced understanding of the larger gender system in which such relationships are embedded. In Chapter 8, I turn to this larger context.

8

Breadwinning and the Web of Gender

This book has used the gender construction model and the conceptualization of the gender system as a web of gender boundaries to focus on one particular boundary in that web, breadwinning. Analyzing breadwinning as a gender boundary has illuminated the distinction between breadwinning and paid employment. My research has confirmed that the two are distinct, replicating the finding that employed wives are not necessarily regarded as family breadwinners (Haas, 1986; Hood, 1983; Perry-Jenkins and Crouter, 1990). Indeed, only 15 percent of wives and 26 percent of husbands in this study reported both that they fully shared responsibility for breadwinning and that they considered such sharing appropriate. Moreover, in only twelve of these dual-earner couples (8 percent of the sample) were husband and wife in agreement that breadwinning was and should be a shared responsibility in their marriage. In most of the remaining cases, a husband's status as breadwinner was modified in varied, complex, and dynamic ways by his wife's employment, but it was not eliminated. In this age of dual-earner marriages, paid employment no longer serves as a readily available gender boundary, as it has in the past. But breadwinning is still widespread as an interpretive boundary, one involving the meaning attached to the behavior of paid employment rather than the behavior itself.

Why has the use of breadwinning as a gender boundary persisted even as labor force participation has ceased to serve as a meaningful divider between men and women? The interviews analyzed here have suggested that one important reason is the institutionalization of the breadwinning boundary in the structure of paid work. One form that this institutionalization takes is absorptive occupations that require enormous commitments of time and energy and that cannot be combined easily with domestic responsibilities; such occupations exert pressure on dual-earner families to have one partner who gives higher priority to employment responsibilities (a primary breadwinner) and one who gives higher priority to domestic responsibilities. But why is it disproportionately husbands who embrace the commitment to paid work that breadwinning seems to require? The answer can be found, at least in part, in two other forms of institutionalization of male breadwinning, occupational segregation (which often defines those jobs that can more easily be combined with domestic responsibilities as women's jobs) and the gender wage gap (which leaves the vast majority of dual-earner wives earning less than their husbands).

If this research has shown that the breadwinning boundary is widespread and institutionalized, however, it has also demonstrated that it is fairly relaxed and highly permeable. It can be maintained at the same time that many exceptions to it are made, and it allows a great deal of room for individual interpretation. Thus, both Charlene (Chapter 3) and Roseanne (Chapter 5) were able to maintain breadwinning as a gender boundary despite their own considerable financial contributions. They did so by downplaying the importance of those contributions and by insisting that it was their husbands' incomes that were used to cover "major" expenses and "really" support the family. Brad (Chapter 4) and Bernard (Chapter 7) both maintained the breadwinning boundary by defining their wives' financial contributions as necessary (and, ideally, temporary) exceptions that did not negate the rule of male responsibility for breadwinning.

One reflection of the flexibility and permeability of the breadwinning boundary is the relative absence of sanctions for breaching it. In the past, male responsibility for breadwinning was enforced indirectly, via negative sanctions attached to married women's presence in the paid labor force. An employer might refuse to hire women workers for certain jobs or lay them off first when work was short. Women might be required to leave the job when they married (airline stewardesses) or when they became pregnant (teachers). Neighbors and relatives might let a mother with a job outside the home know that they thought she was being selfish and neglecting her children. In recent decades, antidiscrimination laws have made many of these barriers to wives' labor force participation illegal, and a large portion of the population now embraces married women's right to paid employment as a principle of gender equity. As prohibitions against married women's employment have waned, they have not been replaced with similar negative sanctions for interpreting that employment as breadwinning. This is, in part, because interpretive boundaries (such as breadwinning) are more difficult to police than behavioral boundaries (such as employment). It is also, however, because the same economic conditions that have drawn married women into the labor force have made it possible for them to define breadwinning as something they do in their capacity as mothers, to ensure a better life for their children.

Men seem to be somewhat more subject to negative sanctions for breaching the breadwinning boundary, reflecting the asymmetrical permeability of this boundary noted in Chapter 4. Even for men, however, there seems to be considerable leeway. A man has to abdicate virtually all responsibility for breadwinning before he triggers formal or informal sanctions. Indeed, a negative response may only be prompted when a man's rejection of breadwinning responsibility is manifest in his behavior. A man may be subject to legal sanctions for refusing to contribute any financial resources to the support of his family (as in the recent campaign against "deadbeat dads"), but not for defining his wife as his co-breadwinner. Men who visibly assign primary (rather than shared) responsibility for breadwinning to their wives (for example, by working considerably fewer hours than their wives) are likely to reap social disapproval. For example, you may have felt angry or uncomfortable as you read about Denis, the handyman in Chapter 6 who dropped back to part-time work and left primary responsibility for breadwinning to his wife, and you may have sympathized with her objections to this arrangement. Another man in the study who had, for a time, held only a part-time job also experienced negative sanctions from his wife. Their seriousness became apparent when I asked this man why he was employed: "To save my marriage," he replied.

This study has also suggested that breadwinning is a dynamic strand in the web of gender. Like all gender boundaries, breadwinning is actively constructed and negotiated through the social interactions of daily life. In a time of gender change, particularly in the workplace and the family, it is perhaps not surprising that this gender boundary is a particularly active site of negotiation. Both the quantitative statistical analyses and the qualitative case studies in this book have provided evidence of couples' active construction and negotiation of the meanings attached to their employment. These are evident not only in the wide array of constructions of breadwinning present in this sample, but also in the way that those constructions are developed in the context of material conditions, current circumstances, and adult experiences. The results of the follow-up study demonstrate that the construction of gender is an ongoing process and that renegotiation and reconstruction of the breadwinning boundary is commonplace in the lives of these dual-earner couples.

The multidimensional nature of breadwinning is an important reason that couples' constructions of it are complex and dynamic. Epstein (1992) has distinguished between "real" and "conceptual" dimensions of gender boundaries and argued that "even when the real boundaries . . . change, the conceptual boundaries remain, as when women take jobs not considered traditional for their sex and the jobs remain labeled as men's" (Epstein, 1992: 234). The analyses presented in Chapters 3 and 4 have provided evidence of just such distinct dimensions. They have also provided some support for Epstein's (1992) observation that these dimensions do not necessarily change in tandem, that individuals may act to protect their own social-psychological investment in gender difference by maintaining the conceptual boundaries in the face of behavior to the contrary. This seems to be what male reluctant co-providers are doing when they cling particularly strongly to the ideal of male breadwinning, even as they acknowledge their wives' sharing of this responsibility in daily life. It is the relative independence of the dimensions of breadwinning and the complex ways that people combine them that create so many richly varied permutations in the construction of the breadwinning boundary.

Another contributor to the dynamism of the breadwinning boundary is the fact that it is highly contested. Fewer than one-third of the couples in this sample (31 percent) were in complete agreement about this boundary at the time of their original interviews, and almost half (46 percent) were in substantial disagreement. The analysis in Chapter 6 has provided evidence that such disagreement is a catalyst for continued negotiation and reconstruction. Moreover, this book has also shown that, even when couples agree about breadwinning, that agreement may be challenged by the changing circumstances of their lives.

If this research has shed considerable light on the universality, permeability, institutionalization, sanctions, contestation, and dynamism of breadwinning as a gender boundary, it has revealed less about the salience of that boundary, about the conditions under which it looms particularly large in the construction of gender difference. I assume that breadwinning is more salient a gender difference in some times and places than in others, but this research does not address these differences. It does, however, provide some clues about the conditions under which the breadwinning boundary becomes more or less salient for individuals and couples in the late-twentieth-century United States. This analysis has shown, for example, that the use of breadwinning as a gender boundary is consistently related to husbands' and wives' incomes. This suggests that the material conditions of people's lives, by constraining the ways that they can construct gender difference, influence the salience of particular gender boundaries. Similarly, the analysis has consistently revealed that family circumstances affect the importance of breadwinning as a gender boundary. Both the regression analyses in Chapters 3 and 4 and the high proportion of childless couples among the co-breadwinners (43.5 percent) and the role sharers (25 percent) suggest that breadwinning is more salient as a gender boundary when children, particularly young children, are present in the family. Finally, the finding that men in blue-collar jobs are more likely to emphasize breadwinning as a gender boundary, at least ideologically, than are those in white-collar jobs suggests that some gender boundaries may become more salient when other related boundaries are unavailable. Men whose occupations do not provide the means for defining their masculinity through social success and superiority (high pay and prestige) may instead emphasize breadwinning to highlight their difference from women.

These clues about the salience of breadwinning as a gender boundary point once again to the image of the web and provide a reminder that breadwinning does not stand alone, but is interrelated with other gender boundaries. Chapter 7 explored one of those relationships, that of the breadwinning and mothering boundaries, in some detail, and this exploration, too, helped to explain the persistence of the breadwinning boundary. The analysis revealed that the relationship between the breadwinning and mothering boundaries tends to be complementary; where one of these boundaries is salient, then, the other is also likely to be. Although the measures used indicated considerable relinquishing of mothering as a gender boundary, they were relatively crude indicators and almost surely underestimated the extent to which the mothering boundary is deployed. It seems likely that constructions of mothering have dimensions and complexities not tapped in this exploration, and that these influence constructions of the breadwinning boundary. Indeed, the case studies suggest that some of the effects of situational factors on the negotiation and construction of breadwinning are probably indirect effects, mediated through their impact on mothering.

The relationship of the breadwinning and mothering boundaries also helps to explain the dynamism of the breadwinning boundary. The interrelations of these boundaries introduce dynamism into the system because conflicts about one are often played out in constructions of the other. The analysis in Chapter 7 revealed, for example, that when the normative and interpretive dimensions of breadwinning were in tension, constructions of mothering were often adjusted to compensate for violated norms about breadwinning. Similarly, contention over the mothering boundary may influence how and when the breadwinning boundary is deployed.

Clearly, understanding breadwinning as a gendered phenomenon will require a fuller examination of its place in the web of gender. Mothering is only one of many gender boundaries whose relationships with the breadwinning boundary should be examined. Hochschild's (1989) work on the "second shift" suggests a relationship between the breadwinning boundary and gendered responsibility for housework. For example, the husband in one of Hochschild's case studies argued that, since his wife's responsibility for breadwinning already constituted one blow to his masculinity, he could not afford to breach yet another gender boundary by sharing responsibility for housework. It is also likely that the use of breadwinning as a gender boundary is related to the deployment of gender boundaries outside the home, in the workplace and in other institutional spheres. These connections deserve further exploration.

The Social Construction of Gender in Families

Scholars (e.g., Berk, 1985; Hochschild, 1989) have repeatedly noted that the family is a critical site for the construction of gender. The analysis presented in this book has not only confirmed that gender is actively constructed in the interactions of daily life, but has also shown that this is an ongoing process. The case studies, in particular, have provided a nuanced picture of how couples negotiate constructions of gender over time, and have clarified why one of the best predictors of agreement between husbands and wives in this study was length of marriage. If the construction of gender in families is an ongoing process, it makes sense that Brad and Michelle (Chapter 4), married only a year, gave totally different accounts of what it was that they had talked through and agreed upon and that many of the couples who disagreed about breadwinning when they were originally interviewed had moved toward agreement by the time of the follow-up study five years later.

This analysis has also demonstrated just how dynamic the process of gender construction is. It is not simply a matter of developing a shared construction of gender and then maintaining it; gendered practices and meanings are continually negotiated, constructed, challenged, renegotiated, and reconstructed. Chapters 3 and 4 demonstrated that such constructions are shaped primarily by adult experiences and circumstances (not by childhood socialization and deeply internalized gender attitudes), and Chapters 5 and 6 showed that these circumstances are themselves continually changing.

Gender is also dynamic because it is contested terrain, and this study has confirmed that the social construction of gender in families is fraught with challenge and conflict. It would be a mistake, however, to assume that this conflict necessarily takes the form of a "battle of the sexes" in which men and women are divided into hostile camps. The picture of gender contention provided by this study is much more subtle and complex. Here, men and women challenge and contest one another's particular constructions of gender but also cooperate in constructing the web of gender. Rather than emphasizing contention, they work to resolve disagreement or to mute its effects. Chapter 6 revealed just how often disagreement about the construction of breadwinning led husband, wife, or both to reconsider that construction. And Chapter 7 showed that, even when individuals were not willing to take the steps necessary to resolve disagreement about one gender boundary, they often compensated for that disagreement by cooperating in the construction (or relaxation) of a different boundary.

It would be unwise to overstate the importance of these cooperative and compensatory dynamics as steps on the road to gender equality, however. This analysis has suggested that many of these efforts at cooperation and compensation are more symbolic than real. In this way, they are much like the "family myths" identified by Arlie Hochschild in *The Second Shift* (1989)—egalitarian glosses rather than substantive moves toward equality. Over and over again in this study, husbands, in particular, moved to ease conflict by adopting gender ideologies designed to please their wives. This might represent real change if gender attitudes provided the basis for behaviors, but this study has not supported the widespread assumption that changed attitudes are precursors of changed behaviors. On the contrary, the plasticity of expressed gender ideology was one of the most striking findings of this research. These ideological shifts often seemed to be symbolic substitutes, rather than scaffolding, for behavioral changes.

Moreover, ideological shifts are not always moves toward compromise and compensation. Faced with contention in the construction of gender, not everyone acts to reduce tensions and increase harmony. Instead, some reconstructions of gender seem designed to protect individuals' interests and resist change. In some cases, when one partner tries to blur a gender boundary more than the other partner is comfortable with, the latter moves in the direction of retrenchment, trying to shore up that boundary (or a related one) and bring the spouse back into line. For example, one uncommitted provider in this sample who was quite open to the *idea* of shared breadwinning, and indeed claimed it as his ideal so long as his wife's earnings were so low as to make it a moot point, changed his mind when she was promoted from a clerical position into management and his position as the family breadwinner was threatened. Although he acknowledged that she was now sharing the responsibility for providing, he no longer claimed this as his ideal; he moved instead to the position of reluctant co-provider, defining his wife's breadwinning as a problem. Similarly, a wife who was content in the role of co-breadwinner—as long as her husband was earning a little more than she was—had second thoughts when he decided to drop back to part-time work. She concluded that he ought to be primary provider and redefined herself as a reluctant provider.

What motivates such resistance to change? Negotiation of gendered behaviors and meanings in families takes place within an existing system of gender inequality, and this context shapes the ways that men and women contest and construct gender boundaries. Both women and men adopt gender strategies that protect their prerogatives within the existing system even as they challenge that system, respond to challenges, or work together to negotiate a shared construction of gender. Thus, men may move to deflect conflict by making a peace offering of more egalitarian attitudes while they maintain nonegalitarian behaviors.

Women, too, may move to protect their privileges within the existing system even though those privileges come at the cost of constraints and inequality. For the gender system does not simply constrain and devalue women; it also defines the ways that women, qua women, are valued and special, and it gives them some prerogatives (such as the right to financial support from a husband and the right to put domestic responsibilities before financial ones). In negotiating the construction of gender, women, like men, make strategic moves. But because women's subordinate position in the gender system typically leaves them with less room to maneuver than men have, their strategies may reinforce the existing system of inequality. Thus, a woman may insist on her right to stay home for a time with her children, even though her assertion of this feminine prerogative reinforces the definition of men as primary breadwinners and men's (but not women's) right to a family wage, and thereby shores up the very gender boundaries that produce her economic disadvantage.

For some, participation in this study was itself a strategic move in the ongoing process of gender construction. I originally assumed that I controlled the research agenda and that participants were doing me a favor by participating. Thus, I was at first confused when respondents frequently thanked me for including them in the study. Eventually, however, I came to understand that mine was not the only view of the research process. It was common for one partner in a couple (most often the wife) to indicate that she had been much more eager to participate in the research than her spouse, and that he had acquiesced as a favor to her. Clearly, the enthusiastic spouses were hoping to gain something from their participation. What benefits were they pursuing? Some, I think, were looking for ways to increase the flow of verbal communication in their marriages. Others were hoping that the interviews would provide an opening for renegotiation of specific issues—the household division of labor, breadwinning, or the construction of gender more generally. For some spouses who were reluctant to participate, acquiescing may have served as another of those symbolic peace offerings that help to maintain a spirit of cooperation in the midst of conflict. In some cases where gender issues were sharply contested in the marriage (and I am thinking here particularly about the cases of Rod and Anita in Chapter 4 and Patricia and Denis in Chapter 6), one spouse may have hoped that the research or the researcher would add weight to his or her side of the dispute. Participants did not necessarily gain what they hoped for from their research experience. Neither, however, were those hopes naive; the follow-up study suggests that participation did sometimes act as a catalyst for change in couples' constructions of gender.

Implications for a Theory of Gender Construction

The most important contribution of this research to the development of gender construction theory has been the elaboration and explication of the concept of gender boundaries. The conceptualization of gender as a web of boundaries provides a way to link a number of seemingly divergent approaches to theorizing gender. The gender boundaries concept illuminates many of the phenomena (behaviors, attitudes, etc.) that have been analyzed under the rubric of gender roles, but it provides a very different reading of these phenomena by emphasizing dynamism rather than stability, contradictions rather than consistency, and adult circumstances and experiences rather than childhood socialization. Similarly, in its focus on the continual and active construction, contestation, and reconstruction of gender by human beings in interaction, the gender boundaries conceptualization is similar to West and Zimmerman's (1987) "doing gender," but it goes beyond their ethnomethodological account by providing conceptual tools to separate out and analyze specific elements of the process. At the same time, analyzing such variable properties of gender boundaries as institutionalization and severity of sanctions provides the means for linking microsociological processes to the macrosociological structures highlighted by more structural and institutional conceptualizations of gender (Lorber, 1994).

Even as it makes connections to other important conceptualizations of gender, the gender boundaries concept combines specificity and complexity in a way that helps to avoid many of the recurrent problems of gender theory. For example, a theory of gender construction based on the concept of gender boundaries would not be a totalizing theory that treats all women or all men as alike. On the contrary, this conceptualization assumes that both the amount and the content of gender differentiation are historically, culturally, subculturally, and situationally specific, and it provides tools for examining variations across time and space. Similarly, the thorny issue of the biological foundations of gender and the relationship between sex and gender (Nicholson, 1994) is left open; the extent to which biological characteristics are used as boundaries to differentiate women and men is treated as an empirical question—and one to which a variable response is expected.

The gender boundaries conceptualization also deals well with another recurrent issue in both gender theory and sociological theory more generally, the structure and agency or micro-macro problem (Wharton, 1991). To what extent are people's actions shaped by environmental constraints and to what extent are they freely chosen? How are the interpersonal social interactions of our daily lives related to larger social structures and social institutions? The gender boundaries conceptualization is complex enough to analyze multiple levels (e.g., social-psychological, structural, cultural) in the process of constructing gender and thus can help to identify both elements of choice (agency) and elements of constraint (structure). Analyzing such variable properties of gender boundaries as permeability, institutionalization, universality, and severity of sanctions also helps to locate the links between social-psychological and interactional processes on the one hand and cultural and structural aspects of gender on the other. Moreover, the emphasis on an active construction of gender that is shaped, but not determined, by situational factors provides a reminder that even highly constraining structures leave room for agency; individuals do choose to breach gender boundaries, even ones that are virtually universal, highly institutionalized, and enforced by severe sanctions.

Emphasizing the links between structure and agency and the ways that gender boundaries operate simultaneously on multiple levels also helps us to deal with one of the problems that often attends social constructionist approaches to gender: explaining why women choose to actively participate in constructing a system of gender inequality. Should we chalk this up to false consciousness or to some kind of collective delusional thinking? I think we can make better sense of women's participation in the construction of a system that disadvantages them if we remember that women, like men, live lives embedded in social interaction, and that the social world in which women live and interact is one in which one's gender category is a critical foundation of social identity. Women, too, have a stake in the gender system.

Paradoxically, the feminist movement of the past two decades has, in some ways, enhanced women's investment in the system of gender boundaries. If one outcome of women's active and collective contesting of the gender system has been the relaxation, or even elimination, of some gender boundaries, another has been the consolidation of womanhood as an identity to be proud of and the reinterpretation of some boundaries that once defined male superiority so that they now define female superiority. The boundary that defines real women as more emotional than real men provides an interesting example; what was once interpreted as women's unfortunate inability to control their emotions has been rearticulated as women's positive capacity for emotional expression. In this and other instances, male superiority has been contested while gender difference has been reinforced. Thus, many women have come to value their differences from men and to have a stake in maintaining the gender boundaries that define those differences.

Considering women's stake in the gender system can also help students of gender to rethink the place of socialization in the gender construction process. During the 1970s and 1980s, both lay and scholarly analyses of gender tended to focus on childhood socialization as a primary causative agent. The gender construction model and the analysis of breadwinning presented in this book have questioned this centrality. A theory of gender focused on the process of gender construction does not deny the existence of gender socialization, but it does suggest a need to reconsider the place of childhood socialization in the construction of gender. I would argue that what is learned and deeply internalized as a core element of culture during the primary socialization of childhood is not so much the content of what it means to be a man or a woman (specific gender boundaries) as the principle of gender dimorphism and its fundamental importance in social relations (the existence of the web). While children certainly learn something about the content of gender-dimorphic categories during childhood, there is no reason to believe that these specifics are deeply internalized and stable over time. Much evidence suggests, to the contrary, that they are remarkably open to challenge and change, and most adults would have no difficulty naming features of what it means to be a man or a woman that have changed dramatically during their lifetimes. Highlighting the distinction between the deeply internalized principle of gender dimorphism and the dynamic, actively constructed content of gender difference elucidates the relative stability of gender dimorphism as a feature of social organization even as the gender boundaries that define that dimorphism are shifting.

New Questions

Many of the new insights into the gender system promised by this conceptualization of gender are, at this point, possibilities that have not yet been realized and that must be pursued in future studies. The theory of gender construction that has been developed here suggests directions for further research on gender boundaries: How permeable, institutionalized, universally deployed, severely sanctioned, stable, or contested are particular boundaries? Under what conditions are they salient? These variables can be used to study individual gender boundaries or to compare them. Systematic examination of the interconnections of gender boundaries should also prove fruitful, addressing such questions as when the relaxation of one boundary leads to the relaxation or the reinforcement of others.

Gender scholars must learn more about the process by which gender boundaries are constructed, and particularly about contention and negotiation in the construction of gender. How typical is the amount of contention found in this study of breadwinning? Does the amount of contention in the gender system vary greatly across time and space? Are all boundaries equally likely to be contested? Does the extent to which a gender boundary is contested depend on characteristics of that boundary, such as its universality, its degree of institutionalization, or the severity of sanctions for its breach? Are more permeable boundaries more or less likely to be contested than less permeable ones? How are disagreements about the construction of gender resolved? How explicit are negotiations about gender boundaries? Who usually initiates them? When are negotiations characterized largely by agreement and when are they contentious? Are there characteristic stages in the process of negotiation or distinct, identifiable types of negotiation? How typical is the degree of cooperation in the construction of gender found in this study? Is such cooperation equally likely at other sites of gender construction (e.g., the workplace) or between actors who are not in close personal relationships with one another?

This study has raised questions about the stability and dynamism of the gender system. Is the extraordinary amount of change over time found here in the construction of breadwinning typical of other gender boundaries? What conditions encourage or inhibit change in the gender system? How are changes in individual boundaries related to changes in the system as a whole? Does such change represent an overall reduction in gender dimorphism or a shift in the content of that dimorphism? Is the propensity for change in particular gender boundaries related to such variables as their universality, institutionalization, permeability, severity of sanctions, and salience? When is the gender system maintained in the face of challenge by increasing the permeability of particular boundaries and when by making them more rigid and impenetrable?

The gender boundaries framework also raises new questions about how the gender system varies cross-culturally, across historical periods, and by social location within a given culture. How do the density and dynamism of the web of gender boundaries differ across time, space, and circumstances? How does the construction of gender differ depending on race, ethnicity, social class, and sexual orientation? Are differences primarily in the amount of gender differentiation, in the content of that differentiation, or in the processes of gender construction? If members of subordinated groups are characterized by distinctive constructions of gender, to what extent do these represent strategic choices on the part of those groups and to what extent constraints imposed on them by members of dominant groups? These questions suggest rich possibilities for using this conceptualization of gender to explore intersections of inequality.

Clearly, those of us who specialize in the study of gender have a great deal of work to do as we develop our understanding and analysis of the gender system. Nevertheless, a theory of gender construction that conceptualizes that system as a complex and dynamic web of interrelated gender boundaries is an important step in that development. The gender boundaries conceptualization has helped to disentangle breadwinning from employment and to explore the complex mix of circumstances and negotiation that shapes and reshapes the use of breadwinning as a gender boundary. This theoretical approach holds similar promise for examining other parts of the gender system. With it, we can reframe old questions, formulate important new ones, and advance our understanding of gender.

Appendixes

Methodology

Research is always a process of compromise and trade-off; there is no such thing as perfect methodology. Rather, good research design involves being self-conscious about the goals of the research and then choosing strategies that optimize those goals within the inevitable constraints of doing research in the real world. This appendix provides a detailed discussion of my goals for this research, the constraints I encountered, and the strategies I adopted.

From the earliest stages of planning the research, I had a number of clear goals in mind. First, I knew that I wanted to study not just behavior, but the subjective meanings attached to that behavior. Second, I knew that I wanted to focus on couples, not individuals. Finally, since many of the studies available were small exploratory studies of a handful of couples or were focused only on upper-middle-class dual-career couples, I knew that I wanted to choose a more broadly representative sample, and one that would be large enough to draw generalizations from.

These goals implied a number of methodological choices. The goal of studying subjective meanings meant that I would need a fairly sensitive data collection method. The goal of studying couples meant that I would have to collect data from both members of the couple, since previous research had shown that individual partners do not give the same responses to questions about their lives together. The goal of generalizability meant that I would need a fairly large sample, and one that was carefully chosen.

These choices, in turn, posed a series of trade-offs. The most sensitive data collection strategy would probably be to conduct in-depth semi-structured or unstructured interviews, but the time- and labor-intensiveness of such interviews would seriously limit the size of the sample and, therefore, its representativeness. Moreover, since interviewer salaries are the single greatest expense of interview studies, sample size and representativeness would also be limited by the funds available. The most representative sample would cover a wide geographic range, but such a range would greatly increase costs—either to hire interviewers in multiple locations or for transportation costs for relatively few interviewers. The need to study couples was likely to lower the participation rate of those chosen for the sample (because both partners would have to agree to participate). This, too, would lower the representativeness of the sample, by introducing selection bias. A structured mail questionnaire or telephone interview would allow for the largest sample and the greatest geographic coverage (both boons to representativeness), but these methods were likely to have higher refusal rates and to be less sensitive to nuance than would personal interviews.

In response to these trade-offs, I chose to do structured personal interviews with a randomly chosen sample of couples from a single community. Personal interviews provided a sensitive data collection tool, while making those interviews structured allowed a fairly large number of interviews, thus maintaining the possibility of representativeness. The decision to limit the sample to a single community reduced representativeness in one way by introducing the bias of the community's peculiar characteristics, but increased it in another by making it easier to use a random sampling method. (These issues are discussed in more detail below.) My original target sample size was 250 couples, large enough for making generalizations with considerable statistical confidence and a fairly small margin of error, but small enough to require the labor of no more than four interviewers. When no major funding was forthcoming for the project, however, I scaled the sample size back to 150 couples, a number that could be reasonably interviewed by myself and one student research assistant but that was still large enough for multivariate statistical analyses.

The Interview Study

The Interview Schedule

Designing a structured interview schedule that would be a sufficiently sensitive research instrument required careful attention. I therefore developed the questions for the interview schedule by doing a preliminary round of in-depth, semistructured interviews with a convenience sample of ten men and ten women in dual-earner marriages. These interviews covered a range of topics, including a description of the employment histories of the interviewee and his or her spouse, a discussion of why both the interviewee and the spouse worked for pay, an examination of who in the family was responsible for financial support, a detailed account of how family finances were managed, and responses to hypothetical situations. Both the questions included on the interview schedule and the response categories provided as options were guided by the results of these exploratory interviews, and the draft interview schedule was pretested on the twenty participants in the preliminary study and their spouses. The final version of the interview schedule can be found at the end of this appendix.

Sampling

To locate a representative sample of dual-earner couples, I used random-digit-dialing sampling. Random-digit dialing involves calling randomly generated telephone numbers from a given exchange or set of exchanges. In this case, the numbers chosen were from the five residential exchanges of the Lewiston-Auburn metropolitan area, and the telephone calls were used not to collect data, but to screen potential participants. When a random call reached a residential number, the caller introduced herself, asked if a married couple lived in the household, and, if so, did a brief screening interview with one member of the couple to see if they were eligible for the study. If they were, the caller briefly described the study and asked if they would be willing to receive a letter with more detailed information. If they agreed, their name and address were ascertained and a letter was put in the mail. Approximately one week after the letter went out, a follow-up telephone call was made to see if interviews could be scheduled. Sampling and interviewing were carried out simultaneously over a period of fifteen months, with random-digit dialing ending only when the target sample size of 150 couples had been reached. The sampling process was a tedious one; many of the numbers dialed turned out to be unassigned, while others were business rather than residential numbers. On average, every ten numbers called yielded one eligible couple, and by the time the sampling was completed, more than 3,000 numbers had been dialed.

A number of criteria were used to determine eligibility for participation in the study. First, I limited the sample to married couples, because previous research (Blumstein and Schwartz, 1983) had shown that co-habiting couples and married couples handled the financial aspects of their relationships differently. Second, I stipulated that both partners had to be currently employed. Finally, to select couples who had established dual-earner patterns, I included only those in which each partner had been employed for at least six months out of the past year.

Selecting the sample from a single community had both advantages and disadvantages. A local focus made it feasible for me, as a solo re-searcher who was not part of a large survey research operation, to draw a random, and therefore representative, sample. At the same time, though, the sample reflected the distinctive characteristics of the locality from which it was drawn. For example, a representative sample from Lewiston-Auburn included a greater proportion of working-class couples than would a national sample because, in its vital statistics, Lewiston-Auburn continues to reflect its industrial past. Its work force has fewer professionals and managers (20 percent) and more blue-collar workers (49 percent) than is typical of either the state of Maine or the nation as a whole. Education and income levels are also below average. In 1990, only 12.6 percent of adults age 25 or over had completed bachelor's de-grees, compared with 19 percent for the state and 21 percent for the na-tion. At $31,953, the median family income was more than $3,000 be-low the national median, despite the fact that Lewiston-Auburn families were more likely than average to have multiple wage-earners. The great-est limitation of a sample from this community is the virtual absence of national minority groups in Maine. In 1990, African Americans, Asian Americans, and Hispanics each made up only one-half of one percent of the population of Lewiston-Auburn. At the same time, Lewiston-Auburn continues to be a center for a regional minority group, Franco-Ameri-cans. In the 1990 census, almost half the population of the metropolitan area identified themselves as of either French-Canadian or French ances-try, and more than 20,000 (22 percent) reported speaking a language other than English (usually French) at home (U.S. Bureau of the Census, 1992).

The sample interviewed for this study, however, was not perfectly rep-resentative of dual-earner couples in Lewiston-Auburn. Rather, a fairly high refusal rate introduced bias into the sample. Of the 347 dual-earner couples located through the random-digit-dialing screening process, only 44 percent (153) agreed to participate in the study. Of those remaining, 177 (51 percent) refused to participate in the study and 17 (5 percent) were lost to the study in some manner other than refusal. This fairly high refusal rate is neither surprising nor unusual for a study of this type. The target population was made up of very busy people who often found it difficult to make time for an interview.* In addition, a couple could not be included in the sample unless both husband and wife were willing to be interviewed.

So that we could assess how those who agreed to participate in the study might be systematically different from those who did not, refusers were asked to provide some demographic information over the telephone. Eighty-nine percent of the 177 refusers agreed to answer these questions, and the data thus collected make it possible to assess the bias introduced by the high refusal rate. The refusers were like the study participants in age. They were more likely to have children (89 percent) than were the interviewees (81 percent), but they were also more likely to have only one or two children (34.2 percent of the refusers, compared with 41.3 percent of the interviewees, had three or more children). The refusers also tended, on average, to be at a somewhat later stage of the family life cycle.

The most pronounced difference between the refusers and the participants, however, was in the higher socioeconomic characteristics of the latter group. The interviewees were more highly educated (median years of school = 13 for interviewees, 12 for refusers). They were also more likely to be in professional and managerial occupations. (For the interviewees, 34.6 percent of the husbands and 36.6 percent of the wives were in such occupations; the comparable figures for the refusers were 33.1 percent and 27.6 percent.) Finally, the refusers estimated their incomes to be much lower than those reported by the interviewees. The median couple income for respondents was $40,500; the median reported by refusers was in the $20,001–$30,000 range. This figure may be skewed by the fact that 12 percent of those who completed refusers' interviews refused to disclose their income. Even if we place all of these unreported incomes in the "above $40,000" category, however, we are still left with a median income for refusers that is $10,000 below that for interviewees. All of this means there is a bias in the sample that makes it more highly educated, more white-collar, and better off economically than the community from which it was gathered. However, because that

---

* One strategy that I adopted to reduce the refusal rate was to offer participants a token payment of $5.00 for their time.

community differs from the nation in being less educated, more blue-collar, and lower-income, the middle-class bias in the sample moves it in the direction of national averages on these variables.

The Interview Process

All participants in this study were interviewed in person. The interviews were structured and based on an interview schedule made up primarily of closed-ended questions. Interviews were tape-recorded,* a strategy that I adopted for quality control purposes since I was not doing all the interviewing myself. Tape-recording allowed me to edit the completed interview schedules, checking for accuracy and doing some preliminary coding, by listening to the tapes of the interviews.

Tape-recording also turned out to have some serendipitous consequences. The presence of the tape recorder gave respondents a sense that what they had to say was important and that the interviewer was interested in more than their one-word responses to closed-ended questions. As a result, they tended to be more expansive in their responses than is typical in standardized interviews. It was these narratives that respondents constructed around their responses to closed-ended questions, along with their responses to the open-ended questions included in the interview schedule, that made the qualitative analyses in this book possible.

The Follow-Up Survey

Throughout the months of interviewing, respondents repeatedly asked how they could get information about the results of the study. After a number of such inquiries, I found myself promising to send out a brief summary when preliminary analyses of data had been completed. In the fall of 1992, a little more than five years after the first interviews, I was finally able to fulfill this promise. A mailing was sent to all the participants in the original study (at the addresses recorded at the time of their interviews). This mailing consisted of a two-page summary of preliminary results and two brief, color-coded questionnaires, one for husbands and one for wives. These brief questionnaires could not possibly replicate the original interviews. Instead, they focused on measures of breadwinning and on changes in circumstances. Because the variables measuring the use of breadwinning as a gender boundary differed for husbands and

---

* Only one interviewee declined to give permission for tape-recording.

wives, the follow-up questionnaires, too, differed. The questionnaires can be found at the end of this appendix.

Of the 153 couples in the original study, 77 (50 percent) sent some response to the follow-up survey. Twenty-five of the 153 follow-up packets were returned by the post office as undeliverable because respondents had moved and no forwarding address was available; an additional 51 couples presumably received the mailing, but they did not respond. Of those who did respond, not all could be included in the follow-up sample. Many were no longer in dual-earner marriages, either because the marriage had ended (four couples) or because one or both partners were no longer employed (ten couples). Of the remaining 63 couples, 13 were excluded from the analysis either because only one spouse had responded (seven couples) or because not all questions about breadwinning had been completed (six couples). The remaining 50 couples (about one-third of the original sample) constitute the follow-up subsample.

Research Instruments

Interview Schedule

Date _____

Interviewer _____

Couple I.D. No. _____

Time Begin _____

Time End _____

[INTERVIEWER INSTRUCTIONS for beginning interview:
  1. Introduce self
  2. Find suitable place to conduct interview (express need for as much privacy as possible)
  3. Assure respondent of confidentiality
  4. Get permission to tape-record; set up recorder]

Let me begin by asking you a few routine questions about yourself:

1. What was your date of birth?

  month _____ day _____ year _____

2. How many years of school have you completed? _____

3. When did you and your (husband/wife) get married?

  month _____ year _____

4. Is this your first marriage?

  ☐ yes
  ☐ no

[INTERVIEWER: If *no*, ask the following; otherwise, skip to 5.]

How long were you married previously?

    1. _____ years _____ months

    2. _____ years _____ months

5. Do you have any children?

    ☐ yes

    ☐ no

[INTERVIEWER: If *yes*, ask the following; otherwise, skip to 6.]

    How many children do you have? _____

    [Ascertain the following for each child:]

        birth month and year

        living at home?

6. Now I'd like to ask you about your work history. Let's begin with your current job and work backward.

[INTERVIEWER: Whenever possible, ascertain both month and year for starting and ending dates. Leave a blank line for any hiatus of more than six months.]

Dates	Occupation	Ave. no. of hours per wk.	Reason for leaving

7. [Asked of wives only]

Some people see employment as a constant part of their adult life; others enter and leave the labor force in response to events in their family lives. Do you plan to work outside the home continuously until retirement?

    ☐ yes

    ☐ no

[INTERVIEWER: If *no*, ask the following; otherwise, skip to 8.]

    Why would you expect to stop working?

8. What are your average earnings (before taxes) in your current job?

[INTERVIEWER: Obtain gross earnings before taxes; specify whether unit of time is weekly, monthly, or annual.]

9. Now I'd like to ask you about how important job advancement (being promoted or being able to move up to increasingly better jobs) is to you in your work. Which of these statements would you say best describes your feelings about job advancement? Would you say that

    ☐ you want to advance as far as possible

    ☐ you would like to advance within the limits imposed by family and other interests in your life

    ☐ you are interested in advancing, but think it's unlikely

    ☐ you are not interested in advancing

    ☐ other: _____

10. When you were a child, was your mother ever employed outside the home?
   ☐ no
   ☐ yes
[INTERVIEWER: If *yes*, ascertain respondent's ages when mother was employed and check whether mother's employment was full or part time. Begin by asking, "How old were you when your mother first went back to work? Did she work full or part time? How long did she stay at that job?"]

R's age at beginning	R's age at end	Full time	Part time

11. When you were a child, did you have chores that you were regularly assigned to do?
   ☐ no
   ☐ yes
[INTERVIEWER: If *yes*, ask the following. Probe; list all that respondent mentions.]
   What were they?
Now I'd like to ask you some questions about your current family financial arrangements:

12. Who is the financial provider for your family? Would you say that
   ☐ you mostly provide
   ☐ your (husband/wife) mostly provides
   ☐ you share providing equally
   ☐ other: _____

13. Whose job would you say is considered more important in your family? Would you say that
   ☐ your job is considered more important
   ☐ your (husband's/wife's) job is considered more important
   ☐ both are considered equally important

14. This card lists a number of reasons why a person might be employed.
[INTERVIEWER: Hand Card A to respondent]
   I'd like to ask you for each of these reasons how important it is *to you* as a reason for being employed. How important to you is _____ as a reason for being employed? Would you say that it is very important, somewhat important, or not important?
   earning money for basic family needs
   earning money for family extras
   a feeling of accomplishment
   being more independent
   having more money for yourself to spend as you want

contact with other people

keeping busy

15. Now I would like you to rank these according to how important they are as reasons for you to be employed. What would you say is the most important? Second most important? (Etc.) Are there any reasons that are important to you that aren't on this list? (How would that rank with the others?)

[INTERVIEWER: Rank only those reasons which were described by the respondent as very or somewhat important. Probe to break ties.]

☐ to earn money for basic family needs

☐ to earn money for family extras

☐ because the work provides me with a feeling of accomplishment

☐ in order to be more independent

☐ to have money for myself to spend as I want

☐ to have contact with other people

☐ to keep busy

☐ other: _____

16. Now I'd like to ask you for each of these reasons how important you think it is to your (husband/wife) as a reason for being employed. How important to (him/her) do you think _____ is as a reason for being employed? Would you say that it is very important, somewhat important, or not important?

earning money for basic family needs

earning money for family extras

a feeling of accomplishment

being more independent

having more money for (him/her)self to spend as (he/she) wants

contact with other people

keeping busy

17. How do you think your (husband/wife) would rank these in importance as reasons for (him/her) to be employed? What would (he/she) say is the most important? Second most important? (Etc.) Are there any reasons that are important to (him/her) that aren't on this list? (How would that rank with the others?)

[INTERVIEWER: Rank only those reasons which were described by the respondent as very or somewhat important. Probe to break ties.]

☐ to earn money for basic family needs

☐ to earn money for family extras

☐ because the work provides (him/her) with a feeling of accomplishment

☐ in order to be more independent

☐ to have money for (him/her)self to spend as (he/she) wants

☐ to have contact with other people

☐ to keep busy

☐ other: _____

18. Who in your family do you think feels an *obligation* to earn money to support the family? Would you say that

    ☐ you mostly feel it

    ☐ you feel it a little more than your (husband/wife)

    ☐ you and your (husband/wife) feel it equally

    ☐ your (husband/wife) feels it a little more than you

    ☐ your (husband/wife) mostly feels it

19. Ideally, who do you think should be the financial provider for your family?

    ☐ you only

    ☐ you more than your (husband/wife)

    ☐ you and your (husband/wife) equally

    ☐ your (husband/wife) more than you

    ☐ your (husband/wife) only

    ☐ other: _____

20. How do you and your (husband/wife) divide up the money that you both bring in to meet the family's financial needs? Do you

    ☐ each have specific basic expenses that you are responsible for

    ☐ put all the money into one financial pot that is used to meet basic expenses

    ☐ use (your husband's/your) income to meet basic expenses and earmark (your/your wife's) income for special items or projects

    ☐ use (your husband's/your) income to meet family expenses and leave (you/your wife) free to spend (your/her) income however (you/she) wants

    ☐ other: _____

Could you tell me a little more about how that works in your family?

21. Who actually pays the bills?

    ☐ husband

    ☐ wife

    ☐ whoever has the time

    ☐ each pays certain assigned bills

    ☐ other: _____

22. Imagine a family (friends of yours, perhaps) in which both the husband and wife are employed full time. The family has young children. The husband earns the same income that (your husband does / you do) and the wife earns a little more than her husband. One of their children, an eight-year-old, becomes ill and is going to need full-time care at home for the next eighteen months. The child does not need skilled nursing care, but does need someone at home. There are no extended family or relatives nearby to help. What should the family do to provide the care?

[INTERVIEWER: If respondent asks for clarification, say, "Should one of the parents quit work to stay home with the child, should they hire someone to care for the child, or what?" If respondent has trouble being specific, ask, "What do you think the *best* solution would be?"]

23. This card lists a number of roles which you might play in your life.

[INTERVIEWER: Hand respondent Card (B/C).]

I'm going to ask you separately for each role how important it is to you to do it well.

How important is it to you to be a good _____? Is it very important, somewhat important, or not important?

    wife/husband
    worker or professional
    friend
    mother/father
    houseworker
    daughter/son
    financial provider for the family

24. Now I'd like you to rank order these roles according to how important they are in your life. Which is the most important? Second most important? (Etc.)

☐ wife/husband
☐ worker or professional
☐ friend
☐ mother/father
☐ houseworker
☐ daughter/son
☐ financial provider for the family

25. Now I'd like to get some sense of how much these various parts of your life conflict with one another. How often do you feel that your other obligations interfere with your ability to be a good _____? Would you say that that happens frequently, sometimes, seldom, or never?

[INTERVIEWER: Ask only for roles which were listed as somewhat or very important in Question 23 above.]

    wife/husband
    worker or professional
    friend
    mother/father
    houseworker
    daughter/son
    financial provider for the family

26. In general, how do you feel about your time—would you say that you always feel rushed even to do the things you have to do, only sometimes feel rushed, or almost never feel rushed?

☐ always feel rushed
☐ sometimes feel rushed
☐ almost never feel rushed

27. This card lists a number of roles which your (husband/wife) might play in (his/her) life.

[INTERVIEWER: Hand respondent Card (C/B).]

I'd like you to rank order your (husband's/wife's) roles according to how important they are to *you*. Which would you say is the most important? Second most important? (Etc.)

☐ husband/wife
☐ worker or professional
☐ friend
☐ father/mother
☐ houseworker
☐ son/daughter
☐ financial provider for the family

28. Can you imagine any circumstances, other than serious illness, under which you would leave the labor force and your (husband/wife) would be the sole financial provider for the family?

☐ no
☐ yes

[INTERVIEWER: If *yes*, ask the following. Probe for whether circumstances would be clearly limited or indefinite.]

What are they?

29. Can you imagine any circumstances, other than serious illness, under which your (husband/wife) would leave the labor force and you would be the sole financial provider for the family?

☐ no
☐ yes

[INTERVIEWER: If *yes*, ask the following. Probe for whether circumstances would be clearly limited or indefinite.]

What are they?

30. Imagine that you bought a Megabucks ticket and won a $3 million jackpot. Would you quit your job?

☐ yes
☐ no

[INTERVIEWER: If *yes*, ask, "Why?" "What would you do instead?" If *no*, ask, "Why not?"]

31. Now I'm going to read several statements to you. For each statement, I'd like you to tell me whether you strongly agree, agree, disagree, or strongly disagree.

There is some work that is men's and some that is women's and they shouldn't be doing each other's.

A woman who works full time can establish just as warm and secure a relationship with her children as a mother who does not work.

Most of the important decisions in the life of the family should be made by the man of the house.

If a wife works on the job as many hours as her husband, he should spend as much time in housework and child care as she does.

Women should take care of running their homes and leave running the country up to men.

A married woman should not work outside the home if her husband can comfortably support her.

That's all. Thank you very much for your help.

[INTERVIEWER: Be sure to mark ending time on front of interview.]

Wife's Follow-Up Questionnaire

1. Are you still married to the husband who participated in this study with you?
   ☐ yes
   ☐ no

If yes, please complete questions 2–12; if no, please skip to question 13.

2. If you have children, are any of them still living at home?
   ☐ yes
   ☐ no

If yes, how many? _____

3. Are you employed?
   ☐ yes

   If you are employed, what is the average number of hours per week that you work? _____

   ☐ no

   If you are not employed, is it because
   ☐ you have retired
   ☐ you choose not to be
   ☐ you want to be but cannot find a job
   ☐ other: _____

4. What are your average earnings (before taxes) in your current job? Please specify either weekly, monthly, or annually.

————————

Please answer the following questions ONLY if you and your husband are both currently employed. OTHERWISE, SKIP TO QUESTION 10.

5. Who is the financial provider for the family?
   ☐ you mostly provide
   ☐ your husband mostly provides
   ☐ you share providing equally

6. Whose job is considered more important in the family?
   ☐ your job
   ☐ your husband's job
   ☐ both are equally important

7. To what extent is *your* income used to meet basic family expenses?
   ☐ it is not used at all for basic expenses
   ☐ some is used for basic expenses, but most is used for family extras
   ☐ it is used primarily for basic expenses, but your husband's income pays for most of the basics
   ☐ it is just as important as your husband's income for meeting basic family expenses

8. The following is a list of reasons why a person might be employed. Please rank order them according to how important they are *to you* as reasons for being employed. (Put a '1' in front of the most important, a '2' in front of the second most important, etc.)
   ☐ to earn money for basic family needs
   ☐ to earn money for family extras
   ☐ because the work provides me with a feeling of accomplishment
   ☐ in order to be more independent
   ☐ to have money for myself to spend as I want
   ☐ to have contact with other people
   ☐ to keep busy

9. How important to you is earning money for basic family needs as a reason for being employed?
   ☐ very important
   ☐ somewhat important
   ☐ not important

10. *Ideally*, who do you think should be the financial provider for your family?
   ☐ you only
   ☐ you more than your husband
   ☐ you and your husband equally

☐ your husband more than you
☐ your husband only

Having read the descriptions of the types of husbands' and wives' orientations to breadwinning, please complete the following questions.

11. Which type of orientation do you feel best describes your husband?
    ☐ traditional breadwinner
    ☐ role sharer
    ☐ reluctant co-provider
    ☐ uncommitted provider

12. Which type of orientation do you feel best describes yourself?
    ☐ employed homemaker
    ☐ co-breadwinner
    ☐ reluctant traditional
    ☐ reluctant provider
    ☐ helper
    ☐ supplementary provider
    ☐ family-centered worker
    ☐ committed worker

13. Who filled out this questionnaire?
    ☐ husband
    ☐ wife
    ☐ other: _____

Husband's Follow-Up Questionnaire

1. Are you still married to the wife who participated in this study with you?
    ☐ yes
    ☐ no

If yes, please complete questions 2–13; if no, please skip to question 14.

2. If you have children, are any of them still living at home?
    ☐ yes
    ☐ no
        If yes, how many? _____

3. Are you employed?
    ☐ yes
    ☐ no
        If you are not employed, is it because
        ☐ you have retired
        ☐ you choose not to be
        ☐ you want to be but cannot find a job
        ☐ other: _____

4. What are your average earnings (before taxes) in your current job? Please specify either weekly, monthly, or annually.

————————

Please answer the following questions ONLY if you and your wife are both currently employed. OTHERWISE, SKIP TO QUESTION 9.

5. Who is the financial provider for your family?
   ☐ you mostly provide
   ☐ you and your wife share providing equally
   ☐ your wife mostly provides

6. Whose job would you say is considered more important in your family?
   ☐ your job
   ☐ your wife's job
   ☐ both are equally important

7. Who in your family do you think feels an obligation to earn money to support the family? Would you say that
   ☐ you mostly feel it
   ☐ you feel it a little more than your wife
   ☐ you and your wife feel it equally
   ☐ your wife feels it a little more than you
   ☐ your wife mostly feels it

8. To what extent is your wife's income used to meet basic family expenses?
   ☐ it is not used at all for basic expenses
   ☐ some is used for basic expenses, but most is used for family extras
   ☐ it is used primarily for basic expenses, but your income pays for most of the basics
   ☐ it is just as important as your income for meeting basic family expenses

9. *Ideally*, who do you think should be the financial provider for your family?
   ☐ you only
   ☐ you more than your wife
   ☐ you and your wife equally
   ☐ your wife more than you
   ☐ your wife only

10. This is a list of roles you might play in your life. Please rank them according to how important they are in your life. (Put a '1' in front of the most important, a '2' in front of the second most important, etc. If any do not apply, leave them blank.)
    ☐ husband
    ☐ worker or professional
    ☐ friend
    ☐ father

☐ houseworker
☐ son
☐ financial provider for the family

11. This is a list of roles which your wife might play in her life. Please rank order them according to how important they are *to you*. (Place a '1' in front of the most important, a '2' in front of the second most important, etc.)

☐ wife
☐ worker or professional
☐ friend
☐ mother
☐ houseworker
☐ daughter
☐ financial provider for the family

Having read the descriptions of the types of husbands' and wives' orientations to breadwinning, please complete the following questions.

12. Which type of orientation do you feel best describes your wife?

☐ employed homemaker
☐ co-breadwinner
☐ reluctant traditional
☐ reluctant provider
☐ helper
☐ supplementary provider
☐ family-centered worker
☐ committed worker

13. Which type of orientation do you feel best describes yourself?

☐ traditional breadwinner
☐ role sharer
☐ reluctant co-provider
☐ uncommitted provider

14. Who filled out this questionnaire?

☐ husband
☐ wife
☐ other: _____

Statistical Analyses

Although much of the analysis presented in this book is in the form of qualitative case studies, quantitative statistical analyses form the backdrop for those case studies and are critical to my analysis of breadwinning in dual-earner marriages. In the interests of accessibility, however, these statistical analyses are described only briefly in the main text of the book. This appendix supplies a more detailed discussion of the statistical procedures used and presents statistical tables for Chapters 3–5.

In analyzing the data from this study, I have taken a pragmatic approach to the use of statistical techniques. By this, I mean that I have taken advantage of the power of parametric statistical tools even though my data did not meet all of their statistical assumptions, but I have done so cautiously, using more conservative nonparametric techniques to cross-check the results. Thus, I have used factor analysis and least-squares multiple regression analysis, but I have not relied on these analyses alone in drawing conclusions. The most important results of the parametric statistical analyses in this book (e.g., the low explanatory power of socialization variables) have proven to be robust, confirmed by nonparametric checks such as bivariate tables. In addition, the statistical analyses are intertwined with qualitative analyses that provide another method of cross-checking and another source of confirmation.

Statistical Procedures and Analytical Strategies

Chapter 3

The primary statistical tools used in developing the analysis of Chapter 3 were factor analysis and multiple regression analysis. Factor analysis was used to confirm and refine the results of a preliminary nonparametric analysis suggesting that wives' responses to questions about breadwinning fell along three distinct dimensions. The factor analysis began with eleven indicators of breadwinning available in the data set:

1. Why Work: How important to you is earning money for basic family needs as a reason to be employed?
2. Rank Work: The respondent's ranking of earning money for basic family needs in importance among a list of reasons for being employed.
3. Provider: Who is the financial provider for your family?
4. Job Importance: Whose job would you say is considered more important in your family?
5. Obligation: Who in your family do you think feels an *obligation* to earn money to support the family?
6. Hours: Average number of hours per week that the respondent is currently employed.
7. Finances: Extent to which the respondent's income is used to meet basic family expenses.
8. Role Importance: How important is it to you to be a good financial provider for the family?
9. Role Rank: Respondent's ranking of financial provider for the family in importance among a list of social roles that respondent plays.
10. Spouse Rank: Respondent's ranking of spouse's financial provider role in importance to respondent among a list of social roles that spouse plays.
11. Ideals: Ideally, who do you think should be the financial provider for your family?

Although all of these had face validity as indicators of breadwinning, not all were included in the analysis. One, ranking of the husband's provider role (Spouse Rank), was eliminated because it was uncorrelated with the other indicators. Two additional indicators, Obligation and Role Rank, were included in early versions of the factor analysis but later excluded because they did not load primarily on a single factor. Factor analysis of the remaining eight indicators, using principal components extraction and varimax rotation, confirmed the presence of three distinct dimensions of breadwinning, as presented in Table B1.

The rest of the analysis in Chapter 3 was based on the dimensions identified through the factor analysis. First, the results of the factor analysis were used to create scores for each of the three dimensions of

TABLE B1
Wives' Dimensions of Breadwinning and Factor Loadings

Variable	Financial support	Job centrality	Norms
Why work	.90058	.09108	−.10241
Rank work	−.87882	−.08208	.18522
Role importance	.64386	.08247	.20597
Finances	.62678	.23869	.24681
Job importance	.10523	.78385	.18729
Hours	.02883	.72195	−.24888
Provider	.43726	.67120	.30618
Ideals	.01662	.03614	.90751
Eigenvalue	3.062	1.324	1.038
Variance explained	38.3%	16.5%	13.0%

breadwinning. This was accomplished by combining the indicators of each dimension, using the factor loadings as weights. Before this procedure could be carried out, however, the variables being combined had to have similar coding schemes. Thus, each indicator was recoded into three possible values, ranging from 0 for responses that did not indicate female responsibility for breadwinning to 2 for responses that indicated such responsibility. The exception was the third dimension, norms, whose single indicator was used in its original form. The resulting scores ranged from 0 to 6 for the financial support dimension, 0 to 4.4 for the job centrality dimension, and 1 to 6 for the norms dimension.

Next, these dimension scores were used as the dependent variables in multiple regression analyses designed to examine factors that influence the construction of breadwinning. This analysis used a hierarchical regression procedure in which the background characteristics of age and education (measured in years of school completed) were entered in the analysis first. These were followed by socialization variables: the total number of years that a respondent's mother had been employed during her childhood, a series of dichotomous variables to represent whether or not her mother had been employed full time during five different childhood periods, and a dichotomous variable that measured whether or not the respondent had been assigned sex-atypical chores as a child. The third block of variables entered into the equation consisted of gender attitude variables, Likert-type responses to six different gender attitude statements. These were coded so that high scores represented egalitarian responses and low scores indicated conventionally gendered responses.

After the background, socialization, and attitude variables were allowed to explain as much variation as possible in the dependent variables (Table B2, partial equations), situational variables were added (Table B2, full equations). These included the respondent's earnings for the past year, her husband's earnings for the past year,* the length of the current marriage, the number of children the respondent has, a series of dummy variables to represent stage in the family life cycle, an aggregate measure of role conflict, dummy variables to measure whether the respondent's occupation is (1) professional or managerial or (2) clerical or sales, and a measure of discontinuity in the respondent's work history. Six cases with missing values on one or more independent variables were excluded from the regression analysis, leaving an N of 147.

The final statistical procedure in the analysis for Chapter 3 involved using respondents' scores on the three dimensions of breadwinning as the basis for a typology of breadwinning constructions. Each dimension was dichotomized into high scores and low scores, where high scores represented wives' sharing of responsibility for breadwinning and low scores represented male breadwinning. The cut points for these dichotomies were not simply set at the mean or median; rather, they were chosen to reflect natural divisions in the data and with attention to face validity. (Thus, a respondent could not score high unless she had given responses indicating shared breadwinning on at least half the component variables of that dimension.) The cut point of the financial support dimension was set at 3.7, and the 60 percent of respondents who scored higher than this were classified as high on this dimension. The cut point for the job centrality dimension was set at 2.1, with 37 percent of respondents scoring high on this dimension. The third dimension, norms, was dichotomized so that those who indicated that the husband should have a special responsibility for breadwinning were scored low and all others (42 percent) were scored high. The cross-classification of these three dichotomized dimensions produced the eight constructions of breadwinning presented in the case studies of Chapter 3.

Chapter 4

The statistical analysis of husbands' constructions of breadwinning in Chapter 4 parallels that for wives in Chapter 3. Once again, factor analysis has been used to identify dimensions of breadwinning, the results of this analysis have been used to compute scores for each dimension, these

---

* Total family income and husband-wife wage ratio were not included because they were multicollinear with these two variables and had less explanatory power.

Influences on Wives' Dimensions of Breadwinning

Independent variable	Financial support Partial equation beta	Financial support Full equation beta	Job centrality Partial equation beta	Job centrality Full equation beta	Norms Partial equation beta	Norms Full equation beta
Background						
Age	−.266**	.065	−.061	.062	−.012	.009
Education	.072	.024	.127	.097	.006	.025
Socialization						
No. of years mother worked	.118	.128	.237	.124	.271	.373
Mother worked—infant	.015	.086	−.023	.044	.069	−.031
Mother worked—preschool	−.018	−.119	−.079	−.031	−.247	−.125
Mother worked—elementary	−.192	−.272*	−.035	.006	.036	−.014
Mother worked—junior high	.081	.116	−.073	.044	.021	−.037
Mother worked—high school	−.171	−.077	−.008	−.010	−.205	−.195
Gender-atypical chores	−.005	−.075	.115	.093	.157*	.135
Gender attitudes						
Attitude item 1[a]	.057	.031	−.033	−.017	−.020	−.035
Attitude item 2[b]	.230*	.165*	.256**	.170*	.176*	.115
Attitude item 3[c]	.038	.056	.051	.125	.290**	.212*
Attitude item 4[d]	−.193*	−.166*	.055	.043	−.084	−.032
Attitude item 5[e]	.104	.061	.054	−.052	.078	.118
Attitude item 6[f]	−.158	−.137	−.064	−.0007	.154	.170
Current situation						
Wife's income		.163*		.376***		.074
Husband's income		−.225**		−.218**		.023
Length of marriage		−.448***		−.106		−.194
Has children		−.131		.332		−.077
Family stage—infant		.057		−.325**		−.104
Family stage—preschool		−.144		−.407**		−.062
Family stage—school		−.003		−.564***		−.118
Family stage—adolescent		−.0003		−.434**		.100
Family stage—nest leaving		.091		−.320*		−.148
Number of children		.130		−.157		.347*
Role conflict		−.005		.131		.005
Professional occupation		−.230		.017		−.051
Clerical occupation		−.276*		.021		.083
Work discontinuity		−.087		−.126		−.147
R^2 (adjusted)	.08	.32	.04	.39	.21	.22

NOTE: $N = 147$.

[a] There is some work that is men's and some that is women's and they shouldn't be doing each other's.

[b] A woman who works full time can establish just as warm and secure a relationship with her children as a mother who does not work.

[c] Most of the important decisions in the life of the family should be made by the man of the house.

[d] If a wife works on the job as many hours as her husband, he should spend as much time in housework and child care as she does.

[e] Women should take care of running their homes and leave running the country up to men.

[f] A married woman should not work outside the home if her husband can comfortably support her.

$*p < .05.$ $**p < .01.$ $***p < .001.$

scores have been used as dependent variables in regression analyses, and the scores have been dichotomized and cross-classified to create a typology of husbands' constructions of breadwinning. The results of these statistical procedures, however, are not the same for husbands as for wives.

The specification of breadwinning dimensions in Chapter 4 was both similar to and different from that in Chapter 3. The analysis began with the same eleven indicators of breadwinning that were initially included in the analysis for wives. In the analysis for husbands, however, three of these indicators (Why Work, Rank Work, and Role Importance) were eliminated because they lacked variation, and a fourth, Hours, was excluded because it was uncorrelated with the others. Factor analysis of the remaining seven indicators identified two distinct dimensions, as shown in Table B3. Scores for these dimensions, like those for wives', were computed by standardizing the coding of component variables and using the factor loadings as weights. As in the analysis for wives, variables were coded so that high scores indicated shared responsibility for breadwinning and low scores denoted male responsibility for breadwinning.

The multiple regression analysis of influences on the dimensions of breadwinning for husbands was also parallel to that for wives, using a hierarchical least-squares regression procedure and beginning with the same four blocks of variables. Once again, however, the two analyses were not identical. The current situation variables included in the analysis for husbands were somewhat different; the aggregate measure of role conflict (which did not prove useful in preliminary analyses) was omitted, the dummy variables for family stage were coded somewhat differently (with no children as the index category), and two additional

TABLE B3

Husbands' Dimensions of Breadwinning and Factor Loadings

Variable	Behavioral interpretation	Norms
Provider	.81216	.12592
Finances	.73506	.08673
Obligation	.72545	.18279
Spouse rank	.68275	.42222
Job importance	.64662	.41860
Role rank	.08561	.82635
Ideals	.11738	.68067
Eigenvalue	2.78	1.40
Variance explained	39.8%	20.1%

dummy variables, to indicate whether a husband holds either (1) a professional or managerial position or (2) a blue-collar job, were added. In addition, this analysis included a fifth block of variables, measures of husband-wife negotiation about gender issues. The steps used in the regression analysis were also different for husbands than for wives. Because the number of variables (37) was large relative to the number of cases, not all of these variables could be included in the equation simultaneously, and the multiple regression analysis was done in four steps, as presented in Table B4. Model 1 in Table B4 is parallel to the partial equation in Table B2 and includes the background, socialization, and attitude variables. Model 2, like the full equation in Table B2, adds the current situation variables. Model 3 includes only the current situation variables and indicates what is lost by omitting the background, socialization, and attitude variables. Model 4 adds the negotiation variables.

In the final statistical analysis for Chapter 4, husbands' breadwinner dimensions, like those for wives, were dichotomized and cross-classified to create a typology of breadwinning constructions. Scores on the behavioral interpretation dimension of breadwinning for husbands ranged from 0 to 7, and the cut point for dichotomization was set at 3. Forty-nine percent of husbands scored higher than this cut point and were classified as high (shared breadwinning) on this dimension. For the second dimension of breadwinning, norms, scores ranged from 0 to 3, and the cut point was set at 2, requiring that a man embrace shared breadwinning on at least one of the two indicators of this dimension to be put in the high classification. Forty-one percent of the husbands in the sample met this criterion. Because the factor analysis identified only two distinct dimensions of breadwinning for husbands, the cross-classification of dichotomized scores yielded only four breadwinner types.

Chapter 5

The analysis for Chapter 5, more than for any other chapter in the book, involved difficult decisions about the use of statistical tools. Three factors made the analytical choices for this chapter particularly complex: First, the analysis itself was complex, involving both cross-sectional and longitudinal comparisons and two very different dependent variables, agreement between husband and wife and change over time. Second, because much of this chapter is based on a longitudinal comparison of constructions of breadwinning at t_1 (1987–88) and t_2 (1992–93), measures of breadwinning at t_2 had to be constructed to parallel those for t_1. Third, the small number of cases at t_2 ($N = 50$; see Table B5 for a

Influences on Husbands' Dimensions of Breadwinning

Independent variable	Model 1 (N = 143)	Model 2 (N = 143)	Model 3 (N = 148)	Model 4 (N = 148)
Behavioral interpretation				
Background characteristics				
Age	−.04	.10		
Education	−.24*	.04		
Socialization				
No. of years mother worked	−.10	−.03		
Mother worked—infant	−.20	−.17		
Mother worked—preschool	.21	.18		
Mother worked—elementary	.08	.03		
Mother worked—junior high	−.003	.08		
Mother worked—high school	.06	−.03		
Gender-atypical chores	−.04	−.04		
Gender attitudes				
Attitude item 1[a]	−.02	−.08		
Attitude item 2[b]	.27**	.28***		
Attitude item 3[c]	.11	.08		
Attitude item 4[d]	.08	−.01		
Attitude item 5[e]	.07	.04		
Attitude item 6[f]	.01	.03		
Current situation				
Length of marriage		−.17	−.11	−.08
Number of children		.24+	.27**	.22*
Family stage—infant		−.13	−.13	−.11
Family stage—preschool		−.13	−.13	−.11
Family stage—school		−:32**	−.30**	−.29*
Family stage—adolescent		−.13	−.08	−.09
Family stage—nest leaving		−.26	−.27+	−.25
Family stage—empty nest		−.10	−.10	−.11
Husband professional		−.07	−.007	.01
Husband blue-collar		.04	−.03	−.02
Husband's income		−.14	−.39***	−.41***
Wife's income		.27***	.26***	.23**
Wife professional		.04	.07	.07
Wife clerical		−.05	−.03	−.03
Wife's work discontinuity		−.14	−.19*	−.18*
Negotiation				
Wife's norms				.08
Wife's attitude item 1[a]				.07
Wife's attitude item 2[b]				.12
Wife's attitude item 3[c]				−.08
Wife's attitude item 4[d]				−.02
Wife's attitude item 5[e]				−.02
Wife's attitude item 6[f]				.07
R^2 (adjusted)	.09*	.37***	.37***	.37***
Norms				
Background characteristics				
Age	−.09	−.005		
Education	.08	.001		
Socialization				
No. of years mother worked	.17	.23		

Independent variable	Model 1 (N = 143)	Model 2 (N = 143)	Model 3 (N = 148)	Model 4 (N = 148)
Norms, socialization (*continued*)				
Mother worked—infant	−.04	.01		
Mother worked—preschool	.007	−.04		
Mother worked—elementary	.09	.03		
Mother worked—junior high	−.08	−.06		
Mother worked—high school	.11	.04		
Gender-atypical chores	.03	.10		
Gender attitudes				
Attitude item 1[a]	−.005	−.07		
Attitude item 2[b]	.02	.02		
Attitude item 3[c]	−.05	−.10		
Attitude item 4[d]	.17*	.16+		
Attitude item 5[e]	.09	.05		
Attitude item 6[f]	.29**	.30**		
Current situation				
Length of marriage		.001	−.03	.03
Number of children		.11	.02	−.02
Family stage—infant		−.17+	−.12	−.09
Family stage—preschool		−.05	.03	.07
Family stage—school		−.007	.02	.06
Family stage—adolescent		.14	−.07	−.08
Family stage—nest leaving		−.22	−.12	−.12
Family stage—empty nest		−.13	−.11	−.14
Husband professional		.12	.08	.11
Husband blue-collar		−.04	−.19	−.20+
Husband's income		−.12	−.15+	−.16+
Wife's income		.12	.15+	.12
Wife professional		.32**	.30**	.32**
Wife clerical		.26*	.24*	.23*
Wife's work discontinuity		−.06	−.09	−.11
Negotiation				
Wife's norms				.21*
Wife's attitude item 1[a]				.04
Wife's attitude item 2[b]				.11
Wife's attitude item 3[c]				−.22*
Wife's attitude item 4[d]				−.02
Wife's attitude item 5[e]				−.01
Wife's attitude item 6[f]				.10
R^2 (adjusted)	.18***	.24***	.18***	.23***

[a] There is some work that is men's and some that is women's and they shouldn't be doing each other's.
[b] A woman who works full time can establish just as warm and secure a relationship with her children as a mother who does not work.
[c] Most of the important decisions in the life of the family should be made by the man of the house.
[d] If a wife works on the job as many hours as her husband, he should spend as much time in housework and child care as she does.
[e] Women should take care of running their homes and leave running the country up to men.
[f] A married woman should not work outside the home if her husband can comfortably support her.
+$p < .10$.   *$p < .05$.   **$p < .01$.   ***$p < .001$.

TABLE B 5

Comparison of Original Sample and Follow-up Subsample

Characteristics (in 1987–88)	Original sample (N = 153)	Follow-up respondents (N = 77)	Follow-up subsample (N = 50)
Median length of marriage	14 yrs.	17 yrs.	14.5 yrs.
Franco-American	37%	42%	42%
Wife's median age	37 yrs.	39 yrs.	37 yrs.
Husband's median age	41 yrs.	41 yrs.	39 yrs.
Wife's median education	13 yrs.	13 yrs.	14 yrs.
Husband's median education	13 yrs.	14 yrs.	14 yrs.
Professional or managerial wives	37%	49%	58%
Clerical worker wives	40%	32%	28%
Professional or managerial husbands	35%	42%	40%
Blue-collar husbands	49%	47%	48%
Wife's median annual earnings	$13,700	$13,500	$13,700
Husband's median annual earnings	$24,000	$24,700	$24,800
Median husband-wife wage ratio	1.7	1.8	1.8
With no children	19%	14%	14%
With preschool-age children	15%	15%	20%

comparison of the main sample and the subsample) rendered the use of parametric statistical techniques more problematic.

The first analyses for this chapter, those of husband-wife agreement about breadwinning, were the least complicated because they were based only on data from the original 1987–88 interviews. The main tasks were to create a measure of husband-wife agreement and to analyze factors that influence that agreement. Husband-wife agreement was created as an ordinal-level variable with four values, ranging from complete agreement to complete disagreement. The coding of this variable, which was based on a comparison of wife and husband breadwinner types as defined in Chapters 3 and 4, was straightforward and is described fully in the text of Chapter 5.

This ordinal-level variable was then used as the dependent variable for a regression analysis designed to identify factors that influence husband-wife agreement about breadwinning. Once again, the large number of variables to be considered relative to the number of cases posed a problem. This problem was dealt with by adapting an analytical strategy, recommended by Cohen and Cohen (1975), that involves grouping independent variables into logically or structurally defined sets and treating each set as a unit in the analysis. In this case, analysis of sets was used to reduce the number of variables included in the regression equation. At the first stage of analysis, ten sets of variables were entered, one by one, into the equation. These were (in order of inclusion) wife's breadwinner dimensions,* family income characteristics, wife's occupational characteristics, husband's occupational characteristics, family characteristics, wife's gender attitudes, husband's gender attitudes, wife's background and socialization variables, husband's background and socialization variables, and Franco-American ethnicity. At the second stage, only those sets that showed some significant contribution ($p < .10$) at the first stage were retained. These were wife's background and socialization variables, wife's gender attitudes, husband's gender attitudes, wife's occupational characteristics, family characteristics, and Franco-American ethnicity. At the next stage, only those individual variables whose contributions to the second-stage equation reached or approached statistical significance at the .10 level were retained. A backward-elimination procedure was then used to identify the best predictive equation. This equation, which is presented in Table B6, includes six variables and explains 15 percent of the variation in husband-wife agreement about breadwinning.

I found it surprising that income characteristics were not significant predictors of agreement, given their strong influence on constructions of breadwinning. Because least-squares regression is sensitive only to linear relationships, I decided to check for a curvilinear relationship between income characteristics and agreement about breadwinning. This was done by taking the three variables of wife's annual income, husband's annual income and husband-wife wage ratio, dividing each into three categories at the first and third quartiles, and analyzing the relationship of each categorized income variable to husband-wife agreement. The results showed some curvilinear relationship with agreement about breadwinning for all three income variables, but this relationship was most striking for husband-wife wage ratio, as presented in Chapter 5, Table 4.

Moving from analysis of husband-wife agreement about breadwinning to analysis of change over time in couples' constructions of breadwinning introduced an added complication, constructing measures of breadwinning from responses to the 1992–93 follow-up survey. For this purpose, the follow-up questionnaires included the questions used to measure constructions of breadwinning in the original interview data. I used the

---

* Husband's breadwinner dimensions were not included because, by definition, husband's and wife's dimensions together would account for all of the variation in agreement.

TABLE B6

Best Predictors of Level of Agreement About Breadwinning

Independent variables	B	beta
Length of marriage	.024	.25**
Number of children	−.089	−.14[+]
Wife's gender attitude item 6[a]	−.467	−.31***
Husband's gender attitude item 3[b]	.339	.27**
Husband's gender attitude item 5[c]	−.229	−.16[+]
Franco-American	.310	.15*
(Constant)	2.005	
R^2 (adjusted)	.15***	

NOTE: $N = 152$. All gender attitude items are coded so that high scores denote egalitarian attitudes.
[a] A married woman should not work outside the home if her husband can comfortably support her.
[b] Most of the important decisions in the life of the family should be made by the man of the house.
[c] Women should take care of running their homes and leave running the country up to men.
$+p < .10.$ $*p < .05.$ $**p < .01.$ $***p < .001.$

dimensions of breadwinning developed through analysis of the 1987–88 data and the formulas derived from the factor analyses of those data to compute the 1992–93 scores, thus ensuring the comparability of the two sets of measures. The financial support dimension of breadwinning for wives required a modification of this procedure, however, because one of the indicators of this dimension, Role Importance, was inadvertently omitted from the follow-up questionnaire for wives. An abridged score for this dimension was computed by combining the remaining three indicators. For the 1987–88 data, the correlation of the abridged measure with the original measure was $r = .98$, and, when the abridged score was dichotomized, 97 percent of the cases fell into the same category (high or low) as they had originally. Thus, it seems likely that the use of the abridged measure of wives' financial support for 1992–93 has introduced little distortion into the analysis.

The final statistical procedure for Chapter 5 involved using multiple regression analysis to identify influences on the dimensions of breadwinning as measured at t_2. This could not be done by simply replicating the regression analyses in Chapters 3 and 4, both because the number of cases in the follow-up subsample was too small and because not all the independent variables used in the original analyses were available in the follow-up data set. Once again, I turned to a multistage procedure in which sets of related variables were entered into the equation one at a time and retained only if they had significant predictive value ($p < .10$).

The variables included and the order of consideration were as follows: respondent's background characteristics (age and education) as measured at t_1, husband's and wife's income at t_2, family characteristics at t_2, respondent's breadwinner dimensions at t_1, and level of husband-wife agreement about breadwinning at t_1. Variables that met the criteria for being retained in the equation throughout this process are presented in Table B7 as the best predictors of husbands' and wives' 1992–93 breadwinner dimensions.

TABLE B7

Best Predictors of 1992–93 Breadwinning Dimensions

Husbands		Wives	
Behavioral interpretation ($N = 48$)	*beta*	Financial support ($N = 49$)	*beta*
Length of marriage	−.23	Length of marriage	−.32
Family stage—preschool	−.08	Family stage—preschool	.23
Family stage—school	.27	Family stage—school	.38
Family stage—adolescent	.27	Family stage—adolescent	.44
Family stage—nest leaving	.32+	Family stage—nest leaving	.60*
Family stage—empty nest	.51*	Family stage—empty nest	.33
Husband's earnings	−.23*	Wife's earnings	.33*
Wife's earnings	.65***	Husband's earnings	−.31*
1987 behavioral interpretation	.21	R^2 (adjusted)	.15+
R^2 (adjusted)	.67***		
		Job centrality ($N = 48$)	
Norms ($N = 49$)		Length of marriage	−.14
Family stage—preschool	−.20	Family stage—preschool	−.20
Family stage—school	−.39	Family stage—school	.14
Family stage—adolescent	−.59*	Family stage—adolescent	.19
Family stage—nest leaving	−.30	Family stage—nest leaving	.31+
Family stage—empty nest	−.37	Family stage—empty nest	.34
Husband's earnings	.25+	Wife's earnings	.49**
Wife's earnings	.34*	Husband's earnings	−.11
R^2 (adjusted)	.19*	1987 financial support	−.10
		1987 job centrality	.44**
		1987 disagreement	.20+
		R^2 (adjusted)	.69***
		Norms ($N = 51$)	
		Wife's earnings	−.08
		Husband's earnings	.17
		1987 financial support	.29+
		1987 job centrality	.13
		1987 Norms	.38**
		R^2 (adjusted)	.23**

+$p < .10$.   *$p < .05$.   **$p < .01$.   ***$p < .001$.

Chapter 6

The examination of contested constructions of breadwinning in Chapter 6 required very little new statistical analysis. The consideration of factors that predict disagreement about breadwinning was based on the same regression analysis already discussed regarding Chapter 5 and presented in Table B6. The only other quantitative analyses in Chapter 6 are the examinations of change over time in constructions of breadwinning and the relationship of those changes to husband-wife disagreement at the time of the original interviews. These analyses are presented in the form of straightforward bivariate tables (Chapter 6, Table 6).

Chapter 7

The exploratory analysis of the relationship between breadwinning and mothering presented in Chapter 7 does not use any parametric, multivariate statistical techniques, but relies instead on simple nonparametric tools, particularly frequency distributions and bivariate tables. The most critical part of this analysis is not the choice of statistical techniques, but the selection and coding of the four measures of mothering used as dependent variables. The first measure, importance of the father role, was taken directly from the rankings of social roles that respondents were asked to do during the interview. I have coded this variable into three categories—most important, second most important, and third or lower in importance—and have regarded the last of these as an indicator that mothering is being used as a gender boundary. The second measure, relative importance of the mother role, was based on the same series of questions in the original interviews and was computed by subtracting a respondent's ranking of the mother role from his or her ranking of the father role. Since a higher score on this ranking represented a lower ranking (the most important role was scored '1,' the second most important '2,' etc.), a difference score of 0 or less means that the mother role was not ranked higher in importance than the father role, a difference score of 1 means that the mother role was ranked somewhat higher than the father role, and a difference score of 2 or more means that the mother role was ranked much higher than the father role. I have regarded any value greater than 0 as indicating use of mothering as a gender boundary.

The third measure of mothering as a gender boundary was based on responses to the hypothetical situation about the dual-earner couple with a higher-earning wife and a sick child. Responses were coded into six categories: the mother should definitely stay home with the child, the mother should stay home if possible, the parents should hire someone to care for the child while they continue to work, the parents should arrange their work schedules so that they can share care of the child, the father should stay home with the child, and other responses. I have coded the first two of these as indicating the use of mothering as a gender boundary. The final measure of mothering is an aggregate of the first three; it simply counts how many of the first three measures indicate the use of mothering as a gender boundary, with scores ranging from 0 to 3. Frequency distributions by gender of the first three indicators can be found in Table 8, Chapter 7. Frequencies on the aggregate measure are displayed in Table 7, Chapter 7.

These four measures of mothering provide the foundation for the rest of the analysis in Chapter 7. Table 9 examines the relationship between each of these measures and constructions of breadwinning. Table 10 documents the relationship between disagreement about the mothering boundary and disagreement about the breadwinning boundary. Other analysis in the chapter is based on more rudimentary inspections of the data and on the qualitative case studies.

Reference Matter

References

Babbie, Earl. 1986. *The Practice of Social Research*. 4th ed. Belmont, Calif.: Wadsworth.

Bem, Sandra Lipsitz. 1993. *The Lenses of Gender: Transforming the Debate on Sexual Inequality*. New Haven, Conn.: Yale University Press.

Berk, Sarah Fenstermaker. 1985. *The Gender Factory: The Apportionment of Work in American Households*. New York: Plenum.

Bernard, Jessie. 1976. "Change and Stability in Sex-Role Norms and Behavior." *Journal of Social Issues*, 32, no. 3: 207–23.

———. 1981. "The Good-Provider Role: Its Rise and Fall." *American Psychologist* 36, no. 1: 1–12.

Blumstein, Philip, and Pepper Schwartz. 1983. *American Couples: Money, Work, Sex*. New York: William Morrow.

Bose, Christine E. 1987. "Dual Spheres." In Beth B. Hess and Myra Marx Ferree, eds., *Analyzing Gender: A Handbook of Social Science Research*, pp. 267–85. Newbury Park, Calif.: Sage.

Carrigan, Tim, Bob Connell, and John Lee. 1987. "Toward a New Sociology of Masculinity." In Harry Brod, ed., *The Making of Masculinities: The New Men's Studies*, pp. 63–100. Boston: Allen & Unwin.

Chodorow, Nancy. 1978. *The Reproduction of Mothering: Psychoanalysis and the Sociology of Gender*. Berkeley: University of California Press.

Cohen, Jacob, and Patricia Cohen. 1975. *Applied Multiple Regression/Correlation Analysis for the Behavioral Sciences*. Hillsdale, N.J.: Lawrence Erlbaum Associates.

Condry, John, and Sandra Condry. 1976. "Sex Differences: A Study of the Eye of the Beholder." *Child Development* 47, no. 3: 812–19.

Connell, R. W. 1987. *Gender and Power: Society, the Person and Sexual Politics*. Stanford, Calif.: Stanford University Press.

Ehrenreich, Barbara. 1983. *The Hearts of Men: American Dreams and the Flight from Commitment*. Garden City, N.Y.: Anchor.

Epstein, Cynthia Fuchs. 1989. "Workplace Boundaries: Conceptions and Creations." *Social Research* 56, no. 3: 571–90.

———. 1992. "Tinkerbells and Pinups: The Construction and Reconstruction of Gender Boundaries at Work." In Michèle Lamont and Marcel Fournier, eds., *Cultivating Differences: Symbolic Boundaries and the Making of Inequality*, pp. 232–56. Chicago: University of Chicago Press.

Ferree, Myra Marx. 1990. "Beyond Separate Spheres: Feminism and Family Research." *Journal of Marriage and the Family* 52, no. 4: 866–84.

Ferree, Myra Marx, and Beth B. Hess. 1987. "Introduction." In Beth B. Hess and Myra Marx Ferree, eds., *Analyzing Gender: A Handbook of Social Science Research*, pp. 9–30. Newbury Park, Calif.: Sage.

Filene, Peter. 1981. "Introducing Ourselves." In Peter Filene, ed., *Men in the Middle: Coping with the Problems of Work and Family in the Lives of Middle-Aged Men*, pp. 1–31. Englewood Cliffs, N.J.: Prentice-Hall.

Gerson, Judith M., and Kathy Peiss. 1985. "Boundaries, Negotiation, Consciousness: Reconceptualizing Gender Relations." *Social Problems* 32, no. 4: 317–31.

Gerson, Kathleen. 1993. *No Man's Land: Men's Changing Commitments to Family and Work*. New York: Basic Books.

Gilligan, Carol. 1981. *In a Different Voice: Psychological Theory and Women's Development*. Cambridge, Mass.: Harvard University Press.

Grønseth, Erick. 1972. "The Breadwinner Trap." In Louise Kapp Howe, ed., *The Future of the Family*, pp. 175–91. New York: Simon and Schuster.

Haas, Linda. 1982. "Determinants of Role-Sharing Behavior: A Study of Egalitarian Couples." *Sex Roles* 8, no. 7: 747–60.

———. 1986. "Wives' Orientation Toward Breadwinning: Sweden and the United States." *Journal of Family Issues* 7, no. 4: 358–81.

Hall, Elaine. 1994. "Developing the Gender Perspective: A Critical Evaluation of Four Definitions of Gender over Two Decades." Department of Sociology, Kent State University. Unpublished manuscript.

Hareven, Tamara K. 1982. *Family Time and Industrial Time: The Relationship Between the Family and Work in a New England Industrial Community*. Cambridge, Eng.: Cambridge University Press.

Hartley, Marsden. 1940. *Androscoggin*. Portland, Maine: Falmouth.

Hertz, Rosanna. 1986. *More Equal than Others: Women and Men in Dual-Career Marriages*. Berkeley: University of California Press.

Hochschild, Arlie (with Anne Machung). 1989. *The Second Shift: Working Parents and the Revolution at Home*. New York: Viking.

Hood, Jane C. 1983. *Becoming a Two-Job Family*. New York: Praeger.

———. 1986. "The Provider Role: Its Meaning and Measurement." *Journal of Marriage and the Family* 48, no. 2: 349–59.

Josefowitz, Natasha. 1980. *Paths to Power: A Woman's Guide from First Job to Top Executive*. Reading, Mass.: Addison-Wesley.

Kessler, Suzanne J., and Wendy McKenna. 1978. *Gender: An Ethnomethodological Approach*. Chicago: University of Chicago Press.

Leamon, James S. 1976. *Historic Lewiston: A Textile City in Transition.* Lewiston, Maine: Lewiston Historical Commission.

Lein, Laura. 1983. *Families Without Villains.* Lexington, Mass.: Lexington Books.

Lopata, Helena Z., and Barrie Thorne. 1978. "On the Term 'Sex Roles'." *Signs* 3, no. 3: 718–21.

Lorber, Judith. 1994. *Paradoxes of Gender.* New Haven, Conn.: Yale University Press.

Margolis, Maxine L. 1984. *Mothers and Such: Views of American Women and Why They Changed.* Berkeley: University of California Press.

Model, Suzanne. 1982. "Housework by Husbands: Determinants and Implications." In Joan Aldous, ed., *Two Paychecks: Life in Dual Earner Families,* pp. 193–205. Beverly Hills, Calif.: Sage.

Nicholson, Linda. 1994. "Interpreting *Gender.*" *Signs* 20, no. 1: 79–105.

Nyhan, Pat. 1984. "French is Not a Foreign Language in Maine, So Why Is It Taught Like One?" *Maine Times* 17, no. 11: 2–5.

Oakley, Ann. 1972. *Sex, Gender, and Society.* New York: Harper & Row.

———. 1981. "Interviewing Women: A Contradiction in Terms." In Helen Roberts, ed., *Doing Feminist Research,* pp. 30–61. London: Routledge & Kegan Paul.

Perry-Jenkins, Maureen, and Ann C. Crouter. 1990. "Men's Provider-Role Attitudes: Implications for Household Work and Marital Satisfaction." *Journal of Family Issues* 11, no. 2: 136–56.

Pleck, Joseph H. 1983. "Husbands' Paid Work and Family Roles: Current Research Issues." In Helena Z. Lopata and Joseph H. Pleck, eds., *Research in the Interweave of Social Roles: Jobs and Families,* vol. 3, pp. 251–333. Greenwich, Conn.: JAI.

———. 1985. *Working Wives / Working Husbands.* Beverly Hills, Calif.: Sage.

Potuchek, Jean L. 1992. "Employed Wives' Orientations to Breadwinning: A Gender Theory Analysis." *Journal of Marriage and the Family* 54, no. 3: 548–58.

Rand, John A. 1975. *The Peoples Lewiston-Auburn, Maine, 1875–1975.* Freeport, Maine: Bond Wheelwright.

Reinharz, Shulamit. 1992. *Feminist Methods in Social Research.* New York: Oxford University Press.

Rodman, Hyman, and Constantina Safilios-Rothschild. 1983. "Weak Links in Men's Worker-Earner Roles: A Descriptive Model." In Helena Z. Lopata and Joseph H. Pleck, eds., *Research in the Interweave of Social Roles: Jobs and Families,* vol. 3, pp. 219–38. Greenwich, Conn.: JAI.

Rosen, Ellen Israel. 1987. *Bitter Choices: Blue-Collar Women In and Out of Work.* Chicago: University of Chicago Press.

Slocum, Walter L., and F. Ivan Nye. 1976. "Provider and Housekeeper Roles." In F. Ivan Nye, ed., *Role Structure and Analysis for the Family,* pp. 81–100. Beverly Hills, Calif.: Sage.

Smith, Audrey D., and William J. Reid. 1986. *Role-Sharing Marriage.* New York: Columbia University Press.

Stacey, Judith. 1990. *Brave New Families: Stories of Domestic Upheaval in Late Twentieth Century America.* New York: Basic Books.

Stacey, Judith, and Barrie Thorne. 1985. "The Missing Feminist Revolution in Sociology." *Social Problems* 32, no. 4: 301–16.

Tannen, Deborah. 1990. *You Just Don't Understand: Women and Men in Conversation.* New York: Morrow.

Thorne, Barrie. 1993. *Gender Play: Girls and Boys in School.* New Brunswick, N.J.: Rutgers University Press.

Tilly, Louise A., and Joan W. Scott. 1978. *Women, Work and Family.* New York: Holt, Rinehart and Winston.

U.S. Bureau of the Census. 1990. *Statistical Abstract of the United States: 1990.* Washington, D.C.: U.S. Government Printing Office.

———. 1992. *1990 Census of Population and Housing.* Washington, D.C.: U.S. Government Printing Office.

———. 1993a. *Current Population Reports: Household and Family Characteristics, March 1992.* Washington, D.C.: U.S. Government Printing Office.

———. 1993b. *1990 Census of Population: Social and Economic Characteristics, United States.* Washington, D.C.: U.S. Government Printing Office.

West, Candace, and Don H. Zimmerman. 1987. "Doing Gender." *Gender & Society* 1, no. 2: 125–51.

Wharton, Amy S. 1991. "Structure and Agency in Socialist-Feminist Theory." *Gender & Society* 5, no. 3: 373–89.

Young, Michael, and Peter Willmott. 1975. *The Symmetrical Family.* New York: Penguin.

Index

In this index an "f" after a number indicates a separate reference on the next page, and an "ff" indicates separate references on the next two pages. A continuous discussion over two or more pages is indicated by a span of page numbers, e.g., "57–59." *Passim* is used for a cluster of references in close but not consecutive sequence.

Who supports the family : gender and breadwinning in dual-earner
marriages / Jean L. Potuchek.
    p.   cm.
Includes bibliographical references and index.
ISBN 0-8047-2835-6 (cl.)
ISBN 0-8047-2836-4 (pb.)
    1. Dual-career families—United States.   2. Married people—
Employment—Social aspects—United States.   2. Married women—
Employment—Social aspects—United States.   4. Sex role—Economic
aspects—United States.   I. Title.
HQ536.P668   1997
306.872—dc20
                                                        96-34115
                                                           CIP

⊗ This book is printed on acid-free, recycled paper.

Original printing 1997
Last figure below indicates year of this printing:
06 05 04 03 02 01 00 99 98 97